THE TIMELINE OF THE VIETNAM WAR

THE TIMELINE OF THE VIETNAM WAR

THE ULTIMATE GUIDE TO THIS DIVISIVE CONFLICT IN AMERICAN HISTORY

Kevin Dougherty & Jason Stewart

THUNDER BAY
P · R · E · S · S

San Diego, California

Thunder Bay Press
An imprint of the Advantage Publishers Group
10350 Barnes Canyon Road, San Diego, CA 92121
www.thunderbaybooks.com

All notations of errors or omissions should be addressed to Thunder Bay Press,
Editorial Department, at the above address. All other correspondence (author inquiries,
permissions) concerning the content of this book should be addressed to
Amber Books Ltd., Bradley's Close, 74–77 White Lion Street, London N1 9PF,
United Kingdom. www.amberbooks.co.uk.

ISBN-13: 978-1-59223-860-6
ISBN-10: 1-59223-860-2

Project Editor: Sarah Uttridge
Picture Research: Terry Forshaw
Design: Hawes Design

Printed in China

1 2 3 4 5 12 11 10 09 08

Contents

Introduction

Vietnam is best known for the period between 1965 and 1973 when the U.S. military was involved in an unsuccessful effort to support its South Vietnamese allies in a war against the Communist forces of North Vietnam and the Vietcong. The roots of this conflict stretch deeper.

The struggle in the second half of the twentieth century was merely the continuation of a much longer quest for a Vietnamese nation that can be traced at least as far back as 208 BC. Then, Trieu Da, a renegade Chinese general, conquered Au Lac, a location in the northern mountains of Vietnam populated by the Viets, a people of Mongolian origin who had migrated south. The Chinese therefore became the traditional rival of the Vietnamese, and the two

Left: Marines wait to board CH-46 helicopters at Vandergrift Combat base. They are on their way to the demilitarized zone during the Battle of Khe Sanh. Right: A foot soldier, also known as a "grunt."

Asian powers remained in a nearly continual state of tension until the nineteenth century, when European imperialism brought a French presence to Vietnam. In 1859 the French captured Saigon and soon established direct rule. Although the nationalist struggle of the Vietnamese people is long and complicated, any history must have a starting point, and this particular study begins with this period of French involvement.

World War II brought a new foreign power to Vietnam with Japan's victory over French forces in Indochina in 1941. The defeat of Japan by the Allied powers in 1945 ushered in a renewed sense of hope for the forces of

Although lacking the equipment and firepower of their enemies, the Viet Minh excelled in the hit-and-run tactics of guerrilla warfare.

....

Vietnamese nationalism. Ho Chi Minh, a charismatic Communist who had cooperated with the Allied forces against the Japanese, declared Vietnam's independence on September 2, 1945. France, however, refused to yield its claim to its colonial interest, and Ho and his Viet Minh forces began a revolutionary war, sometimes called the First Indochina War, against the French, which resulted in the French withdrawal from Vietnam in 1955.

However, the Viet Minh battlefield victory was offset by a diplomatic defeat at the Geneva Conference of 1954. The Viet Minh were forced to accept a partition that gave them control of Vietnam only north of the seventeenth parallel, while a government led by Ngo Dinh Diem and backed by the United States would govern the southern part of Vietnam. This period from the Japanese occupation of Vietnam in World War II to the expulsion of the French and the partition of Vietnam is covered in chapter one.

1940

SEPTEMBER

September 22 Vichy France permits Japan to station troops in northern Vietnam. Although French administrators are left in their positions, the Japanese consolidate their rule and Vietnam becomes a virtual colony of Japan until the end of World War II.

1941

MAY

May 10 The Viet Minh (Vietnam Independence League) is formed. To win popular support, Ho Chi Minh advocates a policy of collaboration with other nationalist groups.

1942

AUGUST

August 13 Ho Chi Minh goes to China to procure aid in the fight against the Japanese, but he is arrested and held prisoner for thirteen months.

1944

SEPTEMBER

September 20 Ho Chi Minh returns to Vietnam from China and, with the help of the American Office of Strategic Services (OSS), the Viet Minh harass Japanese troops and help rescue downed U.S. pilots.

DECEMBER

December 22 Viet Minh troops begin to attack French outposts in northern Vietnam. These attacks mark the beginning of the Viet Minh's armed struggle against the French.

1945

MARCH

March 9 Japan grants independence to Vietnam under Japanese protection and installs Bao Dai as the head of the state. However, Bao Dai is never able to gain the support of the people.

AUGUST

August 16–29 Ho Chi Minh creates the National Liberation Committee of Vietnam to form a provisional government and Japan transfers power in Indochina to the Viet Minh.

The long-standing nature of Vietnam's nationalist struggle and Ho Chi Minh's Communist politics led the North Vietnamese to adopt readily the Maoist doctrine of revolutionary war. According to this model, objectives are achieved through a protracted guerrilla war. The classic Maoist formula involves three phases: a latent and incipient stage marked by organizational and clandestine activities; a guerrilla phase in which hit-and-run tactics are used to put the government on the defensive; and a climactic war of movement phase in which final victory is achieved. The North Vietnamese would adapt the Maoist doctrine to their own particular needs, including an increased emphasis on external support that manifested itself through Chinese and Russian aid, and Laos and Cambodia's acquiescence to the use of the Ho Chi Minh Trail. General Vo Nguyen Giap would emerge as the architect of the North Vietnamese military effort, combining the resources of the National Liberation Front's (NLF) military arm—the Vietcong (VC)—as guerrilla fighters, and the People's Army of North Vietnam (PAVN) or North Vietnamese Army (NVA) as the conventional military force.

International Geopolitics

What thrust Vietnam to the forefront of international geopolitics was the Cold War between the democratic countries of the world led by the United States and the Communist ones led by the Soviet Union. The United States had established a foreign policy of containment, which insisted that unless met by force, Soviet aggression would be unchecked and insatiable. The "domino theory" held that if one Southeast Asian country fell to Communism, others would follow. Based on this logic, the United States could ill afford to not fill the vacuum left by the French withdrawal from Vietnam. Nonetheless, direct involvement of the United States in Vietnam was a gradual process. As early as 1955, President Dwight D. Eisenhower had deployed American military advisers to begin training South Vietnam's army, the Army of the Republic of Vietnam (ARVN). However, it was under the leadership of President John F. Kennedy that the United States began increasing markedly its economic and military support to

South Vietnam. By 1962, the U.S. Military Assistance Command, Vietnam (MACV) was established in Saigon and the number of U.S. advisers had tripled from the Eisenhower era to more than 11,000 troops. For the first time, it was possible to attach advisers to most ARVN

This aspect of the Vietnam War is the subject of chapter two.

The Viet Minh exuberance over the French withdrawal in 1955 gave way to disappointment with a peace settlement that left Vietnam partitioned.

September 2 Ho Chi Minh proclaims the independent Democratic Republic of Vietnam (DRV).

September 12 British troops arrive in Saigon to accept the surrender of the Japanese, in accordance with the Potsdam Peace Conference.

September 21–24 Violence flares as various factions, including the Viet Minh and French colonial forces, try to assert power over Vietnam.

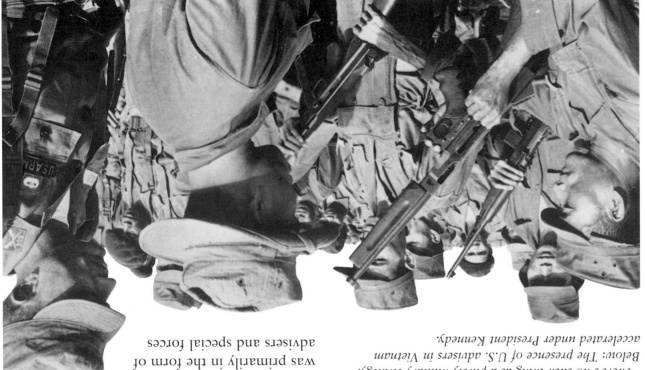

support during operations. In August 1964, North Vietnamese patrol boats engaged U.S. Navy forces in the Gulf of Tonkin, an incident that led President Lyndon B. Johnson to authorize Operation Rolling Thunder, a strategic bombing campaign designed to punish North Vietnam. When the bombing failed to achieve its desired results, Johnson decided to commit ground combat troops. Until then, however, the American contribution to the war effort was primarily in the form of advisers and special forces

Left: Vo Nguyen Giap said of a people's war, "There's no such thing as a purely military strategy." Below: The presence of U.S. advisers in Vietnam accelerated under President Kennedy.

personnel. This period, from 1955 to 1965, is covered in chapter three.

Reliance on Nuclear Weapons

The war in Vietnam was one that the United States was underprepared to fight. Much of its post–World War II strategy had relied on nuclear weapons, including the notion of massive retaliation, as called for in 1954 by Secretary of State John Foster Dulles. As the Soviets improved their nuclear capability, the United States moved toward a strategy of flexible response, which relied on more of a balance between nuclear and conventional forces. The United States was much more focused on a conventional war in Europe than a guerrilla war in Asia, where the Korean War had recently shown the difficulties of fighting a limited war in which the United States could not bring to bear the full weight of its technological and firepower advantage. Nonetheless, under the leadership of MACV Commander General William Westmoreland, the United States opted to fight the Vietnam War using a strategy of attrition, which did not prove effective against the North Vietnamese protracted war strategy of

exhaustion. The United States experienced much frustration in translating tactical victories on the battlefield into anything of a larger strategic consequence. These issues are addressed in chapter four.

South Vietnamese Ally

One serious flaw in the United States' strategic approach to the war was an underutilization of its South Vietnamese ally. Although the South Vietnamese government was plagued by corruption and in some cases South Vietnamese units performed poorly on the battlefield, the South Vietnamese were nonetheless relegated to junior partners in a war for their very survival as a nation. They became overly reliant on U.S. leadership and support, and failed to develop the self-sufficiency and initiative needed to contribute significantly during the years of American involvement or to carry on alone after the American withdrawal. Nonetheless, at its height the ARVN numbered about half a million

During the Vietnam War, the United States tried unsuccessfully to replicate the effectiveness of its strategic bombing campaigns of World War II.

September 24 Viet Minh forces successfully organize a general strike in Saigon, shutting down all commercial, electrical, and water services.

September 26 OSS officer Lieutenant Colonel Peter Dewey is killed by Viet Minh soldiers. Dewey becomes the first American to die in Vietnam.

OCTOBER

October 9 French soldiers begin to arrive in South Vietnam to restore French rule.

men. Around 250,000 South Vietnamese lost their lives in the fighting and over a million more were wounded. Their experience has been underreported, and this book makes a concerted effort to tell their story in chapter five.

The People's War

Because the Vietnam War was a people's war, the struggle for the support of the South Vietnamese people was critical to the U.S. effort. A host of programs grouped under the rubric of "pacification" was designed to win the hearts and minds of the people by weakening the VC infrastructure, or "shadow government," in South Vietnam and strengthening the people's confidence in the South Vietnamese government. Plagued by inadequate resources and arguments that it detracted from the "Big War," the pacification effort showed much promise but could largely be summed up as offering too little, too late. This missed opportunity of the Vietnam War is chronicled in chapter six.

....

William Westmoreland, a veteran of World War II and Korea, commanded the Military Assistance Command, Vietnam (MACV) from 1964 to 1968.

Instead of the civic-oriented pacification program, many in the U.S. military preferred to create opportunities to defeat the North Vietnamese on the battlefield. Unfortunately, the nature of guerrilla warfare made the North Vietnamese and Vietcong unwilling to fight the Americans in open battle. The United States was required to "find, fix, flush, and finish" the enemy through search-and-destroy operations, which often made use of the superior mobility offered by the helicopter. However, the search-and-destroy operations also committed the United States to a strategy of attrition that proved frustrating and slow, and failed to achieve lasting results. As the large U.S. forces would sweep through an area, the more agile North Vietnamese and Vietcong would escape in large numbers, often to cross-border sanctuaries, only to return when the Americans moved on to other areas. Chapter seven covers this tactic and also examines selected search-and-destroy operations in detail.

The desire to leverage U.S. firepower and technology also manifested itself in the bombing campaign. By 1967 the total tonnage of bombs dropped on North Vietnam exceeded that

1946

FEBRUARY

February 20 The Chinese agree to withdraw from North Vietnam in exchange for French concessions in Shanghai and other Chinese port cities.

MARCH

March 5 Ho Chi Minh agrees to allow French troops to return to Hanoi temporarily in exchange for recognition of the Democratic Republic of Vietnam.

MAY

May 30–October 18 Ho Chi Minh travels to France and spends four months attempting to negotiate full independence for Vietnam, but his efforts fail.

dropped on Germany, Italy, and Japan during World War II, but the United States found it had seriously overestimated the capabilities of strategic bombing. Difficulties in targeting, strict rules of engagement, gradualism, and an uncanny ability of the North Vietnamese to repair and recover made the bombing campaign frustrating. The tactical effectiveness of close air support of ground troops was also minimized by the North Vietnamese tactic of "clinging to the GI's belts" and "clutching the people to their breast," which increased the likelihood of American fratricide or civilian casualties. Nonetheless, many air-power advocates credit the massive Linebacker II bombings of late 1972 with ultimately motivating the North Vietnamese to sign a peace agreement. Issues such as these are addressed in chapter eight.

Conventional Warfare

In January 1968 the United States finally got its long-awaited chance to engage the North Vietnamese in conventional warfare. During the Tet holiday, the VC and PAVN forces launched a massive series of attacks across the length of South Vietnam. Initially caught off guard, the

Americans and South Vietnamese soon rallied and used their superior mobility and firepower to hand the North Vietnamese a stunning defeat. Nonetheless, this tactical U.S. victory turned into a strategic defeat, as Tet marked a turning point for U.S. domestic support for the war. The very idea that the North Vietnamese could mount such a huge offensive made many Americans question the progress of the war. Chapter nine explains the double-edged nature of this significant battle.

The strategic importance of Tet on the U.S. home front also indicates the inseparable relationship between the domestic situation in the United States and the war in Vietnam. The 1960s and early 1970s were tumultuous periods in the United States, in which all manners of traditional authority were subject to challenge. The assassination of President Kennedy, the civil rights movement, the sexual revolution, the drug and hippie cultures, unrest on college campuses, and the Watergate scandal all rocked America and impacted on Vietnam. A significant antiwar movement developed in the United States and, especially after Tet, relations between the media and the military became increasingly strained, if

Combat operations were just one part of U.S. involvement in Vietnam. Soldiers also performed other civic services, including providing medical care.

not openly hostile. The Vietnam War polarized the country, and the decision ultimately to withdraw was a reflection of waning popular support for the war. The North Vietnamese strategy of exhaustion had taken its toll. The profound effects of these home-front issues are analyzed in chapter ten.

JUNE

June 22 The French high commissioner for Vietnam, Georges Thierry d'Argenlieu, announces a separate French-controlled government for South Vietnam (Cochin China).

NOVEMBER

November 23 French naval forces bombard Haiphong harbor and drive the Viet Minh from the port city.

November 28 French troops push the Viet Minh out of Hanoi and drive them into the surrounding jungles.

DECEMBER

December 19 The Viet Minh launch their first attack on the French at Hanoi. This begins what is to become the eight-year-long First Indochina War.

While many search-and-destroy operations took place in the remote areas of Vietnam, other battles, especially during the 1968 Tet Offensive, raged in urban areas.

As domestic support for the war eroded, the United States embarked on a program of "Vietnamization," through which a phased withdrawal of U.S. troops would be accompanied by a gradual transfer of primary military responsibility to South Vietnam. Richard Nixon had been elected president in 1968 on a platform of "peace with honor," and in June 1969 he announced the withdrawal plan. As part of Vietnamization, U.S. advisers worked frantically to try to increase the effectiveness of the ARVN, but the South Vietnamese remained vulnerable. When the North Vietnamese launched a massive, conventional attack on South Vietnam in the 1972 Easter Offensive, the United States was forced to stem the North Vietnamese onslaught with massive, sustained bombing attacks, mining Haiphong harbor, and establishing a naval blockade of North Vietnam. The result was a military stalemate in which both sides found reasons to compromise. Nonetheless, the negotiations were grueling and inconclusive until an agreement was finally reached in January 1973 for a U.S. withdrawal from South Vietnam. This period of declining U.S. involvement is the subject of chapter eleven.

1947

APRIL

April 1 By this time, French forces have pushed the Viet Minh out of nearly all of the towns of Tonkin and northern Annam. The Viet Minh move into the Viet Bac region, the mountainous area north of Hanoi.

OCTOBER

October 7–December 22 The French launch Operation Lea, a series of assaults on Viet Minh positions near the Chinese border. Despite suffering 9,000 casualties, Ho Chi Minh and most of the Viet Minh forces slip away.

But the American withdrawal did not end the war. Left to fend for themselves, the South Vietnamese struggled on for two more years until early 1975, when the North Vietnamese launched their final offensive. On April 30, the South Vietnamese capital of Saigon fell to North Vietnamese forces.

Vietnam Syndrome

The war was over but there was no peace. The North Vietnamese treated the defeated South Vietnamese with vengeance, killing or imprisoning many. Those who could became "boat people," risking life and limb to escape. Even as the United States tried to move past the failed war, a "Vietnam Syndrome" made the nation reluctant to again become involved militarily. But if the United States and its South Vietnamese allies lost the war, they seem to be on their way to winning the peace. Although still Communist, Vietnam is today becoming increasingly capitalistic. The United States and Vietnam established formal diplomatic relations in 1995, and since then there has been increased cooperation on issues such as efforts to recover the remains of missing American soldiers. Many American tourists, especially Vietnam veterans, visit Vietnam each year. The United States is also recovering, thanks in part to the 1982 dedication of the Vietnam Veterans Memorial, which has been called "the wall that heals." Chapter twelve covers the period after the American withdrawal, the ultimate North Vietnamese victory, and the war's legacy.

The Vietnam War was always an ambiguous, messy affair, so it remains a controversial and emotional event. It was the United States' longest and most socially divisive war since the Civil War. Some 2.5 million Americans served in Southeast Asia and over 56,000 lost their lives. Literally millions of North and South Vietnamese were killed in the fighting. It is an event seared into the U.S. consciousness and a war that has become a yardstick by which all subsequent U.S. military endeavors have been measured. Without becoming embroiled in the controversy, this book attempts to chronicle the contributions, efforts, and impacts of all those involved.

....

America's experience in Vietnam was painful and divisive. The Vietnam Veterans Memorial serves as a powerful tribute to those who died in the war.

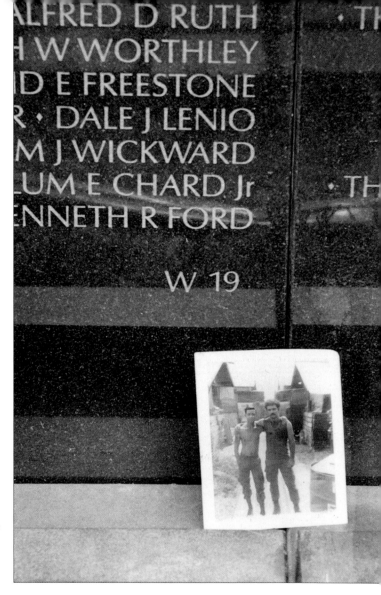

1949		
MARCH	**JULY**	**OCTOBER**
March 8 The French make Bao Dai head of state in South Vietnam.	**July 1** The French establish the Vietnamese National Army (VNA), an anti-Communist army, in an attempt to gain native support against the Viet Minh.	**October 1** Mao Tse-tung's Chinese Communist forces win the Chinese Civil War. This ignites U.S. anti-Communist concerns in Southeast Asia and means the Viet Minh now have a powerful ally in their war against the French.

Colonialism Defeated: The French Years

From the seventeenth century to the nineteenth, the imperial powers of Europe carved up large sections of Asia for colonization. In extending imperial control, the Europeans sought to convert inhabitants of the region to Christianity and exploit newly acquired territories for their natural resources.

Vietnam, endowed with an ample supply of raw materials such as silk, rubber, spices, coal, and timber, attracted the imperial designs of France, which controlled Vietnam until Japan occupied the colony during World War II. Following the defeat of Japan, France attempted to return to Vietnam, but the Viet Minh, a revolutionary group led by Ho Chi Minh, began a war of independence. Using guerrilla tactics and a superior strategy, the Viet Minh defeated the French on the battlefield and forced the end of French colonization. However, Cold War politics complicated the peace negotiations and ensured that Vietnam would become embroiled in warfare once again.

The Arrival of the French

The French came to Vietnam in two separate time periods: first in the seventeenth century and later in the nineteenth. Alexandre de Rhodes, a Jesuit priest and missionary, arrived in Vietnam in 1627 and began laying the groundwork for imperial conquest. While in Vietnam, de Rhodes converted many Vietnamese to Catholicism and created a Latin alphabet for the Vietnamese language. Later missionaries succeeded in converting about 8 percent of the population

Left: The destruction of villages under an official French policy became a recruiting tool for the Viet Minh.
Right: Nguyen Ai Quoc changed his name to Ho Chi Minh to mask his Communist background.

to Catholicism, which created a small but influential pro-French contingent in Vietnam.

The second wave of the French interest in Vietnam began in 1847, when Emperor Napoleon III sent a French naval expedition to Vietnam to establish a military base at the coastal city of Tourane (later called Da Nang). The Vietnamese effectively resisted the first French attempts to capture the port city, but the French succeeded in capturing Tourane in 1858. Soon after, French forces began to conquer large sections of Vietnamese territory, and by 1883 France had achieved military control over all three regions that made up Vietnam: Tonkin in the north, Annam in the center, and Cochin China in the south. By 1893 France had added Laos and Cambodia to its territory and consolidated its gains in an expansive French Indochinese Union.

French rule was often cruel and brutal, focusing entirely on the exploitation of natural resources and labor for profit. French

In 1883 France established a protectorate over Annam and Tonkin and began ruling Cochin China as a colony.

administrators cared little for their Vietnamese subjects, viewing them and their land as expendable resources that existed solely for French benefit. The French also imposed high taxes, forcing many peasants to lose land that their ancestors had owned for centuries. The loss of land forced many families to become tenants or day laborers who made little money but still had to pay high taxes. Overall, French colonial rule brought about many negative changes in Vietnamese life and society, driving a large percentage of the population into poverty and servitude.

Vietnamese Response

From the beginning, the Vietnamese fiercely resisted the establishment of French colonialism, but disunity and a lack of modern weaponry prevented them from expelling the invaders. By the 1920s, however, the Vietnamese began to form various nationalist organizations to challenge French rule. Of these groups, the most significant was the Revolutionary Youth League of Vietnam, the first purely Marxist organization in Indochina. It was founded in 1925 by Nguyen Ai Quoc, who would later

1950

JANUARY

January 14 Communist China and the Soviet Union officially recognize Ho Chi Minh's Democratic Republic of Vietnam. China begins to send military advisers and modern weapons to help the Viet Minh.

FEBRUARY

February 1 The Viet Minh launch an offensive to destroy French outposts near the Chinese border and to open supply routes from China.

February 7 The United States and Britain officially recognize Bao Dai's French-controlled South Vietnamese regime.

JUNE

June 30 U.S. president Harry S. Truman sends ground troops into Korea after Communist North Korea's invasion of the south.

come to be known as Ho Chi Minh.

Highly intelligent, goal-oriented, and charismatic, Ho Chi Minh would become the embodiment of the Vietnamese resistance movement. His main passion in life was Vietnamese independence, and he never missed an opportunity to further his cause. In 1911 Ho left Vietnam to travel around the world and, while on this journey, he developed the skills needed to achieve his goal. He visited Boston and New York, but a stay in Paris during World War I proved to be a turning point in his life. While in Paris, Ho became heavily involved in the political activities of Vietnamese expatriates living in France. During the Versailles Peace Conference of 1919, he sought the opportunity to press the victorious Allied leaders for Vietnamese independence, but none of the Big Four would meet with him.

In 1920 Ho became a founding member of the French Communist Party. He was attracted to Communism by the writings of Vladimir Lenin and soon became convinced that the only way to expel the French from Vietnam was through violent revolution. To further his studies of Communism, Ho traveled to Russia for training in Marxist ideology and revolutionary tactics.

Two years later, Soviet officials sent him to China to work as an agent of the Comintern. While there, he met exiled Vietnamese nationalists and formed the Vietnamese Revolutionary Youth Movement, which would serve as a precursor to the Indochinese Communist Party.

Vietnam and World War II

Over the next fifteen years, Ho continued to work with exiled Vietnamese nationalists, waiting patiently for the right moment to return to Vietnam and lead its people in revolution. That moment came in the spring of 1940, when Nazi Germany invaded and conquered northern France in a mere six weeks of fighting. In the surrender agreement, the southern portion of France remained unoccupied in exchange for the Vichy French government's collaboration with Nazi Germany. Following the French defeat, imperialist Japan took advantage of the power vacuum and occupied Indochina. Although the Japanese were actually in charge,

The Potsdam Conference decided that the British would disarm Japanese troops south of the sixteenth parallel. French troops slowly began to replace the British forces.

they left nominal control of the colony in the hands of the Vichy French. This dramatic turn of events provided the opportunity that Ho Chi Minh had been waiting for, and in May 1941 he returned to Vietnam to begin his revolution.

JULY

July 26 U.S. military involvement in Vietnam begins when President Truman sends $15 million in military aid to the French.

SEPTEMBER

September 16 The Viet Minh launch their main attack against French outposts on the Chinese border. As the outposts fall, the French lose some 6,000 men and their ability to interdict Viet Minh logistical lines from China.

September 27 The United States establishes the Military Assistance Advisory Group (MAAG) in Saigon to aid the French.

DECEMBER

December 23 The United States signs a Mutual Defense Assistance Agreement with France, Vietnam, Cambodia, and Laos (the French Associated States).

On his return to Vietnam, Ho organized the Viet Nam Doc Lap Dong Minh Hoi (League for the Independence of Vietnam), more commonly referred to as the Viet Minh, which sought to expel the Japanese and French from Vietnam and to set up Vietnamese self-rule. Throughout World War II, the Viet Minh harassed the Japanese and provided aid to the Allies, particularly by rescuing downed American pilots. In consideration of this help, the Viet Minh hoped the Allies would recognize them as the true rulers of Vietnam and aid them in gaining their independence once the war ended.

As World War II progressed and it became obvious that Japan would not be able to hold on to its territories, the situation in Vietnam became more volatile. In March 1945, the French made a failed attempt to seize power from the Japanese, after which the Japanese imprisoned the French colonial administrators and declared Indochina's independence. The Japanese placed power into the hands of the young Vietnamese emperor Bao Dai, but the defeat of Japan in August 1945 allowed Ho Chi Minh and the Viet Minh to seize power for themselves.

On September 2, 1945, Ho Chi Minh declared the independence of Vietnam and the creation of the Democratic Republic of Vietnam, but France ignored the declaration. After disarming the Japanese, British forces withdrew from Vietnam in 1946 and the French quickly returned to reassert their colonial rule. The French easily expelled the Viet Minh officials from government positions in the south, but in the north Ho Chi Minh and the Viet Minh had a much stronger hold. Unable to dislodge Ho and his supporters, the French promised the Viet Minh that the Democratic Republic of Vietnam could exist as a free state in the French Indochinese Union as long as Ho allowed the French to "temporarily" deploy troops in the north. Ho accepted the terms, but the French soon reneged on their promise. In response, Ho informed the French that the Viet Minh were ready to fight for their independence; he issued a warning that "We may lose ten Vietnamese for every Frenchman, but in the end we will win." His words would prove to be prophetic.

The War's Early Years: 1946–50

The First Indochina War began in late November 1946 when the returning French ordered the Viet Minh forces in the port city of Haiphong to lay down their arms. When the Viet Minh refused, the French navy shelled the city on November 23. During the next few weeks, the well-equipped French forces used their advantage in firepower to push the Viet Minh out of the major cities and into the countryside.

To negate the advantage of French firepower, the Viet Minh strategy focused on conducting a guerrilla war. Vo Nguyen Giap, the military commander of the Viet Minh, chose to use hit-and-run tactics rather than face the power of French guns in open battle. Therefore, the first year of the conflict was characterized by a low-level insurgency in the Tonkin, the northern region of Vietnam. The terrain was perfect for this type of warfare and the Viet Minh used the jungles and mountains to conceal their forces in times of weakness and to ambush the French when the Viet Minh had the advantage. Another major advantage that the Viet Minh had was the support of the people. Few Vietnamese favored

1951

JANUARY	MARCH	MAY	JUNE
January 13 Around 20,000 Viet Minh troops begin a series of attacks on the French De Lattre Line in the Red River delta. The French punish the Viet Minh with overwhelming firepower. About 6,000 Viet Minh die while assaulting the town of Vinh Yen.	**March 23–28** In a second attack on the De Lattre Line, the Viet Minh target the French outpost of Mao Khe near Haiphong. General Giap's forces withdraw after being pounded by French naval fire.	**May 29–June 18** The Viet Minh attempt to break through the De Lattre Line again in the Day River area southeast of Hanoi. The French devastate the Viet Minh attack and some 10,000 troops die.	**June 19** General Giap orders the withdrawal of Viet Minh troops from the Red River delta.

the French return to Vietnam, and the Viet Minh gained popular support because they appealed to all nationalist groups, not just Communists. Ho Chi Minh and the rest of the Viet Minh leadership carefully deemphasized Communist goals and focused on the nationalist objective of independence. The resulting support of the population allowed the Viet Minh to move freely throughout the countryside and rely on the people for supplies. Therefore, they were able to travel quickly and lightly, which gave them a distinct advantage over the French, who depended on mechanized infantry units that moved slowly and were restricted to jungle roads.

Given the fact that the population was largely against the French return, perhaps the biggest mistake the French made was not sending enough troops to Vietnam. The French deployed about 200,000 soldiers—hardly enough to defeat the guerrilla insurgency. The French numbers were easily absorbed by the

The Viet Minh were lightly armed, physically tough, and devoted to the cause. They were tough adversaries, first for the French and then for the Americans.

SEPTEMBER

September 1 French general Jean de Lattre de Tassigny travels to Washington, D.C., to request more aid from the United States.

September 7 The United States signs an agreement with Saigon for direct aid to South Vietnam. The U.S. presence in Saigon is increased as civilian government employees arrive to aid the military personnel.

NOVEMBER

November 16 French forces gather at Hoa Binh to the southwest of Hanoi in an attempt to lure the Viet Minh into another major battle.

November 20 General de Lattre is replaced by General Raoul Salan as head of French forces in Indochina.

DECEMBER

December 9 In response to the French buildup at Hoa Binh, Giap's forces launch a counteroffensive on the French outpost at Tu Vu on the Black River. Giap uses hit-and-run tactics to wear down the French.

Vietnamese jungles and mountains, and they did not have the strength required to pacify the Vietnamese countryside. As a result of this shortage of troops, the French presence was largely limited to the major cities, particularly the Tonkinese cities of Hanoi and Haiphong. On the other hand, the Viet Minh flourished in the countryside, where the bulk of the Vietnamese population lived.

French tactics for eliminating the Viet Minh presence in the countryside focused on the "oil-slick" method, in which enemy-controlled territory was divided up into a grid, and each square in the grid was systematically swept by French forces. The trouble with this tactic was that the Viet Minh rarely stayed in one place, so when the French forces moved in, the Viet Minh could simply abandon the territory and return after the French had gone. Generally, the Viet Minh refused to fight when confronted with a superior force, so the French rarely made contact with them during these sweeps.

The rudimentary road system was a great hindrance to French mobility.

1952

JANUARY	FEBRUARY	JULY	OCTOBER	
January 12 The Viet Minh ambush a river convoy and successfully cut French supply lines along the Black River. Land logistical lines along Route Coloniale 6 are also cut.	**February 22–26** French forces withdraw from Hoa Binh to the safety of the De Lattre Line.	**July 1** President Truman promotes the U.S. legation in Saigon to embassy status.	**October 11** The Viet Minh try to draw the French out from the De Lattre Line by attacking along the Fan Si Pan mountains between the Red and Black rivers.	**October 29** French forces counter Giap's maneuver by launching Operation Lorraine, a strike against Viet Minh supply bases in the northern Viet Bac region.

However, when the Viet Minh had the advantage of numbers or surprise, they hit quickly and melted back into the countryside.

After fighting this type of war for nearly a year, the French decided to launch a major offensive to try to end the war once and for all. On October 7, 1947, they launched Operation Lea, which was designed to capture Ho Chi Minh and destroy all Viet Minh forces in the Viet Bac region to the northeast of Hanoi. The operation began with a parachute drop directly on the Viet Minh positions of Bac Kan, Cho Moi, and Cho Don. This initial assault caught the Viet Minh completely by surprise, so they had little time to react to it. In the subsequent fighting, 7,200 Viet Minh guerrillas were killed, but Ho Chi Minh escaped through gaps in the French line. A month after Operation Lea began, French forces canceled the mission and withdrew from Viet Bac, leaving behind a string of isolated outposts.

The French achieved greater success in the Red River delta when General Marcel Alessandri deployed twenty battalions to sweep the Viet Minh from the highly contested area. Using oil-slick tactics with land-based and

A shortage of personnel plagued French efforts to control the countryside.

···

1953

NOVEMBER

November 4 Dwight D. Eisenhower is elected president of the United States. The United States views the war in Indochina more as a cold war than a colonial war.

November 14–17 The French cancel Operation Lorraine and withdraw to the De Lattre Line. On the return march, Viet Minh forces ambush the French at Chan Muong.

MAY

May 20 General Henri Navarre assumes command of French forces in Indochina.

JULY

July 27 With the signing of the Korean War armistice, Chinese aid to the Viet Minh increases dramatically.

SEPTEMBER

September 30 President Eisenhower approves an extra $385 million in addition to the $400 million in aid already budgeted for the war in Vietnam.

NOVEMBER

November 20 The French initiate Operation Castor and begin to construct a series of fortified outposts around a small airstrip in Dien Bien Phu. Navarre's hope is to draw the Viet Minh into a set-piece battle.

riverine forces, the French temporarily cleared the delta of guerrillas and cut them off from much-needed rice supplies. However, the French were not able to fully pacify the delta and the Viet Minh would continue to harass them there for the rest of the war.

In response to French success in the Red River delta, General Giap focused on French outposts on the Chinese border. He hoped to destroy these outposts in order to open up the border so the Viet Minh could receive supplies from the Chinese Communists, who had just won the Chinese Civil War. In launching their attacks on the border outposts, the Viet Minh focused primarily on Dong Khe and Cao Bang in the far northeastern corner of Tonkin. Prior to these attacks, the French had the momentum in the war. However, in a major change in tactics, Giap attacked Dong Khe head-on and overwhelmed the French defenders with concentrated artillery and human-wave assaults. French paratroopers recaptured the outpost in a

....

French paratroopers were organized into triple-battalioned Groupes Aeroportees. With their inadequate airlift capability, they performed limited operations.

surprise attack, but the Viet Minh later overran them with more artillery and wave assaults.

Sensing a disaster in the making, French commander General Marcel Carpentier decided to abandon the other border defenses. The subsequent retreat turned out to be an even greater fiasco for the French, as Viet Minh forces ambushed the retreating French columns with devastating success. The guerrillas slaughtered the defenders of Cao Bang and That Khe, killing 6,000 of the 10,000 French defenders and capturing a large number of military stores. Other outposts soon fell, and the Viet Minh came to control nearly all of northeastern Vietnam.

Red River Delta

The loss of the Chinese border territory proved to be catastrophic to the French war effort. Without the French outposts to interdict their logistical lines, the Viet Minh began to receive Chinese supplies and weaponry—including machine guns, mortars, antiaircraft guns, and artillery—from across the border. It would not be long before the Viet Minh could match the French in firepower.

1954

JANUARY

January 25–February 18 Foreign ministers from the United States, Britain, France, and the Soviet Union meet in Berlin. They agree to hold a conference in Geneva on Korea and Vietnam in the spring.

MARCH

March 13 The Viet Minh begin their assault on the French garrison at Dien Bien Phu. Giap's forces quickly knock out the airstrip and then begin to tunnel their way toward the French position.

March 20 News of Dien Bien Phu's impending fall begins to circulate. Chairman of the Joint Chiefs of Staff Arthur Radford proposes nuclear strikes against the Viet Minh but later settles for a massive conventional air strike.

March 25 The U.S. National Security Council approves the Radford Plan and the United States makes a provisional decision to fight in Indochina.

APRIL

April 29 After the British fail to support the Radford Plan, President Eisenhower abandons the idea of intervening at Dien Bien Phu.

MAY

May 7 Dien Bien Phu falls to the Viet Minh. The French survivors are marched to prison camps 500 miles away. Nearly half die during the march or in the prison camps.

After the loss of the border outposts, the French once again withdrew to the Red River delta. There they constructed the De Lattre Line, named after the new French commander, General Jean de Lattre de Tassigny. The De Lattre Line was the most notable of the many defensive fortifications, consisting of hundreds of concrete towers and pillboxes that the French built in order to have some presence in the countryside. The problem with these fixed fortifications was that they tied down the French forces and spread them out in vulnerable positions. The Viet Minh responded to the construction of these outposts by massing their forces against isolated locations and attacking one or two each night to slowly drain the French of manpower and patience.

Encouraged by his victories in Viet Bac, General Giap decided to attack the French defenses in the Red River delta head-on in January 1951. The Viet Minh launched their first attack at Vinh Yen, a key road junction in

Steady casualties and a policy of allowing only volunteers to be sent to Indochina affected French manpower.

JULY

May 8 The Geneva Conference begins. Representatives from the United States, Britain, France, Russia, China, Vietnam, Cambodia, and Laos meet to discuss the fate of Southeast Asia.

July 21 The Geneva accords divide Vietnam in half at the seventeenth parallel, with Ho Chi Minh's Communists in the north and Bao Dai's nationalists in the south. The accords also call for an election to be held within two years, which the United States and South Vietnam later oppose.

AUGUST

August 1 One million refugees from North Vietnam, mostly Catholics, flee to the south to escape Communist oppression.

August 8–12 The U.S. National Security Council concludes that the Geneva settlement is a disaster that could lead to Communist domination of Southeast Asia.

SEPTEMBER

September 8 The Southeast Asia Treaty Organization (SEATO) is created for the defense of Southeast Asia against Communist aggression.

OCTOBER

October 1 Following the French departure from Hanoi, Ho Chi Minh returns to the capital after eight years in the jungle to formally take control of North Vietnam.

the northwestern corner of the Red River delta. In this battle, Giap threw 20,000 men against a French garrison of 6,000. At first, the assault seemed to go well for the Viet Minh, but soon they were beaten back by French firepower. Unlike the jungle terrain of Viet Bac, the topography of the Red River delta did not provide the cover and concealment that the Viet Minh had used to destroy the French garrison at Dong Khe. As the Viet Minh troops assaulted over open ground, the French were able to effectively use the full weight of their superior firepower. The result was a stunning Viet Minh defeat in which some 6,000 were killed and over 500 captured.

In spite of this major defeat, Giap continued his assault on the Red River delta. In subsequent attacks at Mao Khe and the Day River, the Viet Minh suffered the same results as in the Vinh Yen assault. The Viet Minh had overestimated their abilities and paid a heavy price, losing 20,000 men in the Red River delta campaign. However, because of their limited presence in Vietnam, the French did not have the manpower to truly capitalize on their victory.

Operation Lorraine

Despite the victory in the Red River delta, French public opinion was turning against the war. High casualty rates and a war that seemed to drag on with no end in sight served to weaken the French public's resolve. In order to avoid a domestic crisis, they needed to win the war quickly. With this in mind, General de Lattre decided to go on the offensive. He hoped to draw the Viet Minh into a set-piece battle where French firepower could again be used with great effect.

De Lattre's chosen battleground was Hoa Binh, a Viet Minh stronghold south of the Red River delta. On

....

The fixed fortifications of the De Lattre Line tied down the French forces and placed them in vulnerable locations.

1955

JANUARY	MARCH	APRIL	MAY	JUNE
January 1 The first direct shipment of military aid to South Vietnam arrives. The United States begins to send military advisers to South Vietnam to train and organize the South Vietnamese army.	**March 28** South Vietnamese prime minister Ngo Dinh Diem launches a major attack against the Binh Xuyen, an organized crime group that threatens his regime.	**April 28** Diem's forces attack the Bin Xuyen again, driving them out of Saigon and into the Mekong delta. Many of the survivors join forces with the Vietcong.	**May 16** The United States signs an agreement with Cambodia to supply direct military aid.	**June 5** Diem's forces begin offensive operations against the Hoa Hao, a religious sect that opposes the Diem government. Most of the Hoa Hao surrender or rally to the government.

November 14, 1951, three parachute battalions dropped on the airstrip at Hoa Binh. Concurrently, a ground force of fifteen infantry battalions, seven artillery battalions, and two armored groups traveled by land to the objective. Two naval assault divisions known as *divisions navales d'assaut*, or *dinassauts*, sailed down the Black River to provide additional security.

Giap responded to the French plan by withdrawing his troops from Hoa Binh in order to gather a larger force. He then attacked the Red River delta with five divisions, sending the 304th and 312th against the French supply routes to Hoa Binh, and using a third division, the 308th, to attack Hoa Binh itself. The other two divisions, the 320th and the 316th, were used to pin down other French forces in the Red River delta. After the Viet Minh cut the French supply routes, General Raoul Salan, the new French commanding general, decided to withdraw from Hoa Binh,

Operation Lorraine failed to capture Giap's supply bases at Yen Bai in Viet Bac. It also failed to divert the Viet Minh away from their Black River position.

JULY

July 7 China announces that it will provide North Vietnam with $200 million in economic aid following a trip to Beijing by Ho Chi Minh.

July 18 Ho Chi Minh travels to Moscow and procures $100 million in aid from the Soviet Union.

July 20 Diem rejects North Vietnamese calls for an election to unify the country on the grounds that it will "prevent the people from expressing themselves freely."

OCTOBER

October 23 Prime Minister Diem becomes head of state after defeating Emperor Bao Dai in a national referendum.

October 26 Diem proclaims the Republic of South Vietnam with himself as president. In the United States, President Eisenhower immediately recognizes the Diem government and pledges support and military aid.

DECEMBER

December 1 The North Vietnamese leadership initiates a radical agrarian reform program in which several thousand "landlords" are executed or sent to prison camps.

but, in order to do so, he first had to open RC6, the only road that led back to Hanoi. Salan sent twelve infantry battalions to remove the Viet Minh who were blocking the road. At this critical point the battle became desperate, with both forces pummeling each other with infantry attacks. Each side lost more than 5,000 men in the battle, but in the end the French defenders of Hoa Binh escaped.

Despite the fact that both the French and Viet Minh took about the same number of casualties at Hoa Binh, the battle was far more damaging for the French. After Hoa Binh, they no longer had the manpower to operate successfully outside of the Red River delta. On the other hand, the Viet Minh were getting stronger. Sensing the French weakness, General Giap sought to draw the French away from their De Lattre Line defenses, where he could destroy them.

On October 11, 1952, Giap began to move three divisions toward the Fan Si Pan mountain

French troops pass a road bridge that has been demolished by the Viet Minh.

1956

JANUARY

January 11 The Diem administration launches a violent assault against suspected Viet Minh. Many of those who are arrested are tortured or killed.

APRIL

April 28 The last French soldiers leave Vietnam, and the French high command in Indochina is officially dissolved.

JULY

July 20 The deadline passes for the election called for by the Geneva accords. Backed by the United States, South Vietnam refuses to participate.

NOVEMBER

November 10–20 Some 6,000 North Vietnamese peasants are killed or deported after the North Vietnamese government sends its 325th Division to put down an open rebellion.

range between the Red and Black rivers, a move that threatened the Tai tribesmen, allies of the French. In a reaction to the move, General Salan initiated Operation Lorraine, an assault on Giap's supply bases at Yen Bai in Viet Bac. Giap responded to the French move, but not in a way that Salan had predicted. Rather than face the French head-on again, Giap sent two battalions to stop the French advance while the rest of his forces remained in the Black River area.

Fearing stiff opposition from the Viet Minh who blocked the road to Yen Bai, General Salan canceled the operation on November 14. The only real fighting took place when the Viet Minh ambushed the retreating French column on the way back to the Red River delta. After some fierce fighting, the French finally broke through the ambush and returned to the safety of the De Lattre Line. Operation Lorraine ended in complete failure. Not only did the French fail to take Giap's supply base at Yen Bai, they also failed to divert the Viet Minh away from their Black River position. By the autumn of 1953, it was becoming clear that the war was settling into a stalemate. Despite their best efforts, the French had not been able to destroy the Viet

Minh. From the standpoint of the French high command, the problem was that the Viet Minh would not engage them in open combat. Nearly every time the French had tried to force the Viet Minh into a set-piece battle, Giap had outmaneuvered them and cut them to pieces with ambushes. The French needed a victory like the one at Vinh Yen, but on an even larger scale. French public opinion was continuing to plummet and it seemed as if French forces were stretched to the breaking point. The French desperately needed a quick end to the war. To accomplish this, General Henri Navarre, the new French commander, came up with a bold plan to draw the Viet Minh into a major set-piece battle that he hoped would end the war once and for all.

Operation Castor and Dien Bien Phu

Navarre's plan, called Operation Castor, was designed to draw the Viet Minh into open battle so that French forces could destroy them with their artillery and air support. He chose an

The Viet Minh surrounded the remote French outpost at Dien Bien Phu and won a decisive victory.

1957

JANUARY	MAY	OCTOBER		DECEMBER
January 24 The Soviet Union proposes that North and South Vietnam be admitted to the UN as two separate countries. The United States rejects the proposal because it is unwilling to recognize North Vietnam.	**May 8–18** President Diem visits Washington, D.C., to seek more U.S. aid. In their meetings, President Eisenhower assures Diem of the United States' commitment to South Vietnam.	**October 1** Communist insurgent activities in South Vietnam begin. Viet Minh guerrillas launch a widespread campaign of terror bombings and assassinations to undermine the Diem government.	**October 22** Thirteen Americans are wounded in three terrorist bombings of MAAG and U.S. Information Service installations in Saigon.	**December 31** By the end of 1957, approximately 400 South Vietnamese officials have been killed by Communist guerrillas.

isolated village called Dien Bien Phu as the place to fight, both because it was near Viet Minh supply routes that ran out of Laos and because it was so remote that he believed that Giap would see it as a tempting target. The valley itself was twelve miles long and eight miles wide, with two small airstrips. The airstrips were crucial to Navarre's plan because Dien Bien Phu was so isolated that the only way the French could be resupplied was by air.

The battle of Dien Bien Phu began on November 20 when two French airborne battle groups parachuted into the valley and cleared out a small contingent of Viet Minh soldiers in the area. On taking the low ground, the paratroopers immediately began to create fortified positions. However, they surrendered the surrounding hills to the Viet Minh because they believed that Giap's troops would be physically unable to get artillery on top of them. Colonel Charles Piroth, an artilleryman and the deputy commander at Dien Bien Phu, confidently boasted, "Firstly, the Viet Minh won't succeed in getting their artillery through to here. Secondly, if they do get here, we'll smash them. Thirdly, even if they manage to

keep on shooting, they will be unable to supply their pieces with enough ammunition to do us any real harm." When General Navarre expressed concern that the high ground around the French position offered abundant concealment for the enemy's heavy guns, Piroth replied, "No Viet Minh cannon will be able to fire three rounds before being destroyed by artillery."

What Piroth did not understand was how badly Giap wanted to strike a decisive blow against the French, and how he would spare no effort in preparing for the battle.

Preparing for the Assault

Giap spent months getting ready for the assault, and much of his energy was devoted to organizing his artillery into the positions the French had written off. The effort was Herculean. The Viet Minh supply line stretched back some 500 miles from Dien Bien Phu to Mu Nam Quan near the Chinese border. Nearly 20,000 coolies and tribesmen labored for three months to rebuild and widen the road so it would accommodate the artillery pieces and the 800 Russian-built Molotova trucks that were

the backbone of the conventional supply system. The last fifty miles of the road had to be built from scratch and were subjected to French aerial surveillance and bombardment. To keep the artillery supplied, columns of porters pushed bicycles that had been modified to carry heavy loads. It was a remarkable triumph of the human will. No one really knows how much artillery the Viet Minh amassed at Dien Bien

JUNE

June 1 The Communists establish a coordinated command structure in the Mekong delta, where thirty-seven armed companies are being formed.

June 25 Cambodia alleges that South Vietnamese troops have invaded and occupied several Cambodian border towns, but the South Vietnamese government denies the allegations.

Phu because Giap never revealed this information. He did, however, praise the logistical buildup, explaining, "Our troops razed hills, cut roads into mountainsides, and opened the road to the artillery in the prescribed time. The secret was well kept thanks to excellent camouflage, and the

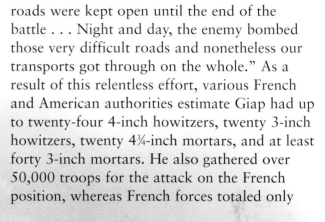

roads were kept open until the end of the battle . . . Night and day, the enemy bombed those very difficult roads and nonetheless our transports got through on the whole." As a result of this relentless effort, various French and American authorities estimate Giap had up to twenty-four 4-inch howitzers, twenty 3-inch howitzers, twenty 4¾-inch mortars, and at least forty 3-inch mortars. He also gathered over 50,000 troops for the attack on the French position, whereas French forces totaled only

Above: At Dien Bien Phu, Giap amassed over 50,000 troops to oppose the 16,000 French isolated there.

Right: Casualties are evacuated from Dien Bien Phu prior to the airfield being closed because of Viet Minh shell fire.

Left: The key to Giap's success at Dien Bien Phu was an army of porters who carried supplies and ammunition through the rugged terrain.

DECEMBER

December 12 The CIA comes into possession of a North Vietnamese directive that calls for armed and overt insurgency.

Viet Minh troops parade through Hanoi after the French withdrawal from Indochina.

....

16,000. In the face of such a disparity, the battle itself was almost a foregone conclusion. Indeed, Bernard Fall, perhaps the most respected scholar of the First Indochina War, wrote, "Essentially, then, the battle of Dien Bien Phu was won along the communications lines."

With everything in readiness, Giap launched his attack on March 13. Almost immediately, the French began to pay a heavy price for Piroth's underestimation of the Viet Minh artillery. Sergeant Kubiak, one of Dien Bien Phu's defenders, recalled, "Shells rained down on us without stopping like a hailstorm on a fall evening. Bunker after bunker, trench after trench, collapsed, burying under them men and weapons." The expert Viet Minh camouflage made it difficult for the French to deliver effective air strikes and counterbattery fire. The Viet Minh artillery soon destroyed the French airstrip, leaving parachute drops as the only method of resupply. By the end of the third day of the bombardment, the French could no longer fight a coordinated battle and were isolated from reinforcements. Belatedly realizing his costly miscalculation of the Viet Minh artillery, Piroth committed suicide.

After further weakening the defenses, Giap began to send infantry wave assaults against the French lines in the first week of April. It soon became obvious that the defenders of Dien Bien Phu could not hold out. Although their firepower took a heavy toll on the Viet Minh, the French were forced to surrender on May 7. The French had 7,000 casualties in the battle, and the rest of the defenders were captured. The Viet Minh also suffered about 25,000 casualties, but the decisive results of the battle made the human cost acceptable to Giap. In the aftermath of Dien Bien Phu, the French had no choice but to recognize that their colonization of Indochina was over.

The Geneva Accords

For the French, defeat at Dien Bien Phu could not have come at a worse time. On the very day that Dien Bien Phu fell, delegates from the former Indochina, France, United States, Russia, China, and Britain met in Geneva, Switzerland, to conduct peace negotiations in order to bring an end to the nine-year-long First Indochina War. Realizing that they had lost all of their bargaining chips in the defeat of Dien Bien Phu, the French decided to relinquish all claims to Vietnam. Cold War politics, however, prevented Ho Chi Minh from gaining control over the entire country. The United States was not about to surrender Vietnam to Communist control. Instead, after two and a half months of peace

1959

MAY

May 1 North Vietnamese leaders decide to take command of the growing insurgency in South Vietnam. North Vietnam establishes the Central Office for South Vietnam (COSVN) to direct the war in the south.

May 1 The Communists begin construction of the Ho Chi Minh Trail, which will become the main infiltration route for Communist guerrillas and material into the south.

May 5 U.S. military personnel are assigned to advise regimental-sized South Vietnamese armed forces.

negotiations, the delegates decided to temporarily divide Vietnam at the seventeenth parallel. The Communist forces of Ho Chi Minh were to take control of the north, whereas the south was placed under the control of U.S.-backed Vietnamese nationalists led by Emperor Bao Dai. According to the agreement, Vietnam was to be divided for a period of two years until elections could be held to peacefully reunify the country under a single government. However, the agreement that brought an end to the First Indochina War only gave birth to a second, and it was not long before the United States became drawn into its own bloody struggle in Vietnam.

....

Defeat at Dien Bien Phu forced the French out of Indochina, but the Geneva accords that ended the war were disappointing to the Viet Minh hopes for nationalism.

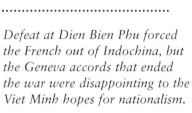

JULY

July 1 About 4,000 Communist guerrillas, originally from the south, are sent from the north to infiltrate South Vietnam.

July 8 Two U.S. military advisers, Major Dale Buis and Sergeant Chester Ovnand, are killed by Communist guerrillas at Bien Hoa, South Vietnam.

AUGUST

August 1 Diem creates a law authorizing the brutal repression of Communists and other dissident factions.

SEPTEMBER

September 26 Vietcong guerrillas ambush South Vietnam's 23rd Division, killing twelve soldiers and capturing their weapons.

The North Vietnamese Military and Strategy

Just as the French appeared to have had an enormous physical advantage at the start of the First Indochina War, an analysis of the resources available to the United States and its South Vietnamese ally compared to those of North Vietnam would clearly indicate a U.S.-South Vietnamese advantage in the next Vietnam War.

Nonetheless, the North Vietnamese ultimately emerged victorious, achieving the objective Ho Chi Minh had announced in 1946 of an independent and unified Vietnam under Communist control. This accomplishment came not from tactical battlefield victories but from a superior North Vietnamese strategy that was carefully planned and expertly executed.

In formulating this strategy, the Communist forces drew on Vietnam's long history of

Left: Ngo Dinh Diem became the first president of the Republic of South Vietnam in October 1955. Right: Nguyen Xuan Phong served in a variety of cabinet-level positions in the Saigon government.

nationalist struggle, and their recent victory over the French had given them practical experience in fighting a larger Western power. Ho Chi Minh had also closely watched Mao Tse-tung's strategy during the Chinese Civil War, which resulted in a Communist victory in 1949. Mao had won that struggle by using a doctrine that emphasized the formation of a broad united front consisting of all elements of the population sharing nationalist goals. He also relied on protracted war to exhaust stronger opponents. Finally, he recognized the close interaction of military and political operations. The North Vietnamese would adapt the Maoist doctrine to their own particular needs, including an increased emphasis on external support that manifested itself through aid from China and Russia, and exploitation of Cambodian and Laotian territory via the Ho Chi Minh Trail.

Vulnerable Population

The Communist movement in South Vietnam benefited greatly from the people's negative reaction to the oppressive and corrupt regime of Ngo Dinh Diem. With a small group of loyal aides and members of his immediate family, Diem had ruled South Vietnam in an autocratic and authoritative fashion since 1954, and many individuals and groups found common cause in their frustration with him. For example, Diem was urban-oriented, which alienated him from the rural population of peasants who were plagued by poverty, poor medical care, and high taxes. The peasants found little relief from officials who were distant and often corrupt. To many South Vietnamese people, the Diem government seemed detached and uncaring.

Land reform was another serious problem. Of all the arable land, 45 percent was owned by just 2 percent of the total population, and the vast majority of landowners were wealthy absentee landlords. Many especially resented

Diem's refusal to redistribute more than 370,000 acres of land owned by the Roman Catholic Church, which highlighted an even bigger problem. Diem was French-educated and Catholic in a country that was 85 percent Buddhist. The overriding goal of everything Diem and his regime did was to preserve their privilege and power. The result was the first prerequisite necessary for an insurgency to occur: a vulnerable and alienated population ready for change.

A United Front

In such fertile ground, a select cohort of Viet Minh soldiers who had remained in the south after the Geneva Conference of 1954 were able to attract thousands of supporters and establish a presence in numerous South Vietnamese villages. In December 1960, the insurgents formed the National Liberation Front (NLF), an organization led by Communists but designed to use the promise of sweeping reforms and genuine independence to unite all those disaffected by Diem. As a southern movement, the NLF allowed North Vietnam to claim it was not violating the Geneva Conference's provision

against sending forces into the south. Nonetheless, the NLF took its orders from the politburo in Hanoi and, recognizing this association, the Diem government gave the NLF the pejorative label Vietcong (VC), or Vietnamese Communists. Through the NLF, the Communists achieved the second prerequisite for an insurgency: a leadership element available to direct the vulnerable population.

Guerrilla War

The classic Maoist formula had three phases. Phase One was the latent and incipient stage in which the insurgents organized themselves and conducted limited subversive activities of a selected, rather than continuous, nature. In this phase, NLF cadres used a combination of agitation and propaganda to arouse people's dislike for the Diem regime. They created special organizations to recognize oppressed groups such as farmers, women, and children. They used songs, skits, and plays to explain their program in terms the people could understand. The results were impressive. In 1958, there were an estimated 12,000 VC in South Vietnam. By 1963, NLF strength had grown to 300,000.

1960

APRIL		AUGUST	NOVEMBER	DECEMBER
April 2 North Vietnam begins universal military conscription. All conscripts are to serve indefinitely.	**April 15** Several distinguished citizens from Saigon send a petition to President Diem demanding that he reform the government. Diem ignores their demands, cracking down on opposition and arresting journalists and intellectuals.	**August 1** U.S. intelligence sources forecast that unless the South Vietnamese government can protect the peasants and win their support soon, Vietcong power will increase dramatically.	**November 11–12** Several South Vietnamese officers launch a coup against Diem but fail in their efforts. Diem has some 50,000 "enemies of the state" arrested. Many are tortured and killed, creating even more opposition to his regime.	**December 20** North Vietnam establishes the National Liberation Front as its Communist political organization for the Vietcong guerrillas in the south.

The NLF also used terror tactics to expand its control. By the end of 1963, it was estimated that the VC had committed more than 13,000 assassinations. Between 1964 and 1967, at least 6,000 more were killed and many more were kidnapped. The victims were the natural community leaders such as hamlet chiefs, schoolteachers, and social workers that the VC eliminated to make the population more vulnerable and to discourage cooperation with the South Vietnamese government. In response, rather than acknowledge an insurgency problem and institute much-needed reforms, Diem merely increased his repressive style of government. The result was that, although cruel, the VC's actions during Phase One were effective in gaining control over much of the population.

Phase Two was the guerrilla warfare phase in which continuous guerrilla warfare and other forms of violence were used to put the government on the defensive. During this phase, the VC sabotaged roads, bridges, power lines,

The National Liberation Front became expert at taking its anti-Diem message to the population and used songs, skits, and plays to reach a popular audience.

1961

JANUARY

January 1 The United States sends a carrier task force to the Gulf of Siam, increasing its presence in Southeast Asia.

January 2 Soviet leader Nikita Khrushchev pledges support for "wars of national liberation" throughout the world, which greatly encourages North Vietnam to escalate its armed struggle to unify Vietnam under Communism.

January 20 John F. Kennedy is inaugurated as the thirty-fifth president of the United States.

MARCH

March 23 A U.S. SC-47 intelligence-gathering plane is shot down over the plain of Jars in Laos. President Kennedy suggests that all U.S. reconnaissance planes should be identified with Laotian markings.

Left: The VC used assassinations and kidnappings to weaken the natural leadership of the South Vietnamese people.

Below: The VC were masters at hit-and-run tactics, using mines and ambushes to harass government forces on terms advantageous to the guerrillas.

1961

APRIL

April 1 Some 400 Vietcong guerrillas attack a village in Kienhoa province and are beaten back by South Vietnamese troops.

April 3 A hundred Vietcong are killed when they launch an attack on Bencat, to the north of Saigon.

MAY

May 11 President Kennedy sends 400 Green Beret special advisers to South Vietnam to train South Vietnamese soldiers in methods of counterinsurgency to fight the Vietcong.

May 12 Vice President Lyndon B. Johnson visits South Vietnam and refers to President Diem as the "Winston Churchill of Asia."

The VC increasingly used terrorist attacks to undermine the legitimacy of the South Vietnamese government.

....

and other vulnerable items of infrastructure. The VC ambushed ARVN forces, and superior VC leadership, tactics, and morale gave them the upper hand over government troops. Before long, security outside major urban areas had disappeared. This was especially true at night, when government security personnel often withdrew into the district and province capitals, leaving the villagers to fend for themselves. All the VC actions during Phase Two further damaged the already-weak legitimacy of the South Vietnamese government and accomplished the final prerequisite necessary for an insurgency: a lack of government control.

Phase Three was a war of movement in which guerrillas were strong enough to directly engage government forces in decisive combat. To prepare for this phase, the North Vietnamese built a capable People's Army of North Vietnam (PAVN) and Vietcong main force units. Once the United States entered the war, however, the North Vietnamese knew that the key to their

success would be avoiding U.S. efforts to draw them into open combat. The North Vietnamese would always fight on their own terms.

This outcome was readily attainable because in guerrilla warfare, movement from one phase

to the next was flexible and opportunistic. The activities that occurred during the earlier phases continued throughout the latter phases. As opportunities presented themselves, the guerrillas could jump from Phase One directly to

---

JUNE

June 9 President Diem requests U.S. aid to expand the South Vietnamese army by 100,000 men. The U.S. agrees to finance an increase of only 30,000 men.

JULY

July 2 North Vietnam captures three members of a clandestine U.S. reconnaissance unit known as the First Observation Group when their C-47 aircraft is shot down.

July 16 South Vietnamese forces launch an attack into Cambodia and kill 170 Communist guerrillas on the plain of Jars.

SEPTEMBER

September 18 About 1,500 Vietcong guerrillas besiege the province capital of Phuoc Vinh, thirty-seven miles to the north of Saigon.

September 21 The U.S. Army's 5th Special Forces Group (Airborne) is activated and takes charge of all Special Forces operations in Vietnam.

Phase Three. Likewise, if the guerrillas did not succeed during Phase Three, it was completely acceptable to revert to an earlier phase. For example, the North Vietnamese practiced this flexibility after their defeat during the Tet Offensive. Having mistakenly attempted to escalate to Phase Three, the North Vietnamese regrouped and returned to Phase Two activities.

Political Integration

Another aspect of the Maoist doctrine used by the North Vietnamese was the well-orchestrated interaction of political and military operations. Especially after the military defeat at Tet, the North Vietnamese maximized the classic "fighting while negotiating" strategy. Closely coordinated military, political, and diplomatic moves were all designed to apply various pressures on the United States and exacerbate differences between the Americans and their South Vietnamese allies. The North Vietnamese showed little interest in substantive negotiations and certainly were not sincere about any real compromise. They rejected U.S. demands for reciprocity and refused any terms that would limit their ability to support the war in the

south while leaving the United States a free hand there. Throughout all negotiations, the North Vietnamese remained keenly aware of U.S. domestic politics, including election cycles. For example, when President Johnson made a focused attempt to reach a negotiated settlement prior to the November 1968 national elections, the North Vietnamese knew they had the upper hand. On October 31, on the basis of informal, unwritten "understandings"—which the North Vietnamese neither officially accepted nor rejected—the United States completely halted

....

The Communists carefully planned their operations and were skilled at integrating military and political activity.

1961

OCTOBER

October 2 Addressing the South Vietnamese National Assembly, President Diem declares that the guerrilla war has grown into "a real war," with the enemy "attacking with regular units fully and completely equipped."

October 5 U.S. intelligence estimates that 80–90 percent of the Vietcong in South Vietnam have been recruited locally and do not depend on supplies from the north.

October 18–24 Top presidential aides Maxwell Taylor and Walt Rostow visit South Vietnam to assess the situation. They inform President Kennedy that "if Vietnam goes, it will be exceedingly difficult to hold Southeast Asia."

October 24 President Kennedy sends additional military advisers and U.S. helicopter units to South Vietnam. Kennedy justifies the United States' expanding military role as a means "to prevent a Communist takeover of Vietnam."

NOVEMBER

November 10 U.S. Special Forces medical specialists are sent to Vietnam to provide assistance to the Montagnard tribes in the central highlands. The Civilian Irregular Defense Group (CIDG), a program of organized paramilitary forces manned by ethnic minorities in South Vietnam, will develop out of this initiative.

November 12 Several U.S. F-101 reconnaissance jets are ordered to engage in monitoring operations against guerrilla units in remote areas of South Vietnam.

its bombing campaign. Having achieved the desired objective, the North Vietnamese then proceeded to ignore the "understandings." Later, when President Nixon tried to negotiate through intermediaries in the summer and fall of 1969, the North Vietnamese merely dragged out the negotiations in order to buy time to recover from Tet and to pressure the United States to make concessions.

Confident that U.S. domestic support would eventually crack, the North Vietnamese knew time was on their side when it came to negotiating. As early as 1962, North Vietnamese premier Pham Van Dong had predicted that "Americans do not like long, inconclusive wars—and this is going to be a long, inconclusive war." Dong was correct, and North Vietnamese negotiating tactics supported his prophecy.

The North Vietnamese were also masterful in manipulating the blue chips held by each side in the negotiating process. For the North Vietnamese, these blue

Testimonies of prisoners released were often of brutal abuse and torture, despite the NLF's denials.

chips were infiltration tactics and prisoners of war, and they guarded them jealously. The United States, on the other hand, was excessively generous in compromising with its blue chip of the bombing campaign. Even when the North Vietnamese were willing to make token concessions, infiltration and bombing were always an unequal trade because of the ease in which bombing could be monitored versus the difficulty in detecting infiltration. The North Vietnamese also recognized prisoners as their major bargaining weapon and tied their release exclusively to a U.S. withdrawal. In nearly every aspect, the North Vietnamese were far superior negotiators than the Americans.

Another component of the political-military dynamic was the existence of a Vietcong infrastructure, or "shadow government," throughout the South Vietnamese countryside. Whenever possible, Communist cadres were secretly assigned positions as village chiefs, police officers, and postal workers, as well as

DECEMBER

December 11 The ferry-carrier USS *Core* arrives in Saigon with a contingent of U.S. helicopters and 400 air and ground crew to operate and maintain them.

December 16 Under Operation Farmgate, U.S. aircrew are authorized by President Kennedy to fly combat missions with South Vietnamese crewmen aboard.

December 20 The *New York Times* reports that 2,000 uniformed U.S. troops are "operating in battle areas with South Vietnamese forces."

December 23 UH-1 Huey helicopters from the 57th Transportation Company (Light Helicopter) and the 8th Transportation Company (Light Helicopter) participate in Operation Chopper, the first airmobile combat action in Vietnam.

December 31 By the end of 1961, U.S. forces in South Vietnam number 3,200.

officers at district, province, and national levels. These officials levied taxes, regulated trade, drafted men, and punished criminals on behalf of the Communist cause. The VC hoped to have a complete government in place when their victory was secure, and these individuals could then step forward and formally claim their offices. When the shadow government did step forward prematurely in anticipation of the popular uprising expected to result from the Tet Offensive, the VC suffered crippling losses to this infrastructure. The shadow government that was years in the making was largely devastated in a matter of weeks. However, this infrastructure was critical to the Communists' control over the most important objective of a guerrilla war: the people.

Military Capability

As the military component of the NLF, the Vietcong were a highly disciplined and potent organization. By 1965, its main forces consisted of forty-seven battalions organized into five regiments with an estimated 80,000 fighters. The VC enjoyed the typical guerrilla strengths of having vast intelligence networks and local knowledge, indigenous characteristics that allowed them to blend in with the local population, the motivation and discipline that comes from near-fanatical devotion to a cause, limited responsibilities that allowed them to focus almost exclusively on insurgency goals, and excellent physical conditioning. The VC were lightly equipped and usually wore black pajamas rather than uniforms. They relied principally on speed, surprise, and deception. One 1966 U.S. Army publication declared that "a more bizarre, eccentric foe than the one in Vietnam is not to be met." Indeed, the VC proved to be a misunderstood and puzzling enemy for the United States.

In addition to the VC, North Vietnamese forces included the People's Army of North Vietnam (PAVN). Vo Nguyen Giap, a onetime history professor, had built a formidable army fighting the French in the First Indochina War. By 1954, when he defeated the French at Dien Bien Phu, Giap commanded about 50,000 soldiers representing the best army of its size in Asia. The PAVN was trained, organized, and equipped along Chinese lines, and originally employed Mao's doctrine and tactics for a rural-based insurgency. As the Vietnam War progressed, Giap would expand and improve on that model.

The PAVN consisted of as many as half a million men with a ready reserve of nearly the same number. Military training emphasized camouflage, small unit tactics, ambushes, night operations, and the use of explosives. Operations were planned and rehearsed in the greatest detail, and units often took up to a month to prepare for a particular action. A considerable amount of training time was also devoted to political education, and political commissars accompanied every unit above the company level.

Like the VC, the PAVN was lightly armed and equipped to maximize mobility. They would also fight only under favorable conditions. The preferred tactic was to attack and withdraw before the enemy could react, rather than attempting to hold captured ground. In 1965, Vietnam scholar Bernard Fall proclaimed the North Vietnamese army to be "one of the best infantry combat forces in the world, capable of incredible feats of endurance and raw courage even against vastly superior firepower and under

1962

JANUARY

January 2 The United States deploys a tactical air group in South Vietnam and furnishes several aircraft for combat and airlift operations.

January 4 The United States and South Vietnam announce a "broad economic and social program aimed at providing every Vietnamese with the means for improving his standard of living."

January 12 The U.S. Air Force launches Operation Ranch Hand, a program designed to defoliate jungle cover and eliminate Vietcong hideouts and ambush areas. U.S. C-123s spray Agent Orange over large areas of the Vietnamese jungle until 1971.

January 13 In Operation Farmgate's first combat mission, T-28 fighter-bombers are called in to support a South Vietnamese outpost under attack.

January 15 During a press conference, reporters ask President Kennedy if any Americans are engaged in fighting in Vietnam. The president responds with a simple no.

Left: A former VC sapper approaches a U.S. Claymore mine on the perimeter of landing zone Stinston.

Below: An NVA platoon leader demonstrating the use of the "S" hook in holding open a path through barbed wire.

FEBRUARY

February 1 The 39th Signal Battalion, a communications unit, is the first U.S. regular ground force to arrive in South Vietnam.

February 4 The first U.S. helicopter is shot down in Vietnam during an assault against the village of Hong My.

February 8 The U.S. Military Assistance Command, Vietnam (MACV) is established. It replaces the Military Assistance Advisory Group (MAAG) created in 1950. From this point on, the conduct of the war is directed by the MACV.

February 11 The first Operation Farmgate casualties occur when nine U.S. and South Vietnamese crew are killed after their SC-47 crashes north of Saigon.

February 27 Two renegade South Vietnamese pilots flying U.S.-made AD-6 fighter planes bomb the presidential palace in Saigon. The attack confirms Diem's belief that his main enemies are within the South Vietnamese military.

the worst physical conditions." These were the exact skills needed to battle the more powerful U.S. military.

Giap was able to combine the resources of the VC as guerrilla fighters and the PAVN as the conventional military force. In so doing, he achieved unity of effort on the part of the North Vietnamese in a manner that stood in stark contrast to the disjointed alliance between the United States and South Vietnam. Giap recognized that the key to North Vietnamese success would be avoiding the U.S. strengths through guerrilla warfare rather than open combat. Therefore, until the 1968 Tet Offensive, the VC served as North Vietnam's principal field force, allowing the PAVN to conserve its strength and wait for an opportune moment to strike. The VC's tasks were to draw U.S. military units away from populated areas in order to allow continued North Vietnamese access to its logistical bases among the local population, to generate U.S. casualties in order

The PAVN served as the Communists' conventional military force while the Vietcong served as the guerrilla fighters.

to erode the will of the United States to continue the war, and to keep the U.S. forces in remote, static positions when possible in order to inhibit their organizational effectiveness. It was the VC who harassed and distracted both the U.S. and South Vietnamese forces so that the PAVN could ultimately fight decisive conventional battles.

When the North Vietnamese finally felt that the right conditions had been achieved, they launched the massive Tet Offensive. The strategy was to lure U.S. troops away from major population centers and inflict high casualties with a series of large-scale diversionary attacks on remote areas. Then the VC would launch coordinated assaults on major South Vietnamese cities to weaken the government and ignite a general uprising among the people. At the same time, North Vietnam would initiate new efforts to open negotiations. Although Tet turned out to be a tactical failure, it showed the flexibility of the Maoist doctrine because, rather than collapsing in defeat, the North Vietnamese merely reverted to Phase Two guerrilla warfare.

Tet also marked a transition point in the war from the VC to the PAVN in terms of the level

1962

MARCH

March 22 President Diem initiates Operation Sunrise, a program in which scattered rural communities in South Vietnam are removed from their ancestral lands and resettled in fortified villages. The program is very unpopular with large sections of the population.

APRIL

April 9 Two U.S. soldiers are killed in a Vietcong ambush while on a combat mission with South Vietnamese troops.

April 15 The first U.S. Marine air units land in Vietnam when fifteen UH-34D combat helicopters arrive from the aircraft carrier USS *Princeton*.

April 22 Twenty-nine U.S. helicopters airlift 600 South Vietnamese troops into battle in the Mekong delta.

of activity. By miscalculating the willingness of the South Vietnamese to join in a general uprising and by coming out to fight in the open, the lightly equipped VC suffered horrendous casualties. Therefore, after Tet, most of the day-to-day combat in Vietnam was undertaken by the PAVN as the VC had been reduced to no more than 20 percent of the Communist fighting force. Nonetheless, the VC continued to serve its strategic purpose, which was always a means rather than an end. The torch, however, had been clearly passed, and the final decision of the Vietnam War would be wrought by the PAVN, and not the VC.

External Support

Critical to the success of North Vietnam's effort was its ability to secure external support. The North Vietnamese and Vietcong received economic, diplomatic, and military aid from both China and the Soviet Union but, as both these Communist "big brothers" were motivated

The North Vietnamese lack of an offensive air capability led them to introduce large-caliber rockets, heavy artillery, and heavy mortars into the south.

MAY

May 1 The Vietcong begin operating in battalion-sized units in central Vietnam.

May 11 Secretary of Defense Robert McNamara travels to Vietnam and reports, "We are winning the war."

May 17 In response to Pathet Lao troop movements near the Thai border, 3,000 U.S. Marines land in Bangkok.

by self-interest, the support was at times inconsistent. Although North Vietnam enjoyed much success in playing the Chinese and Russians against each other to gain the optimal support at any given time, of even greater importance was North Vietnam's ability to exploit territory in the supposedly neutral neighboring countries of Cambodia and Laos.

There, the North Vietnamese built an elaborate communications network, officially called the Truong Son Strategic Supply Route, but more popularly known as the Ho Chi Minh Trail.

In the initial stages of southern insurgency, North Vietnam infiltrated cadres as well as modest logistical shipments through Cambodia and Laos to the Vietcong. By the end of the war, much of the trail was a paved, two-lane highway. Tonnage moving along the trail grew from 89 tons a week in 1963 to over 8,930 tons in 1970. One Vietnamese account claims that 1,586,631 tons of supplies moved down the route between 1965 and 1975. In order to avoid escalating the war, the United States never made a concerted, sustained effort to interdict the trail. It was therefore allowed to become the logistical lifeline for North Vietnamese forces in the south. Furthermore, U.S. reluctance to cross into Cambodia and Laos gave the North Vietnamese a safe haven to flee from search-and-destroy operations and a strategic port at

Although initially caught by surprise, the Americans and South Vietnamese recovered and turned Tet into a tremendous battlefield victory.

1962

JULY

July 23 A declaration of Laotian neutrality is signed in Geneva by the United States and thirteen other nations.

AUGUST

August 1 President Kennedy signs the Foreign Assistance Act of 1962, which calls for "military assistance to countries which are on the rim of the Communist world and under direct attack."

August 5 A U.S. Special Forces camp is set up near the Laotian border to monitor North Vietnamese movements down the Ho Chi Minh Trail.

August 20 The U.S. Army Tactical Mobility Requirements Board, better known as the Howze Board, issues its final report, recommending innovations in the army's pursuit of helicopter air mobility.

Sihanoukville. A major part of the North Vietnamese success was based on this ability to use Cambodia and Laos to their advantage.

A Unified Front

Through the formation of a broad, unified front, close interaction of political and military operations, a commitment to protracted war, and the effective use of external support, the North Vietnamese developed an excellent strategy in the Vietnam War. They exhausted the Americans and effectively eroded the United States' national will. It is a strong testimony to the expertise of the North Vietnamese in executing this strategy that the United States recognized early what was going on, yet still seemed helpless to thwart it. After a visit to Vietnam in 1966, Secretary of Defense Robert McNamara remarked that he saw "no reasonable way to bring the war to an end soon [as the enemy] has adopted a strategy of keeping us busy and waiting us out . . . a strategy of eroding our national will." For North Vietnam, the war was an ongoing, long-term struggle. It was total war in which the entire society was mobilized and willing to win

regardless of how long and at what cost victory would take. In contrast, the United States was fighting a limited war that precluded an open-ended approach and made U.S. resolve a dangerous vulnerability. The North Vietnamese set out to exploit this weakness because, with the Americans gone, they knew they could easily defeat the South Vietnamese alone.

In 1959 Hanoi formed an infiltration network through South Vietnam's vulnerable western flank. The project became the Ho Chi Minh Trail.

The North Vietnamese strategy of exhaustion through guerrilla war was tailor-made for the situation in Vietnam, and their forces executed it expertly.

OCTOBER

October 15 Several media sources report that U.S. helicopter crewmen are initiating combat against the Vietcong, but Washington denies these reports.

October 19 The South Vietnamese launch Operation Morning Star, a major operation to clear Tayninh province of Vietcong. Some 5,000 South Vietnamese troops, carried into battle by U.S. helicopters, kill forty guerrillas in eight days.

NOVEMBER

November 6 The Army Concept Team in Vietnam is established in Saigon to study alternatives for airmobile operations in Vietnam.

Early American Involvement

The United States' involvement in Vietnam was inexorably intertwined with the Cold War. At the end of World War II, the United States began to see the Soviet Union as a major threat to freedom and democracy throughout the world.

The United States adopted a foreign policy of containment to keep the Soviet Union from fostering Communist revolutions all over the globe. U.S. policy makers also embraced the domino theory, which stated that if one country fell to Communism, neighboring nations would soon fall. Given this ideological viewpoint, it is understandable why the United States became involved in Vietnam. American policy makers felt it was necessary to take a stand against Communism wherever possible, and Vietnam became the place to make that stand.

Early U.S.-Vietnamese Relations

Direct U.S. involvement in Vietnam began with the 1954 Geneva peace conference that brought an end to the First Indochina War. However, U.S.-Vietnamese relations stretched back to

Left: The counterinsurgency campaign in Vietnam saw Special Forces soldiers conduct civic action programs. Right: In September 1954, Secretary of State John Foster Dulles signed the Southeast Asia Collective Defense Treaty.

World War II, when President Franklin Roosevelt's administration began providing Ho Chi Minh's Viet Minh with weapons and supplies to fight against Japanese occupation. Roosevelt also supported Ho's bid for Vietnamese independence because he personally believed in the anticolonial ideal of self-determination that stated that all nations are entitled to self-government and autonomy.

Despite the friendly relationship between the United States and Ho Chi Minh during World War II, things began to sour soon after Roosevelt's death in April 1945. Influenced by the developing Cold War ideology, the administration of President Harry S. Truman reevaluated the U.S. stance on Vietnam and soon cut ties with Ho Chi Minh because of his Communist background. Instead, the United States began to aid the French in their bid to restore colonialism in Vietnam.

Aiding the French

At the outbreak of the First Indochina War, the United States began to send weapons, supplies, and money to aid the French war effort. As the war progressed, the United States continually increased the amount of aid, particularly after China fell to Mao's Communist forces in 1949. In the following year, Truman authorized the establishment of the Military Assistance Advisory Group (MAAG), an organization specifically designed to assist in the transfer of U.S. money, weaponry, and supplies to the French. In its first year of existence, the MAAG provided the French with over $100 million in aid. Four years later, in 1954, the MAAG distributed $1 billion in assistance to France. In total, the United States provided over $3 billion in aid to the French cause, which amounted to about 60 percent of the total cost of the war.

Despite the vast amount of monetary and material aid contributed to France during the First Indochina War, the United States stopped short of directly intervening in the conflict. However, during the battle of Dien Bien Phu, U.S. officials considered using air strikes, even nuclear weapons, to save the French forces. In the end, President Dwight D. Eisenhower felt it was best to stay out of the conflict, in part because the United States had only recently signed the armistice to end the Korean War. Eisenhower thought it was unwise to involve the country in another major conflict so soon after one had just ended, particularly one as difficult and dissatisfying as Korea.

Without U.S. military support, the French were consigned to defeat and the Geneva convention of 1954 brought an end to the First Indochina War. Nonetheless, the policy of containment gave the United States a vested interest in the peace settlement. Rather than allowing the Communist forces of Ho Chi Minh to take control all over Vietnam, the United States forced a compromise that divided the country at the seventeenth parallel. The Viet Minh would rule the northern half of the country and U.S.-supported nationalists under Bao Dai would rule the southern half. The Geneva accords also stated that the division of Vietnam was not to be permanent. General elections were to be held in 1956, after which the country was to be unified under the democratically elected government. However, the United States and South Vietnam later rejected the idea of elections because they feared Ho Chi Minh and the Communists would win.

Following the Geneva convention, the United States began working to develop a viable and

1963

JANUARY

January 2 At Ap Bac in the Mekong delta, 2,500 ARVN troops, supported by U.S. helicopters and armored personnel carriers, are defeated by 300 Vietcong guerrillas.

FEBRUARY

February 15 The 11th Air Assault Division is established at Fort Benning, Georgia, as a test division for the airmobile concept.

February 26 U.S. helicopters are ordered to shoot first at enemy soldiers after a U.S. helicopter is downed by Vietcong ground fire on February 24.

independent South Vietnam. The first step the United States took was to create the Southeast Asia Treaty Organization (SEATO), a military alliance organized by Secretary of State John Foster Dulles in 1954 for the purpose of providing a framework to contain Communist expansion in Southeast Asia. SEATO's members included the United States, France, Britain, Australia, New Zealand, the Philippines, Pakistan, and Thailand, and they agreed to provide protection for the nonmember nations of South Vietnam, Laos, and Cambodia. Overall, the alliance proved to be largely ineffective, although some of its members did participate in the Vietnam War.

Ngo Dinh Diem and the ARVN

Following the creation of SEATO, the United States' next task in building up South Vietnam was to choose a new leader for the country. Emperor Bao Dai, the initial leader of South Vietnam, was unpopular among the South

The United States provided a total of $3 billion in aid to the unsuccessful French effort in Indochina.

APRIL

April 11 A hundred U.S. troops from the 25th Infantry Division arrive in Vietnam to reinforce military units and to serve as gunners aboard U.S. helicopters.

April 17 President Diem announces plans for an "Open Arms" program for Vietcong soldiers who are willing to abandon the war against the government. More than 2,500 guerrillas rally to the side of the South Vietnamese government.

MAY

May 8 South Vietnamese forces fire on 20,000 Buddhists gathered in Hue. The South Vietnamese province chief fires on the Buddhists because they are flying the Buddhist flag, which was made illegal under South Vietnamese law. As a result of this incident, Buddhists begin a major protest against Diem that will lead to his eventual downfall.

Vietnamese people because he had served as a puppet to the French and Japanese during their occupations of the country. In his place, the United States chose Ngo Dinh Diem, Bao Dai's prime minister. Diem was an ardent anti-Communist and Roman Catholic who once studied in the United States. With the help of Edward Lansdale, a U.S. Army colonel serving as an officer of the Central Intelligence Agency, Diem used a combination of bribery and force to eliminate all competition except Bao Dai. In an election set up by Lansdale, Diem won by a highly suspect 98 percent of the vote. In Saigon, for example, Diem received one-third more votes than there were registered voters.

As president of the Republic of Vietnam (RVN), Diem embarked on a regime that was autocratic, nepotistic, and corrupt. With his brother Ngo Dinh Nhu serving as his most trusted adviser, Diem ruled South Vietnam with complete authority and established many policies and programs that alienated the population and strengthened government opposition. He persecuted Buddhists, who made up over 85 percent of the population, and had suspected dissidents tortured for being "Communist infiltrators." These policies made international support of Diem difficult, but the United States tolerated his failings in the light of his strong anti-Communist credentials.

After helping to install the Diem government and providing for regional security via SEATO,

Emperor Bao Dai was unpopular with the South Vietnamese people because of his ties to the French. In 1955 Ngo Dinh Diem defeated him to become president.

1963

JUNE

June 7 President Diem's sister-in-law Madam Nhu publicly blames the United States for the ongoing Buddhist crisis, claiming the Buddhists are being manipulated for political reasons.

June 10 MACV commander General Paul Harkins warns U.S. advisers not to associate with Vietnamese units engaged in the suppression of Buddhists.

June 11 Buddhist monk Thich Quang Duc publicly burns himself to death in protest against the Diem government. Despite the Buddhists' call for equality and compassion, Diem refuses to give in to their demands. More Buddhists commit self-immolation over the next few weeks.

June 27 President Kennedy appoints Henry Cabot Lodge as ambassador to Vietnam. Washington begins to seriously question the usefulness of the Diem regime.

the United States' next job was to aid South Vietnam in providing for its national defense. The MAAG had been providing advice and assistance to the Army of the Republic of Vietnam (ARVN) since the end of the First Indochina War. By 1956, the ARVN numbered around 140,000 men supported by about 350 U.S. military advisers. The job of these advisers was to train and organize the ARVN as a conventional fighting force, prepared to repel a North Vietnamese invasion. However, little attention was paid to counterinsurgency, which was the type of warfare that the United States and South Vietnam would later be fighting.

Vietcong

Facing the ARVN was the National Liberation Front (NLF), more commonly referred to by the name of its military component, the Vietcong (VC). The initial VC were natives of South Vietnam who sought to undermine the Diem regime in order to bring about Communist rule in the south. Originally made up of just a few thousand Viet Minh veterans, they created political unrest through assassinations and terrorism. However, as

the war progressed, their number and their operations grew dramatically.

By 1959, the Vietcong began to pose a more serious threat to South Vietnam. It became clear to Ho Chi Minh that the south would not fall on its own, so the north began to support actively the southern insurgents. In order to

Initially, U.S. advisers provided the Army of the Republic of Vietnam with help only in planning, training, and the logistical aspects of operations.

speed up the collapse of the Diem regime, the Communists established the Central Office for South Vietnam (COSVN) to run the war in

---

JULY

July 4 General Tran Van Don contacts the CIA and informs them that several South Vietnamese officers are planning a coup against Diem.

July 30 ARVN forces engage the Vietcong in a four-hour battle in the Camau peninsula. About ninety guerrillas and three South Vietnamese soldiers are killed.

In 1956, about 350 U.S. military advisers were helping to train the ARVN. By the time President Kennedy was assassinated in 1963, the number had grown to 16,700.

the south. The north also authorized the construction of the Ho Chi Minh Trail, a series of infiltration routes that ran through Laos and Cambodia and into South Vietnam. By utilizing the Ho Chi Minh Trail, members of the Vietcong and People's Army of North Vietnam (PAVN)—also called the North Vietnamese Army (NVA)—were able to bypass the heavily defended demilitarized zone (DMZ) and supply the insurgency with hundreds of thousands of soldiers, as well as supplies and weapons.

Despite the increased amount of aid from North Vietnam to the VC in the south, the Eisenhower administration refused to commit combat troops to South Vietnam. The United States did increase the number of advisers, but they were supposed to remain in noncombat roles. For now, the ARVN would have to fight the Vietcong alone. Unfortunately for the ARVN, the North Vietnamese and Vietcong began to filter more troops, supplies, and weapons into South Vietnam. With this increased troop strength, the impact of the Vietcong became more devastating. For example, between 1959 and 1961, the number of assassinations rose from 1,200

1963

AUGUST

August 20 President Diem accepts a proposal by General Tran Van Don that calls for a declaration of martial law to end the Buddhist crisis, but Tran's real purpose for the declaration is to consolidate power in order to launch a coup against Diem.

August 21 Government soldiers raid several Buddhist temples throughout South Vietnam, arresting, beating, and murdering Buddhist monks. Thousands of protests break out in the streets of South Vietnam's cities. The United States denounces the attacks and calls for a peaceful resolution.

August 22 President Diem's foreign minister and ambassador to the United States resign their posts in protest of Diem's actions.

August 24 A U.S. State Department message advises Ambassador Lodge to give President Diem one final chance to resolve the Buddhist crisis. However, Lodge is also told to give his approval for a coup if Diem refuses to make the proper reforms.

a year to more than 4,000. Vietcong military operations became more aggressive as well. In January 1960, a group of about 200 Vietcong soldiers attacked an ARVN headquarters at Trang Sup and completely overran it. The ARVN began to feel the impact of COSVN and the Ho Chi Minh Trail. The tide of the war was turning in favor of the Communists, but it would not be long before the United States dramatically increased its presence in South Vietnam as well.

Kennedy's War

The election of John F. Kennedy as president of the United States in November 1960 marked a turning point in U.S.–South Vietnamese relations. In his inaugural address, Kennedy had warned the world that the United States would "pay any price, bear any burden, meet any hardship, support any friend, oppose any foe, in order to assure the survival and the success of liberty." With the South Vietnamese democracy under increased pressure, Kennedy had a ready target for his promise. Under his leadership, the United States significantly increased its military and economic support to South Vietnam.

With General Paul Harkins as commander of the U.S. Military Assistance Command, Vietnam (MACV), American advisers finally began to go into combat with ARVN units.

August 26 Lodge meets Diem for the first time. Lodge tells Diem to dismiss his brother Nhu, the main perpetrator of Buddhist oppression, and to make reforms to end the Buddhist crisis. However, Diem refuses to even discuss the issue.

August 27 Cambodia severs diplomatic relations with South Vietnam in response to the ongoing Buddhist crisis.

August 29 French President Charles de Gaulle proposes that North and South Vietnam become a unified neutral state. He offers French aid in helping Vietnam rid itself of U.S. and Communist influences.

August 30 Two U.S. pilots are killed when their helicopter is shot down by Vietcong guerrillas in the Tay Ninh area near Saigon.

A U.S. Special Forces heavy weapons adviser instructs CIDG personnel on how to arm and set the fuse on a 3¼-inch mortar round.

....

In October 1961, Kennedy sent his Special Military Adviser, General Maxwell Taylor, and the Deputy Special Assistant to the President for National Security Affairs, Walt Rostow, on a fact-finding mission to South Vietnam. On their return, Taylor and Rostow told Kennedy that South Vietnam was on the verge of collapse, and they recommended that Kennedy send combat troops to Vietnam. Rather than doing this, the president decided to send in several thousand more advisers. When Kennedy took office in January 1961, the U.S. advisory presence was 650 strong. At the time of his assassination in November 1963, there were 16,700 advisers in South Vietnam.

As part of his plan to increase aid to South Vietnam and expand the number of advisers, Kennedy upgraded and replaced the MAAG with the U.S. Military Assistance Command, Vietnam (MACV) in February 1962. General Paul Harkins was named its first commander, and the MACV served as the headquarters of the U.S. military effort in South Vietnam until the American withdrawal in March 1973.

Under the command of General Harkins, U.S. advisers finally started to go into combat with ARVN units. Prior to this development, advisers were limited to the planning, training, and logistical aspects of operations, but now they would be going out into the field to fight beside their South Vietnamese allies. The U.S. Special Forces, the renowned Green Berets, were also becoming heavily involved in the war. Their main task was to organize the Civilian Irregular Defense Group (CIDG), a program to turn the Montagnards—aboriginal peoples from Vietnam's central highlands—into partisan groups to fight against the Vietcong.

Despite increasing amounts of aid and greater numbers of advisers, the situation in South Vietnam continued to deteriorate in the early 1960s. Kennedy's actions forestalled the collapse of the South Vietnamese government, but actually did little to win the war. In fact, the United States and South Vietnam had no real plan for victory. The ARVN's poor showing in the January 1963 battle of Ap Bac caused much consternation about South Vietnam's ability to defend itself. The only positive measure of success was that the South Vietnamese government continued to survive, but even this glimmer of hope was not without challenge.

The Buddhist Crisis

In June 1963, Buddhist monks in South Vietnam started to lead mass protests against

1963

SEPTEMBER

September 2 In a television interview, President Kennedy describes Diem as "out of touch with the people."

September 11 Approximately ninety soldiers and civilians are killed in an ARVN attack on the Vietcong at Dam Doi in the Camau peninsula.

OCTOBER

October 2 President Kennedy informs Ambassador Lodge that "no initiative should now be taken to give any encouragement to a coup," but that Lodge should "identify and build contacts with possible leadership as and when it appears."

the oppressive nature of the Diem regime and the war itself. In a few cases, the monks publicly burned themselves to death in protest. During this Buddhist crisis, the U.S. government begged Diem to make reforms and end the oppression of the Buddhists, but he refused to listen. Eventually, the United States saw Diem's actions as harmful to the war effort and decided that something had to be done. When U.S. ambassador Henry Cabot Lodge was approached by South Vietnamese generals who wanted to overthrow Diem, Lodge tacitly agreed to the plan. On November 1, 1963, ARVN soldiers staged a coup that forced Diem and his brother Nhu from the presidential palace. After only one day in hiding, the two were captured by ARVN officers and later executed in the back of an armored personnel carrier.

The Diem assassination shook Kennedy's confidence in the situation in Vietnam. During his administration, the United States had dramatically increased the numbers of advisers, money, and material to South Vietnam, but the security situation was weakening as the Vietcong were growing stronger. Now the country was in a political crisis as well. Shortly after the assassination of Diem, Kennedy ordered an investigative committee to "complete a very profound review of how we got into this country, what we thought we were doing, and what we now think we can do. I even want to think about whether or not we should be there." Sadly, Kennedy never received the report, as he was assassinated in Dallas on November 23, 1963.

Johnson and the Gulf of Tonkin Incident
Following Kennedy's assassination, Lyndon B. Johnson became president and found himself faced with a dangerously deteriorating situation in Vietnam. After Diem's assassination, the government of South Vietnam underwent a rapid string of coups, perpetually undermining any sense of government stability. Taking advantage of the chaos, Vietcong forces began to step up their operations, and more ARVN soldiers and U.S. advisers were soon killed in the field. Johnson's advisers, notably Secretary

....

Some Buddhist monks burned themselves in protest at what they considered the oppressive nature of the Diem regime.

October 5 The rebellious South Vietnamese generals, led by Duong Van "Big" Minh, ask for U.S. assurances that aid to South Vietnam will continue if Diem is removed. The CIA responds by giving them the go-ahead to proceed.

October 7 Madame Nhu travels to the United States for a visit, but the Kennedy administration refuses to acknowledge or extend diplomatic courtesies to her.

October 28 Ambassador Lodge informs President Kennedy that a coup is imminent.

October 29 The Kennedy administration begins to second-guess its decision for supporting the coup and requests that Ambassador Lodge has it postponed or canceled. Lodge responds by informing the White House that calling off the coup would betray the conspirators to Diem.

The Brinks Hotel was bombed on Christmas Eve in 1964 by Vietcong terrorists, who detonated a bomb in a garage underneath the hotel.

of Defense Robert McNamara, warned him that South Vietnam was on the verge of collapse and called for direct military involvement.

At first, Johnson refused even to consider deeper military commitment. However, his attitude began to change on August 2, 1964, when North Vietnamese patrol boats attacked an American destroyer, the USS *Maddox*, in the

Gulf of Tonkin. Minimal damage was done and the United States did not strike back, but the navy responded by adding another destroyer, the USS *C. Turner Joy*, to the patrols. Two days later, on August 4, the destroyers reported another attack, but the occurrence of this assault is questionable. No visual contact was made with the enemy patrol boats and the radar feedback may have simply been weather interference. Regardless of whether the second attack occurred or not, President Johnson decided to use the incident to escalate U.S. involvement in Vietnam, asking Congress for a resolution empowering him to "take all necessary measures to repel an armed attack against the forces of the United States and to prevent further aggression." On August 7, Congress approved the Gulf of Tonkin Resolution, giving Johnson carte blanche to escalate U.S. involvement in Vietnam.

To the North Vietnamese, the Gulf of Tonkin Resolution was equivalent to an American declaration of war. In the days after the United States passed the resolution, Vietcong operations began specifically targeting U.S. bases and personnel. On November 1, 1964, Vietcong

forces attacked the American air base at Bien Hoa, killing five U.S. servicemen and wounding seventy-five others. Despite the attack, President Johnson refused to respond, primarily because his presidential election campaign was in full swing and he did not want to appear to be escalating the conflict in Vietnam.

After winning the election, Johnson felt free to act more aggressively against the Vietcong. The U.S. began to bomb North Vietnamese supply routes in Laos, and Johnson considered expanding the role of the military in Vietnam even further. He got his chance on February 7, 1965, when the Vietcong attacked the U.S. air

On August 2, 1964, North Vietnamese patrol boats attacked the USS Maddox *in the Gulf of Tonkin. A more questionable incident occurred two days later.*

1963

NOVEMBER

November 1 At 1:30 p.m., rebellious South Vietnamese troops initiate the coup by surrounding the presidential palace and seizing the Saigon police headquarters. Diem tries to talk the generals out of the coup, but he is unsuccessful. That night, he and his brother flee to the Cho Lon district of Saigon.

November 2 At 3:00 a.m., one of Diem's aides betrays him to the rebellious generals. At 6:00 a.m., Diem contacts the generals and begins to negotiate his surrender. A U.S. M113 armored personnel carrier is sent to pick him and Nhu up from a Catholic church in Cho Lon, but Diem and Nhu are murdered on the way back.

November 4 The United States officially recognizes the provisional government of South Vietnam. Former vice president Nguyen Ngoc Tho becomes premier, but the real power is in the hands of the Revolutionary Military Committee led by General Duong Van Minh.

November 15 A U.S. military public relations officer announces that the American presence in South Vietnam will be reduced by 1,000 troops by December 3.

base at Pleiku, killing nine servicemen and wounding 126 others. As a result, General William Westmoreland, the new commander of the MACV, asked Johnson for a small contingent of marines to defend the new bases. Despite some contention from cabinet members, Johnson approved the request, and the first U.S. combat troops came ashore at Da Nang on March 8, 1965. Thousands more would follow.

Right: In October 1961, President Kennedy sent helicopter units to South Vietnam to transport and direct South Vietnamese troops in battle.

Below: The U.S. conducted numerous riverine operations to interdict Communist infiltration efforts in the Mekong delta and other shallow waterways

DECEMBER

November 19 Cambodian leader Prince Sihanouk declares that he is rejecting all U.S. military and economic aid and claims that the CIA is trying to encourage a coup against him.

November 22 President Kennedy is assassinated in Dallas, Texas, and Lyndon B. Johnson is sworn in as president.

November 24 President Johnson announces that the United States will continue its military and economic aid to South Vietnam.

November 25 South Vietnamese government officials announce that 150 Vietcong guerrillas have been killed in heavy fighting in the Mekong delta.

December 24 In response to mounting pressure for further U.S. involvement in Vietnam, President Johnson reportedly tells the Joint Chiefs of Staff to "just let me get elected and then you can have your war."

December 31 By the end of the year, Johnson has increased the U.S. presence in South Vietnam to 16,300 advisers.

The U.S. Strategy and Military

When the United States dropped atomic bombs on Hiroshima and Nagasaki at the end of World War II, the nature of warfare changed. After this impressive display of power, the United States enjoyed a monopoly on the atomic bomb.

The United States made this huge firepower the centerpiece of its defense strategy. They had the monopoly until 1949. In 1954, Secretary of State John Foster Dulles articulated the notion of "massive retaliation" by which nuclear weapons would be considered a viable option to Soviet challenges of U.S. interests. But as the Soviets improved their own nuclear capability, the United States had to adjust its strategy. During his campaign for the presidency

Left: After using atomic bombs on Hiroshima and Nagasaki, the United States developed a post–World War II strategy that relied heavily on nuclear weapons. Right: Army Chief of Staff General Maxwell Taylor.

in 1960, John F. Kennedy had committed himself to replacing President Dwight D. Eisenhower's strategy of massive retaliation with one of "flexible response." This new strategy relied on more of a balance between nuclear and conventional forces. To help with the effort, Kennedy tapped General Maxwell Taylor, who had served as Army Chief of Staff during the previous administration but had become disenchanted with Eisenhower's heavy reliance on nuclear weapons. However, as tensions escalated in Vietnam, the United States was much more

focused on a conventional war in Europe than a guerrilla war in Asia.

Limited War

As an alternative to massive retaliation, flexible response was designed to harness the United States' military power in a way that closely tied it to the achievement of political objectives. Only the minimum amount of force necessary to achieve the political aim would be employed. The objective was not to destroy the opponent but to persuade him to modify his behavior commensurate to the interests of the United States. This construct is known as "limited war" and the United States had been forced to come to grips with its peculiar difficulties during the Korean War. As opposed to the "total war" of World War II, where the United States fought for unconditional surrender, mobilized all aspects of its society, and unleashed its most destructive military weapons, in Korea the United States had fought a limited war in which

The limited war nature of the Korean War was a frustrating experience for the United States. The Vietnam War would prove to be more of the same.

1964

JANUARY

January 4 Ten ARVN battalions move into the Ben Suc region, forty miles west of Saigon, in order to attack a Vietcong force of two battalions. The battle ends when the South Vietnamese units are unable to locate the guerrillas. Two Vietcong and fifteen ARVN soldiers are killed.

January 5 Some 500 Vietcong escape an ARVN encircling movement in Long An province, twenty-five miles to the southwest of Saigon. During the battle, fifteen U.S. planes are damaged by ground fire and nine ARVN are killed.

January 6 General Duong Van Minh, leader of the Military Revolutionary Council, makes a move to centralize government and military power under the control of General Tran Van Don, General Le Van Kim, and himself.

January 13 The Vietcong attack and destroy two strategic hamlets in Pleiku province.

January 14 Lieutenant General William Westmoreland is named deputy to General Paul Harkins in the MACV.

January 14 Vietcong forces down a U.S. B-26 bomber, killing two Americans.

it did not bring to bear the full weight of its technological and firepower advantage. Likewise, in Vietnam, the limited war theory would significantly reduce U.S. military options. Especially fearful of the war escalating into a general conflict directly involving the Soviet Union and China, the U.S. civilian leadership would reject military proposals to invade enemy sanctuaries in Laos, Cambodia, and North Vietnam; severely restrict bombing targets; and deny MACV commander General William Westmoreland's request for additional troops after the Tet Offensive. Instead, the limited war theory argued that "gradual escalation" would, through a steady increase in the level of military pressure, coerce the enemy into compliance. Unfortunately for the Americans, the limited war theory proved to be much more appropriate as an academic rather than a military concept. As history has often shown, when one side is fighting a limited war, as the Americans were, and the other is fighting a total war, as the

On November 22, 1963, President John F. Kennedy was assassinated. Lyndon Johnson was sworn in as president. The inauguration ceremony was on January 20, 1965.

January 17 Five U.S. helicopter crewmen are killed while supporting ARVN units in the Mekong delta.

January 18 The USS *Providence* arrives in Saigon on a goodwill mission to show U.S. commitment to South Vietnam.

January 23 A Vietcong battalion makes a predawn attack on the district capital of Nam Can in the Camau peninsula. This is the first sizable guerrilla action in the southern Mekong delta since November 1962.

January 30 General Minh is removed from power in a bloodless coup by General Nguyen Khanh, who now becomes the leader of South Vietnam.

January 31 General Khanh takes command of the Military Revolutionary Council and moves to gain U.S. support for his government.

North Vietnamese were, the odds are stacked against the side fighting the limited war.

As the limited war theory would suggest, the United States approached the Vietnam War in a cautious manner. Its entry into Vietnam and its prosecution of the war were incremental processes. While Eisenhower was president, the United States began to deploy military advisers to Vietnam, but little progress was made. By the time Eisenhower was preparing to leave office, the situation had worsened. In the short time between Kennedy's election and inauguration, Communist leaders in North Vietnam established the National Liberation Front to fight against Ngo Dinh Diem's anti-Communist regime in South Vietnam. Soviet premier Nikita Khrushchev had also promised Soviet support for unconventional "wars of national liberation." Kennedy responded to these developments by urging the Department of Defense to accelerate its efforts to deal with unconventional war. Kennedy had a personal interest in counterinsurgency warfare and prodded the army to expand the curriculum and the size of the classes of its Special Warfare School at Fort Bragg, North Carolina. Within a

year, the Special Forces grew from 1,500 to 9,000 men. President Kennedy personally authorized them to wear the distinctive headgear that gave birth to their popular name. The Green Berets were highly trained in counterguerrilla warfare, as well as nation-building activities such as community organization, preventive medicine, and construction. It was Kennedy's plan that the Special Forces could share their expertise with the defenders of vulnerable countries such as South Vietnam in a way that would preclude the commitment of large combat forces.

Attrition Warfare

By 1965 it had become obvious that such a limited effort was not working. Insurgents controlled half the population and more than half the territory of South Vietnam. Empowered by the Gulf of Tonkin Resolution, President Johnson authorized Operation Rolling Thunder

General William Westmoreland took command of the MACV in June 1964 and emphasized attrition warfare and search-and-destroy operations.

1964

FEBRUARY

February 1 President Johnson pledges full support for the new South Vietnamese regime.

February 1 One U.S. soldier is killed and five others are injured when a bomb explodes in Saigon.

February 3 A Vietcong squad attacks the U.S. military compound at Kontum. One U.S. soldier is killed.

February 4 Vietcong forces attack the ARVN battalion headquarters at Hau My and kill twenty South Vietnamese troops.

February 4 Vietcong forces ambush an ARVN battalion in Thua Thien province and kill eight South Vietnamese troops.

February 5–6 In Saigon, 1,000 students protest for the return of General Duong Van Minh to power.

February 6 A force of 500 Vietcong cross into South Vietnam from Cambodia and take control of three strategic hamlets at Ben Cau. After a fourteen-hour battle, the Vietcong are forced to retreat, taking more than 100 casualties. ARVN forces take 115 casualties in recapturing the hamlets.

February 7 A bomb explodes in a Saigon bar, killing five Vietnamese and wounding twenty-six Americans.

in February, a gradual escalation of bombing designed to halt the North Vietnamese advance to the south. The first ground combat troops arrived in March, and by the end of the year 180,000 American troops were in Vietnam.

With these new forces, Westmoreland first sought to stem the momentum of Communist advances into the countryside and to secure urban areas. Then he planned to launch large-scale search-and-destroy operations to cripple the Communist regular forces and break the NLF's hold on the countryside. Once this was accomplished, Westmoreland felt the South Vietnamese government could solidify its position and pacify its territory. The North Vietnamese would then be forced to negotiate an acceptable peace.

Westmoreland's model, with the consent of President Johnson, was a marked departure from President Kennedy's vision of a "whole new kind of strategy" for unconventional war. Rather than empowering and assisting the South Vietnamese in defending themselves, the U.S. military would come to dominate the war effort. In the process, the army would fall back on its traditional strategy to annihilate the enemy as it

had in World War II. However, in Vietnam the restraints of limited war would serve to harness the total application of U.S. military might and, instead of the sought-for strategy of annihilation, the United States ended up waging a less effective war of attrition.

The goal of attrition warfare was to steadily erode the enemy's ability to fight. Therefore, a key measure of the war's progress inevitably became enemy casualty figures, and the body count was used to determine the success or failure of the U.S. effort. This system was plagued by a series of inaccuracies, including duplications, exaggerations, and falsifications. More importantly, however, was the reality that a strategy of attrition played right into the hands of the North Vietnamese tactic of exhaustion. In guerrilla warfare, it is the guerrillas who usually choose the time, place, type, and duration of the battle. Therefore, the initiative lay with the North Vietnamese. By 1966, the Joint Chiefs of Staff had realized that "The enemy, by the type of action he adopts, has the predominant share in determining enemy attrition rates." However, Westmoreland relentlessly pursued the crossover point, where

U.S. Army and Navy units conducted several joint operations in the Rung Sat Special Zone, which surrounded the Saigon River.

February 8 General Khanh announces the formation of a new government, with himself as premier and General Duong Van Minh as chief of state.

February 9 Terrorism continues to threaten the city of Saigon as a bomb explodes at a stadium. Two Americans are killed and twenty are wounded.

February 13 General Khanh visits ARVN troops in the field over the lunar new year and announces that all servicemen up to the rank of corporal will receive a 20 percent pay increase.

February 16 Another terrorist bomb explodes in Saigon, killing three Americans and fifty civilians at a theater.

February 19 Vietcong forces shoot down two South Vietnamese planes, killing one U.S. adviser.

February 19 Prince Sihanouk of Cambodia proposes that the United States, South Vietnam, Thailand, and Cambodia sign an agreement to recognize Cambodia's neutrality.

Throughout the Vietnam War, the naval facility at China Lake, California, was part of the American effort to bring technology to the battlefield.

....

the United States and South Vietnam could kill more soldiers than the North Vietnamese could replace through infiltration and recruitment. This elusive point was never reached, even when U.S. troop strength in Vietnam reached its peak in 1968 at nearly 543,400 men. About 200,000 North Vietnamese came of draft age each year, and the enemy proved more than capable of matching each gradual U.S. escalation.

Therefore, Westmoreland was never able to muster the size of force he needed to destroy the PAVN and control the countryside. The U.S. strategy of attrition proved to be a failure.

In another instance of the U.S. failure to understand fully the nature of guerrilla warfare, the United States sought technological solutions to thwart the North Vietnamese effort. Secretary of Defense Robert McNamara was especially enamored with the promise of technology to bring battlefield victory. Again, however, the ability of the guerrillas to dictate the nature of the fighting made it difficult to bring to bear U.S. technology. Finding strategic bombing targets proved much more difficult against a largely agrarian society than it did against the industrialized enemies of World War II. A variety of "James Bond–type" gadgets designed to locate the enemy through heat, light, and sound refraction, as well as one electronic device that could detect human urine, all proved of limited use in the guerrilla war environment. Work even began on a "McNamara Line" of minefields and sensors to serve as a barrier across the demilitarized zone. All these initiatives proved problematic.

More promising were developments in the use of helicopters. First introduced in the Korean War but largely limited to casualty evacuation, helicopters would become the linchpin of American mobility in Vietnam and essential to the search-and-destroy tactic. In June 1965, McNamara activated the 1st Cavalry Division (Airmobile) and in November the division killed some 3,000 North Vietnamese regulars at the battle of Ia Drang while suffering 300 "friendly" deaths. The helicopter appeared to be the solution to bringing the war to the North Vietnamese in a way that would allow American firepower to be employed decisively. Instead, however, the North Vietnamese merely adjusted their tactics by reverting to guerrilla warfare, largely negating the U.S. advantage. However, Ia Drang confirmed Westmoreland's belief that the search-and-destroy strategy was the key to breaking the enemy's will to resist.

Although the search-and-destroy operations and the strategy of attrition failed to show results, the Americans largely ignored an alternative strategy of pacification designed to combine military, economic, and social programs to help the South Vietnamese

1964

FEBRUARY

February 24 Vietcong forces ambush an ARVN convoy near Saigon in an unusual daytime ambush.

February 25 Vietcong forces blow up a train on the Saigon–Da Nang railway, killing eleven.

February 26 About 3,000 ARVN troops encircle and engage 600 Vietcong in an eight-hour battle in Long Dinh. Despite their numerical superiority, the South Vietnamese forces allow most of the Vietcong to escape.

MARCH

March 1 The USS *Craig*, a destroyer, begins the DeSoto mission, an intelligence-gathering operation in the Gulf of Tonkin.

March 3 General U Thant, Secretary-General of the United Nations, states that the UN will play no role in the Vietnam conflict.

March 7 In sporadic fighting, ARVN forces report killing more than fifty Vietcong and capturing thirty-three.

government control its rural population. This lack of emphasis on pacification was another indication that the United States failed to understand the nature of guerrilla warfare, where the true center of gravity is the people. Pacification was designed to win the hearts and minds of the population, but instead the dominant thought in the minds of many was "Grab 'em by the throat, and their hearts and minds will follow." After General Creighton Abrams replaced Westmoreland as commander of the MACV, Abrams approved a new "one-war concept" designed to achieve cooperation and unity of effort between large combat operations and pacification, but by 1969 this effort was too little, too late.

U.S. Forces

With the decision to seek victory on the conventional battlefield, the United States deployed a powerful force to Vietnam. Throughout the duration of the conflict, more

Helicopters were first used in the Korean War, primarily in a casualty evacuation role. In Vietnam they would become essential to American combat tactical mobility.

March 9 Vietcong forces attack the Mekong delta city of Can Tho and destroy several fuel tanks.

March 17 The U.S. National Security Council recommends that President Johnson should initiate a bombing campaign against North Vietnam. However, Johnson approves only the planning phase of the bombing campaign.

March 24 South Vietnamese forces claim two major victories in Kien Phong and Hau Nghia provinces.

March 29 Secretary of Defense McNamara announces that the United States will provide South Vietnam with an additional $50 million each year for the expansion of its military.

March 30 General Khanh initiates a "clear and hold" training program for ARVN forces so that the Vietcong "will not come right back."

than 3 million men and 10,000 women were drafted or volunteered for service and were sent to Vietnam. By the end of 1965, the year ground troops were first committed, some 180,000 U.S. troops had arrived.

At first, these soldiers occupied and secured key positions and existing U.S. installations, and began the logistical buildup necessary to receive additional troops. At the time, South Vietnam had only one major port, Saigon, and it was already crowded with shipping. The country's sole railway was not operating, and the VC made using the roads hazardous. Despite these difficulties, the logistical buildup proceeded at a remarkable pace. Ports, warehouses, cantonments, airfields, maintenance facilities, and communications networks were all built so that by 1967 the logistical system could handle an average of 758,930 tons of supplies each month. The demands were staggering. Troops consumed 10 million field rations each month, fired 71,430 tons of ammunition, and burned 80 million gallons of petroleum products. The individual U.S. soldier in Vietnam received almost $36 of support each day, more than twice the amount per soldier in the Pacific during World War II. As a result of the buildup, by 1967 the United States had nearly 500,000 soldiers—roughly 50 percent of its tactical air power and 30 percent of its naval strength—in Vietnam.

Vietnam was divided into four tactical zones. The U.S. Marine Corps had primary responsibility for the I Corps Tactical Zone, composed of the five northernmost provinces in South Vietnam. The U.S. Army operated mainly in the II and III Corps Tactical Zones, which included the central highlands, adjacent coastal regions, and the area around Saigon. South Vietnamese troops were mainly responsible for the delta region of the IV Corps Tactical Zone. The U.S. Air Force provided tactical air support, airlift, and bombing, and the U.S. Navy provided air support from its carrier-based planes. Air operations against North Vietnam and naval patrols of the U.S. Seventh Fleet were

The 1st Cavalry Division (Airmobile) was activated in June 1965 and deployed to Vietnam to apply the new airmobility doctrine in battle.

1964

APRIL

April 8 ARVN forces capture a Vietcong base in Kontum province and kill seventy-five guerrillas.

April 9–12 ARVN forces engage Vietcong guerrillas in four days of heavy fighting in the Mekong delta. Fifty ARVN soldiers are killed, along with four Americans.

April 11–15 In a five-day battle at Kien Long, 134 miles south of Saigon, South Vietnamese forces kill 175 Vietcong guerrillas but lose 125 of their own men in the process.

April 25 President Johnson announces that General William Westmoreland will replace General Paul Harkins as commander of the MACV.

MAY

May 2 A bomb sinks the USS *Card* at its dock in Saigon. No one is injured and the ship is eventually raised and repaired.

May 3 A hundred ARVN rangers are killed by a Vietcong ambush twenty-five miles northwest of Saigon.

May 5 The United States announces that it is freezing all of North Vietnam's assets and is barring any financial and commercial transactions between the two countries.

controlled by the Commander-in-Chief, Pacific rather than the MACV. In addition to supporting the air war, the navy established the River Patrol Force (RPF) in 1965 to curtail enemy infiltration and logistics along the Mekong River delta's major arteries and the Long Tau shipping channel. Although effective at interdiction operations, the RPF remained vulnerable to enemy attacks from the shore until early in 1967, when the Mobile Riverine Force was established. This organization included the U.S. Army's 2nd Brigade, 9th Infantry Division as a ground component that facilitated search-and-destroy operations launched from bases ashore and afloat.

The Home Front and Other Complications

With all these forces in place, the United States finally got its long-awaited chance to engage the North Vietnamese in open warfare in January 1968. During the Tet holiday, the VC and PAVN forces launched a massive series of attacks

The first American combat troops came ashore at Da Nang on March 8, 1965. By the end of 1965, there were 184,300 ground troops in Vietnam.

JUNE

June 1 As the guerrilla war in South Vietnam continues, North Vietnamese regulars begin pouring down the Ho Chi Minh Trail and into South Vietnam. President Johnson approves Operation Plan 34A, a CIA-run covert operation that uses South Vietnamese commandos in speedboats to harass radar sites along the North Vietnamese coast.

June 6 Lieutenant Charles Klusmann becomes the first U.S. aviator taken prisoner in the Southeast Asian conflict when his Crusader is shot down over eastern Laos. Held captive by the Pathet Lao for eighty-six days, Klusmann eventually escapes.

JULY

July 1 General Maxwell D. Taylor, chairman of the Joint Chiefs of Staff, is appointed as the new U.S. ambassador to South Vietnam.

July 3 The Vietcong overrun an ARVN camp at Kontum, killing forty-four South Vietnamese soldiers and wounding twenty-two.

July 4 The Vietcong attack a U.S. Special Forces training camp at Polei Krong, killing forty-one South Vietnamese and wounding two Americans.

May 9 A terrorist is arrested while trying to plant a bomb under a bridge in Saigon where Defense Secretary McNamara's car is to pass on May 12.

May 15 Premier Khanh signs a decree that abolishes restrictions on Buddhists and grants them the same rights as Roman Catholics.

across the length of South Vietnam. Initially caught off guard, the U.S. and South Vietnamese forces soon rallied and used superior mobility and firepower to hand the North Vietnamese a stunning defeat. However, this tactical U.S. victory turned into a strategic defeat, as Tet marked a turning point for domestic support for the war. Having been led to believe that there was a light at the end of the tunnel, many Americans, including influential newsmen like Walter Cronkite, saw the large-scale North Vietnamese offensive as evidence that the army and the Johnson administration had deceived the public over the war's progress. Furthermore, the North Vietnamese showed their inherent flexibility and, as after Ia Drang, gave up more immediate attempts at a war of movement in favor of renewed guerrilla tactics. Many North Vietnamese troops retreated to sanctuaries across the border to rebuild their strength.

A major flaw in the United States' strategy was its failure to isolate the North Vietnamese

An ARVN soldier with a sentry dog prior to being airlifted by H-21 helicopters of the 57th Trans Company.

from their sources of external support. U.S. naval operations directed against infiltrations of personnel and logistics along the South Vietnamese coast were largely successful but merely motivated the North Vietnamese to seek safer and more reliable means of supply. By 1967 the North Vietnamese had developed a highly effective Ho Chi Minh Trail network, which wound its way through supposedly neutral Cambodia and Laos into South Vietnam and made use of the Cambodian port at Sihanoukville. Although search-and-destroy operations such as the 1967 Operation Junction City targeted enemy activity near the border, the United States, in an effort not to widen the war, largely refused to pursue the enemy into its cross-border sanctuaries.

After a coup against Cambodian prince Norodom Sihanouk by pro-U.S. members of the Cambodian armed forces, President Nixon authorized a limited incursion into Cambodia in April 1970. Even then, Nixon limited the depth of penetration by U.S. troops to twenty miles and specified that all U.S. forces be out of Cambodia within sixty days. In all, 31,000 U.S. and 43,000 South Vietnamese troops entered the

1964

JULY

July 6 A group of 500 Vietcong attacks a U.S. Special Forces training camp at Nam Dong in the central highlands. After five hours of heavy combat, the guerrillas retreat, but the fighting results in the deaths of fifty-seven ARVN, two U.S. advisers, one Australian adviser, and forty Vietcong.

July 9 Communist China pledges to defend North Vietnam if it is invaded by the United States.

July 11–12 In the largest battle to date, 1,000 Vietcong guerrillas attack the South Vietnamese outpost of Chuong Thien and ambush a relief column. About 200 ARVN soldiers are killed or wounded.

July 14 The United States declares that North Vietnamese regular army officers are commanding Vietcong units in the central highlands. General Khanh calls the North Vietnamese participation in the war an "invasion of NVA forces."

July 31 In the Gulf of Tonkin, as part of Operation Plan 34A, South Vietnamese commandos raid two North Vietnamese military bases located on islands just off the coast. The operation takes place in the vicinity of the destroyer USS *Maddox*.

AUGUST

August 2 Three North Vietnamese patrol boats attack the USS *Maddox* in the Gulf of Tonkin, ten miles off the coast of North Vietnam, causing minor damage to the *Maddox*. In response, U.S. naval planes attack the boats, sinking one.

August 3 The USS *Maddox* and C. *Turner Joy* continue to monitor operations in the Gulf of Tonkin. Crew members believe they have come under torpedo attack from North Vietnamese patrol boats, but no evidence can be found. Both destroyers open fire on apparent targets, but there are no actual sightings of any attacking boats.

Above: U.S. naval forces battled waterborne infiltration of Communist supplies along Vietnam's long and vulnerable coast and inland waterways.

Right: A crewman aboard a 7th Fleet ship watches as the guns of the USS New Jersey *fire at targets in Vietnam.*

August 4 Although doubts arise over whether or not the *Maddox* and the *C. Turner Joy* were attacked, the U.S. Joint Chiefs of Staff recommends that President Johnson retaliate with air strikes against the North Vietnamese. Johnson calls for a limited bombing mission against North Vietnam.

August 5 Naval fighter-bombers from the carriers USS *Ticonderoga* and *Constellation* fly sixty-four sorties against North Vietnamese targets along the Gulf of Tonkin. They strike twenty-five North Vietnamese boats in attacks on naval bases. They also strike an oil storage depot at Phuc Loi. Two U.S. planes are damaged and two others are shot down.

August 5 Opinion polls show that 85 percent of Americans are in favor of President Johnson's decision to bomb North Vietnam.

August 6 Secretary of Defense McNamara and Secretary of State Dean Rusk appear before a joint congressional committee on foreign affairs to ask for a resolution authorizing the president to take action against North Vietnam.

August 7 The U.S. Senate (by a vote of 82–2) and House of Representatives (by a vote of 416–0) approve Public Law 88408, which comes to be known as the Tonkin Gulf Resolution. This allows the president "to take all necessary measures" against North Vietnam.

August 21–29 In Saigon, college students and Buddhist activists initiate a series of large-scale protests against the Khanh regime. Khanh resigns as sole leader of South Vietnam but continues to rule with two other generals, Duong Van Minh and Tran Thien Khiem.

August 26 President Johnson is nominated at the Democratic National Convention to run for president. During his campaign he declares, "We are not about to send U.S. boys nine or ten thousand miles away from home to do what Asian boys ought to be doing for themselves."

Cambodian promontories of the Parrot's Beak and the Fishhook. The operation was highly successful, with more than 11,000 enemy killed compared to 337 U.S. casualties. Of particular significance was the fact that the port of Sihanoukville was denied to the enemy.

As with Tet, however, a U.S. tactical battlefield victory caused adverse strategic ramifications on the home front. The incursion into Cambodia reinvigorated the antiwar movement in the United States, especially since it appeared to be an escalation of the war after President Nixon had announced his withdrawal plan. A protest against the Cambodian operation at Kent State University in Ohio turned to tragedy on May 4 when National Guardsmen fired into a crowd, killing four. The deaths at Kent State unleashed further protests across the country, including one at Jackson State College in Mississippi, which resulted in two students being killed. The Vietnam War was tearing the United States apart.

The Impact on the Army

As the U.S. strategy in Vietnam continued to defy solution, the army also began to show signs of strain. Although the army in Vietnam was the best clothed, equipped, and prepared force the United States had ever sent to war, the frustrations of guerrilla warfare, combined with declining support at home, soon took their toll. Reflecting a desire to provide a certain level of comfort and security for the soldiers, as well as showing a misunderstanding of the importance of controlling the countryside, all U.S. divisions and separate brigades had fortified base camps. Units would deploy from these fixed locations,

....

Soldiers fire on North Vietamese army positions while in close contact of the "Y" bridge.

1964

SEPTEMBER

September 12 Two U.S. destroyers, USS *Edwards* and *Morton*, resume monitoring patrols in the Gulf of Tonkin.

September 13 Two South Vietnamese generals attempt to overthrow the Khanh regime, but fail.

September 18–19 Destroyers USS *Edwards* and *Morton* are pursued at night by four unidentified vessels. The U.S. ships fire several shells at them, but never actually see the enemy boats.

September 18 Vietcong artillery sinks two South Vietnamese landing craft in the Mekong River.

September 30 Students from the University of California at Berkeley protest about the United States' deepening involvement in the conflict. However, polls show that most Americans support President Johnson's decisions.

OCTOBER

October 7 Five U.S. servicemen are killed when Vietcong fire brings down their helicopter.

October 14 Soviet leader Nikita Khrushchev is ousted from power. The new Russian leader, Leonid Brezhnev, will increase military aid to North Vietnam.

October 14–November 12 The U.S. Army conducts the final exercise of Air Assault II to test the airmobile concept.

NOVEMBER

November 1 Vietcong forces attack the U.S. air base at Bien Hoa, twelve miles north of Saigon. Five Americans and two South Vietnamese are killed but, because the presidential election is only two days away, President Johnson decides against any retaliatory action at this time.

often relying on helicopters for transportation, firepower, and logistical support. Eventually, especially after the U.S. withdrawal plan was announced, a certain "fire-base psychosis" set in, which further surrendered initiative and control of the countryside to the North Vietnamese. Personnel turbulence, resulting from the one-year tour of duty, adversely affected unit cohesion and meant leaders did not stay in units long enough to have a lasting influence. The result was the famous quip that the United States "wasn't in Vietnam ten years; it was in Vietnam one year, ten times."

Compounding this problem was the fact that the draft produced a mixed bag of soldiers, especially after Project 100,000 forced the services to fill their ranks with a certain percentage of men of lower intelligence ratings. Additional problems that reflected the challenges to traditional authority occurring on the home front manifested themselves in desertions, racial problems, drug use, and "fraggings" (attempts to kill or injure unpopular leaders). This breakdown in discipline and crisis in leadership, as well as frustration with the difficulties posed by guerrilla warfare,

contributed to civilian atrocities such as at My Lai in March 1968. By the time the war entered its "Vietnamization" period, the U.S. Army in Vietnam was a shell of its former self.

In Vietnam, the United States experienced much frustration in translating battlefield tactical victories into anything of larger strategic consequence. In an often-told anecdote, Colonel Harry Summers, author of a critical analysis of the U.S. strategy in Vietnam called *On Strategy: The Vietnam War in Context* (1981), describes a conversation he had with a North Vietnamese colonel after the war. "You know," boasted Summers, "you never defeated us on the battlefield." Undaunted, his North Vietnamese counterpart replied, "That may be so, but it is also irrelevant." The United States simply fought the Vietnam War with a strategy ill suited to the realities of guerrilla warfare. By the time it realized its mistake, the initiative had shifted to the North Vietnamese, and support for the war effort at home had evaporated.

A soldier shows signs of strain and fatigue after completing a grueling mission.

The Forgotten Ally

If the United States failed to effectively incorporate its South Vietnamese ally into the war effort, history has also failed to recognize the contributions of the South Vietnamese and their point of view. This is an overview of their story.

O f the thousands of books written on the Vietnam War since the fall of Saigon in 1975, most focus on the U.S. experience with only a nominal treatment of the Army of the Republic of Vietnam (ARVN). However, it is impossible to fully understand why the Vietnam War ended with a Communist victory without taking the ARVN's role into account.

To ensure the long-term security of South Vietnam, the United States had to help develop

Left: A demonstration commemorating the seventh anniversary of the Vietnamese Airborne.
Right: In the First Indochina War, Frenchmen made up less than 25 percent of the total French force.

a South Vietnamese army and government that could eventually stand without the help of the U.S. military. Yet two short years after the last U.S. soldiers withdrew from Vietnam, the country collapsed under a massive North Vietnamese onslaught. Why? The simple answer is to point to such South Vietnamese deficiencies as corruption and poor performance in the field. Although these reasons were a major part of the problem, they do not tell the whole story. A negative image with the South Vietnamese population, faulty U.S. strategy, improper training, and chronic underutilization all hamstrung the ARVN and played a major role in South Vietnam's collapse.

In the late nineteenth century, French colonial officials created several indigenous units such as the Tonkin Fusiliers and the Annamese Rifles to augment their forces in the colony. By doing so, they hoped to give the indigenous population a role within the French colonial system and create a pro-French contingent among the Vietnamese. Prior to the First Indochina War, the French kept tight control over their indigenous army, but that relationship began to change as the war against the Viet Minh escalated.

Vietnamese National Army

Needing manpower and a larger base of support among the Vietnamese, the French chose to grant a greater amount of independence to Vietnam. Therefore, in June 1948 the French named Emperor Bao Dai head of an "independent" Vietnam within the French Union. The agreement also called for the creation of a Vietnamese National Army (VNA). This association with French colonialism ensured that the VNA would never enjoy the popular support of the Vietnamese people. To the Vietnamese, who followed a long tradition of resistance to foreign intrusion, the VNA appeared to be a puppet army that upheld

colonial rule. It would never overcome this perception of illegitimacy with the population.

Following the defeat of the French in the First Indochina War, the United States sent advisers to Vietnam to build the remnants of the VNA into a South Vietnamese national army capable of protecting South Vietnam's sovereignty against Communist aggression. The task of creating and shaping this Army of the Republic of Vietnam fell to the Military Assistance Advisory Group (MAAG). By 1956, the ARVN numbered around 140,000 men, with 350 MAAG advisers dedicated to training and organizing it as a conventional fighting force that would be prepared to repel a North Vietnamese invasion across the demilitarized zone (DMZ).

However, the South Vietnamese Joint General Staff (JGS) disagreed with the focus of the MAAG's training program and argued that the ARVN should be trained to fight against a Communist insurgency. But because the United States was paying for the ARVN's training and arms, the South Vietnamese JGS's suggestion was ignored. Therefore, the MAAG set out to create a seven-infantry division army that was trained and armed to fight a conventional war.

French and Vietnamese troops on patrol in the northern highlands of Vietnam, 1951.

1965

JANUARY

January 4 In his State of the Union address, President Johnson reaffirms the United States' commitment to South Vietnam. He also states that U.S. security "is tied to the peace of Asia."

January 27 Two of President Johnson's aides, National Security Adviser Bundy and Secretary of Defense McNamara, tell the president that the United States' limited military involvement in Vietnam is not succeeding and that it has reached a "fork in the road" in Vietnam.

FEBRUARY

February 7 Vietcong guerrillas attack the U.S. military compound at Pleiku in the central highlands, killing eight Americans, wounding 126, and destroying several aircraft.

February 7–8 President Johnson approves Operation Flaming Dart, a limited bombing campaign against a North Vietnamese army camp near Dong Hoi by U.S. Navy jets from the aircraft carrier USS *Ranger*.

February 8 A follow-up air raid by South Vietnamese planes targets a North Vietnamese military communications center at Vinh Linh.

February 10 Vietcong guerrillas blow up the U.S. military barracks at Qui Nhon by planting explosives under the building. Twenty-three U.S. personnel are killed in the attack.

The ARVN was more of a political army than a popular one and experienced great difficulty in fighting the growing insurgency.

In training the ARVN, the United States sought to create an army in its own image that could employ sheer firepower to destroy the enemy. The goal of this style of warfare was to find the enemy, fix him in a position, and finish him with superior firepower. This, in turn, would slowly erode the enemy's capability to fight. However, by focusing on this type of attrition warfare, the United States failed to train the ARVN in proper counterinsurgency techniques.

By modeling the ARVN on its own army, the United States made the ARVN wholly dependent on the United States for survival. To fight the U.S. style of warfare, the ARVN needed access to expensive weaponry and equipment, as well a very complex logistical system to keep the troops supplied. Therefore, the U.S. plan for the ARVN created a major problem. For a developing nation like South Vietnam, maintaining and funding the logistical, armament, and training needs of such a military was impossible. To keep the ARVN running,

February 11 Some 160 U.S. and South Vietnamese planes carry out a series of retaliatory attacks against North Vietnamese barracks and staging areas at Chan Hoa and Cha Ple in North Vietnam. In the fighting, three U.S. Navy planes are downed.

February 13 President Johnson decides to commit U.S. aircraft to a sustained bombing campaign against North Vietnam. Named Operation Rolling Thunder, the campaign will continue until October 1968.

February 19–25 Another military coup in Saigon leads to the removal of General Khanh from power. A new military/civilian government, led by Dr. Phan Huy Quat, is installed.

February 22 General Westmoreland cables Washington and asks for two battalions of U.S. marines to protect the air base at Da Nang. Ambassador Taylor disagrees with the plan, but President Johnson approves Westmoreland's request.

South Vietnam would need continuous access to U.S. logistical and economic support. This dependence on the United States meant that the ARVN would never be a self-sufficient army.

Another problem created by the conventional structure of the ARVN was the need for manpower. Few South Vietnamese were willing to volunteer to fight for their country because their first priority lay with their families, and military service often conflicted with this family loyalty. In such a predominantly agrarian society as South Vietnam, most military-age men were needed in the rice fields. Therefore, the South Vietnamese government had to rely on a draft system to fill the ranks of the ARVN. Drafting men into the army served to further alienate the army from South Vietnamese society. The system also created a major desertion problem because many soldiers often went home during the harvest season to help their families bring in the rice crop. Like the VNA before it, the ARVN would never be an army of the people.

In April 1956, the U.S. Military Assistance Advisory Group took over the training of the South Vietnamese armed forces.

1965

MARCH

March 2 Operation Rolling Thunder begins as more than 100 U.S. fighter-bombers attack targets in North Vietnam. Scheduled to last eight weeks, Rolling Thunder will instead continue for more than three years.

March 2 The first U.S. air strikes on the Ho Chi Minh Trail occur.

March 6 The White House confirms that President Johnson is sending 3,500 marines to Vietnam to be deployed in security work at the Da Nang air base.

March 8 The first U.S. combat troops arrive in Vietnam as 3,500 marines land at Red Beach Two, north of Da Nang. They join 23,000 U.S. advisers already in Vietnam.

March 9 President Johnson authorizes the use of napalm by U.S. planes bombing targets in North Vietnam.

March 9 U.S. marines continue to come ashore at Da Nang. Among the arrivals is the first American tank, an M48A3 of the 3rd Marine Tank Battalion. The marines receive scattered fire from Vietcong hidden onshore, but no one is injured.

Instead of being a popular army, the ARVN became a political one, especially among its officer corps. President Diem was unpopular among the South Vietnamese people, so the survival of the regime was fully reliant on the backing of the ARVN to protect him. Diem filled the upper echelons of the ARVN officer corps with men he felt he could trust rather than those who had earned their positions based on merit. In order to reach the highest positions in Diem's army, one had to be unswervingly loyal, have ties to Diem's family or region, and share Diem's Roman Catholicism. Amid these stringent qualifications, those who were well qualified to lead an army but lacked the right background were passed over for promotion.

Political concerns also affected ARVN efforts in the field. Because the army was necessary for the survival of the regime, Diem cautioned his most trusted commanders not to take casualties from the Vietcong. He needed his loyal commanders to keep their divisions at full strength in case disloyal officers tried to overthrow him in a military coup. Therefore, during the Diem years, several ARVN units failed to press their advantage in the face of the

Vietcong because they feared reprimands from Diem for taking too many casualties. This subordination of military action to political purpose set a dangerous precedent that would come back to haunt the ARVN in future engagements.

Early Operations

In spite of these problems, during the first years of its existence, the ARVN did well against such weak and outnumbered opponents as the small and poorly armed religious sects that stood in opposition to Diem's regime. However, the ARVN's task became far more difficult when North Vietnam decided to support the southern-based Vietcong in a guerrilla campaign to destroy Diem's government. As the VC grew stronger and gained control of large sections of the South Vietnamese countryside, the ARVN found itself in a far more tenuous position. Although early engagements against the VC resulted in victories, the tide of the war began to turn against the ARVN when the insurgency gained momentum.

The situation got far worse in February 1962 when South Vietnamese pilots attacked

Major General Matthew K. Diechelmann pays a visit to President Ngo Dinh Diem during Air Force Day ceremonies.

the presidential palace in an attempt to kill President Diem. As a result of the attack, Diem became so paranoid that he moved his best and most loyal ARVN units to areas near Saigon, where they could quickly come to his defense in the event of a coup. The problem with this strategy was that it left much of the countryside, particularly the Mekong delta, vulnerable to the

---

March 10 Marines at Da Nang report making their first contact with Vietcong guerrillas.

March 11 U.S. and South Vietnamese naval forces begin Operation Market Time, designed to disrupt North Vietnamese sea routes carrying supplies to the south. The operation is highly successful in cutting off coastal supply lines and results in the North Vietnamese shifting focus to the more difficult land route along the Ho Chi Minh Trail.

March 12 The last of the 3,500 U.S. marines arrive at Da Nang.

March 24 The first "teach-in" is conducted at the University of Michigan. Around 200 faculty take part in the protest by holding special antiwar seminars. Regular classes are canceled and replaced by rallies and speeches.

March 25 President Johnson makes an offer of "economic and social cooperation" to North Vietnam if peace can be restored, but his offer is ignored.

March 26 Forty U.S. planes bomb radar sites in North Vietnam as Operation Rolling Thunder continues.

Vietcong. American advisers begged Diem "to take the war to the enemy," but Diem was afraid that taking casualties or possibly losing battles would undermine the ability of his trusted ARVN units to protect him. He also feared victories might create popular generals who could become political threats to his regime. As a result of these concerns, the ARVN became a dysfunctional army in the face of a growing insurgency.

Because of Diem's political worries, the ARVN was cautious and conservative as it met the VC in its first major battle on January 2, 1963, at Ap Bac. No other engagement better illustrates the havoc Diem's political fears exacted on the ARVN than this battle. In late December 1962, 200 troops from the Vietcong 514th Battalion set up a defensive position along a canal in Dinh Tuong province, next to the village of Ap Bac. Once intelligence reports confirmed the location of the Vietcong, units from the ARVN 7th Infantry Division, which

President Diem pressured his most trusted commanders to avoid combat casualties in order to husband their personnel strength to defend against a coup.

April 1 President Johnson authorizes sending two more marine battalions and 20,000 logistical personnel to Vietnam. He also authorizes the marines to conduct patrols to root out the Vietcong in the countryside.

April 5–7 After three days of heavy fighting in the Mekong delta, six Americans and 276 Vietcong are killed.

April 10–14 The U.S. marines already stationed at Da Nang are reinforced with the arrival of the 2nd Battalion, 3rd Marines.

April 15 Planes from the USS *Midway*, *Coral Sea*, and *Yorktown* conduct the first carrier-launched attacks against Vietcong positions northwest of Saigon.

included several helicopters, tanks, and a number of U.S. advisers, were deployed to dispatch the guerrillas. However, when the ARVN forces arrived at Ap Bac they discovered they were up against not just the enemy along the canal but an entire Vietcong infantry battalion. From beginning to end, Ap Bac was a total disaster. In the face of withering enemy fire, the ARVN units were hesitant and indecisive, largely because of Diem's orders to

Above: The Communists made expert use of sanctuaries in Cambodia. To avoid widening the war, the United States made only limited excursions across the border, such as in May 1970, when this prisoner was captured.

Right: Helicopters transport marines during an operation south of Da Nang.

April 17 Some 15,000 students gather in Washington, D.C., to protest the United States' bombing campaign.

April 19–20 Several U.S. military and civilian leaders meet in Honolulu to discuss the possibility of doubling the presence of U.S. forces in Vietnam. The meeting concludes with the agreement to send a further 40,000 troops to South Vietnam.

April 24 President Johnson announces that U.S. troops in Vietnam will now receive combat pay.

not take casualties that would weaken the division's ability to protect his regime. In light of this "no-casualty order," the battle quickly spun out of control. Five U.S. helicopters were shot down, and sixty-five ARVN and three Americans were killed. The Vietcong, on the other hand, slipped away during the night with only light casualties. In the wake of the battle, the U.S. media severely criticized the ARVN and the U.S. effort in South Vietnam. As bad as Ap Bac was, things would only get worse as the year progressed.

The End of the Diem Regime

The next challenge the ARVN and the South Vietnamese government faced was one of President Diem's own making. Beginning in June 1963, Buddhist monks started to protest against the religious persecution of the Roman Catholic Diem government. Soon, thousands of South Vietnamese were protesting in the streets of Saigon. As the conflict came to a head, U.S. military advisers began to think that South Vietnam would have a much better chance of survival without Diem. They began to hold secret discussions with top ARVN generals about initiating a coup. Both the generals and the Americans decided that the situation had deteriorated too far and the crisis had to be resolved before it undermined the stability of

Protests against the unpopular Diem government reached new heights in June 1963, when the Buddhist crisis led thousands of protesters to take to the streets.

1965

MAY

May 3 Army troops numbering 3,500 from the 173rd Airborne Brigade begin arriving in Vietnam from Okinawa to provide security for the major air base at Bien Hoa and the airfield at Vung Tau.

May 11 Vietcong forces overrun ARVN troops in a battle in Phuoc Long province north of Saigon.

May 13–18 The United States suspends air raids on North Vietnam to give them a chance to call for peace negotiations. However, the North Vietnamese ignore the peace overtures, using the pause to repair air defenses and send more troops into the south.

May 19 U.S. bombing raids over North Vietnam resume.

JUNE

June 2 U.S. marines and ARVN troops mount a joint operation against Vietcong forces in the area near the Chu Lai air base.

June 18 Air Marshal Nguyen Cao Ky takes power in South Vietnam with Nguyen Van Thieu as his chief of state. They represent the tenth government in the last twenty months.

the entire country. With Communist insurgents constantly working to destroy South Vietnam, the Americans and the generals decided that Diem was no longer worth the risk. On November 1, 1963, ARVN forces launched a military coup that led to the downfall and assassination of Diem.

As a result of the ARVN's role in the removal of Diem, South Vietnamese officers became more heavily involved in politics and distracted from the war effort. U.S. leadership hoped that the new military government would lead to a more effective prosecution of the war, but this was not to be. Infighting among the ARVN generals led to political factions and a number of subsequent coups that undermined the stability of the South Vietnamese government and the effectiveness of the ARVN. The situation became so unstable that Secretary of Defense McNamara described the state of affairs in South Vietnam as "very disturbing," noting that, "Current trends, unless reversed in the

Troops of the 21st Vietnamese Marine Infantry Division at Ha Tien airstrip, waiting to board helicopters to take them into action.

next two to three months, will lead to neutralization at best and more likely to a Communist-controlled state. The new government is the greatest source of concern. It is indecisive and drifting." As the situation in South Vietnam continued to deteriorate,

the United States saw no other recourse than to become more deeply involved in the war. Soon, U.S. forces would come to the forefront of the conflict and the ARVN would be pushed aside.

Enter the United States
As U.S. combat troops began pouring into South Vietnam in March 1965, most members of the ARVN leadership welcomed their arrival. However, some South Vietnamese observers

JULY

July 1 The 1st Cavalry Division (Airmobile) is officially activated as the army's first airmobile division.

July 1 Vietcong guerrillas mortar the U.S. air base at Da Nang, destroying three U.S. aircraft.

July 8 Ambassador Taylor resigns and is replaced by Henry Cabot Lodge as the U.S. ambassador to South Vietnam.

July 9 President Johnson announces that the government is considering a limited military mobilization in response to the deepening crisis.

July 28 President Johnson states that he will send an additional forty-four combat battalions to Vietnam to increase the U.S. presence to 125,000 troops. To fill the rising manpower needs, Johnson will increase the draft calls to 35,000 per month.

July 30 The U.S. Coast Guard establishes Commander Task Force 115 (Market Time). Five coastal surveillance centers are set up at Da Nang, Qui Nhon, Nha Trang, Vung Tau, and An Thoi.

were unhappy with the turn of events. On seeing the large role that the United States was taking in the conflict, one ARVN soldier said, "Why are we fighting at all? If the Americans are going to make all the decisions . . . what kind of country will we be left with?"

Moreover, the fact that U.S. soldiers were in South Vietnam meant that the goal of creating a self-sufficient South Vietnam had failed. Soon, U.S. troops assumed most of the combat responsibilities of the war and most of the ARVN forces were relegated to security operations. While U.S. commitment deepened, ARVN forces found themselves shunted aside and ignored. The early U.S. policy of creating an independent and effective ARVN had now become subordinate to using American muscle to win the war for the South Vietnamese.

Despite the influx of U.S. combat troops in 1965, the situation continued to deteriorate in South Vietnam as the Vietcong made more gains. Since the assassination of Diem, the North Vietnamese had taken advantage of the South Vietnamese government's weakness and sent hundreds of thousands of soldiers to the south. Communist troop numbers rose from 30,000 in November 1953 to 212,000 in July 1965. Facing such large numbers of enemy

As U.S. advisory efforts proved insufficient to shore up the ARVN's fight against the insurgency, the United States saw no alternative but to deepen its involvement.

forces, ARVN troops suffered multiple humiliating defeats. By the end of 1965, U.S. military planners grew impatient with the ARVN and made an effort to further reduce their role in combat operations. The new plan for combat operations called for most offensive operations against the VC to be conducted by the United States and third-country forces, while the bulk of ARVN forces were to "be committed to the defense of GVN [Government of Vietnam] installations and securing operations."

Therefore, after the arrival of U.S. combat troops, 60 percent of all ARVN forces were placed on rural security detail, often referred to as pacification. One ARVN soldier complained of the shift in responsibility, stating, "Instead of taking the war to the enemy, we were turned into security guards." Despite such misgivings, ARVN leaders understood that pacification duties were necessary to winning the war, but they also recognized that their forces were wholly unprepared for that task. Since the ARVN's inception in 1956, they had been trained to fight a conventional war, not pacify the countryside. Furthermore, ARVN pacification efforts suffered because the South

1965

AUGUST

August 1 The U.S. marines form Combined Action Platoons with South Vietnamese militia units to fight against the Vietcong.

August 3 *CBS News* airs video of U.S. marines engaged in burning down the village of Cam Ne, near Da Nang. This footage generates anger and disgust in the United States.

August 1–21 U.S. marine units launch Operation Starlight, the first major ground operation conducted by U.S. forces in Vietnam. The marines attack 1,500 Vietcong guerrillas near the air base of Chu Lai. The action is a major success for the United States.

August 23 Vietcong forces mortar the U.S. air base at Bien Hoa, damaging forty-nine aircraft.

August 26 U.S. B-52 bombers strike Vietcong bases in War Zone D in South Vietnam, while other bombers strike radar stations in North Vietnam.

Above: Vietnamese soldiers rush a wounded comrade to a waiting U.S. helicopter ambulance; the soldier has suffered horrific injuries from stepping on a land mine.

Left: An MACV adviser goes over their position with his Vietnamese counterpart during combat operations in Kien Sing province.

SEPTEMBER

September 7–10 U.S. marines and ARVN forces launch Operation Piranha against Vietcong forces near Chu Lai. About 200 Vietcong guerrillas are killed.

September 11 The 1st Cavalry Division arrives at Qui Nhon, bringing the U.S. troop presence in Vietnam to 125,000.

September 18–21 Troops from the 101st Airborne Division engage a large number of Vietcong forces at An Khe, killing 226 enemy soldiers.

September 30 Two U.S. Air Force jets are shot down by surface-to-air missiles over North Vietnam.

Vietnamese government and the United States placed logistical priority on combat operations.

The 40 percent of ARVN forces that remained on combat operations also suffered as a result of the introduction of U.S. combat units. Initially, U.S. firepower and logistical support increased ARVN effectiveness, but in the long term it made the South Vietnamese troops overly dependent on U.S. support. As a result, the ARVN became tied to a conventional way of fighting that a small developing country like South Vietnam could not financially or socially sustain. By the time the United States left Vietnam, the ARVN had become so dependent on U.S. support that South Vietnam was unable to continue the war alone. ARVN General Ngo Quang Truong described the situation, saying, "Resorting to the use of combat force meant that the U.S. advisory effort and level of military assistance up to that time had either fallen short of their goal or were not enough . . . Entering the war with the posture and disposition of a fire brigade, the Americans rushed about to save the Vietnamese house from destruction but took little interest in caring for the victims. Only after they realized that the victims, too, should be made firefighters to save their own houses did Americans set about to really care for them. Valuable time was lost, and by the time the victims could get onto their feet and began to move forward a few steps after recovery, the fire brigade was called back to the home station."

Due to the ARVN's diminishing role in the war, South Vietnamese units rarely conducted unilateral offensive operations after 1965. They did, however, participate in small-scale search-and-destroy missions with U.S. troops. By 1967, the ARVN had an impressive success rate with these operations; their progress was enough to

Vietnamese junk fleet sailors provide cover for a retreating junk after its raid on Quang Tin province, South Vietnam.

1965

OCTOBER

October 6 U.S. B-52s strike Vietcong bases in Tay Ninh province, near Saigon.

October 19 North Vietnamese soldiers attack the U.S. Special Forces camp at Plei Me.

October 23–November 16 As a result of the attack on the U.S. Special Forces camp at Plei Me, ARVN forces and U.S. troops launch an attack to destroy enemy forces within Pleiku province. The operation concludes with the battle of Ia Drang. During the fighting, seventy-nine Americans are killed and North Vietnamese losses are estimated to be around 2,000.

make the United States believe that the ARVN could match the Vietcong in their abilities. However, the ARVN victories were largely misleading because they were not participating in the "big-unit" battles that they would be required to fight after the U.S. troops had gone. In the meantime, ARVN units continued to beat the VC in small-scale actions in 1967.

Tet and "Vietnamization"

Perhaps the ARVN's greatest success in the war came during the Tet Offensive of 1968. General Westmoreland's plan was to send the Americans out on combat operations and leave the ARVN in the cities to guard South Vietnamese government buildings and military installations, so the ARVN faced the brunt of the Communist assault. During the Tet Offensive, ARVN units participated in bloody house-to-house fighting with much success. As a result of Tet, ARVN and U.S. soldiers virtually destroyed the Vietcong as an effective fighting force. Because of this exceptional performance in some of the most intense combat of the war, ARVN units proved that they could win battles and stand toe-to-toe with the Vietcong. Despite this major

victory for the ARVN, the Tet Offensive also meant serious trouble for South Vietnam. Soon after Tet, U.S. public opinion turned against the war and the military began to look for a way out of Vietnam. Therefore, by late 1968, the United States began to hand over all operations to the ARVN in a program known as "Vietnamization." The plan was to build up the ARVN and turn all aspects of the war over to the South Vietnamese as U.S. forces began to withdraw from the conflict. On hearing of the plan, some ARVN soldiers greeted the news with optimistic anticipation because they would finally get to fight their war. However, many others condemned the plan as the outright abandonment of South Vietnam. They knew they were not prepared to face the onslaught of NVA divisions without U.S. support.

As the United States began to withdraw from the war in Vietnam, the ARVN appeared to be in a favorable situation. The United States stepped up its bombing missions over the Ho

....

Right: A soldier runs to a new position while under fire from North Vietnamese arm positions south of the "Y" bridge.

Chi Minh Trail to disrupt a possible NVA buildup and began to supply the ARVN with state-of-the-art weaponry and equipment. The ARVN held a three-to-one advantage in troop numbers over the North Vietnamese at the end of 1971 and was the fourth-largest army in the world. Because of these factors, the ARVN appeared on paper to be a formidable army, but

several years of neglect could not be rectified overnight. The American decision of pushing the ARVN aside for most of the war had led to a lack of experience on the part of the ARVN in fighting the NVA in big-unit actions.

Operation Lam Son 719

In 1970, ARVN and U.S. forces sought to disrupt the North Vietnamese strategy by taking

the war to their base of external support. In April, U.S. and ARVN forces launched an incursion into Cambodia in order to drive the Communists from their safe haven across the border. In doing so, ARVN and U.S. forces hoped to destroy Communist staging areas so that South Vietnam would have more time to prepare to fight the war alone. In the Cambodian incursion, U.S. and South Vietnamese forces succeeded in destroying many Communist supply areas, but they were unable to deal a devastating blow to the enemy.

In February 1971, ARVN forces launched Operation Lom Son 719, another cross-border assault—this time into Laos—in order to further disrupt the Communist war plans. However, on this occasion, ARVN forces went into battle without the support of U.S. ground troops. American air power was still available, but it would prove to be largely ineffective because ARVN troops did not have the ability to call in close air support. Throughout the earlier stages

....

After Tet, the United States began a program of "Vietnamization," designed to hand over the war effort to the South Vietnamese.

of the war, U.S. advisers had always handled requests for tactical air strikes, but in Laos the ARVN were alone. Without much U.S. support and with little experience in offensive operations, ARVN forces soon found themselves in a desperate situation. After being met with fierce resistance, the mission descended into mass chaos as ARVN troops panicked in the face of the enemy. A month and a half after it began, the attack into Laos ended with a bloody ARVN retreat. U.S. advisers saw that the ARVN forces were not ready to fight the war alone, but the U.S. withdrawal continued nonetheless.

The Easter Offensive

By the beginning of 1972, the bulk of U.S. forces had withdrawn from Vietnam and the ARVN was left with only a small number of advisers to help fight the war. To the North Vietnamese, it seemed as if the time was right to bring an end to the war by defeating the ARVN on the battlefield. With that goal in mind, the North Vietnamese launched the Easter Offensive, their largest offensive to date, in March 1973. Waves of NVA divisions struck the ARVN across the DMZ, at Kontum in the

1965

DECEMBER

December 4 Vietcong terrorists bomb a hotel in Saigon, killing eight and wounding 137.

December 9 The *New York Times* reports that the United States is unable to cut the flow of North Vietnamese soldiers coming down the Ho Chi Minh Trail.

December 18 The U.S. Navy establishes the River Patrol Force, designated Task Force 116, to conduct Operation Game Warden to curtail enemy infiltration and logistics on the Mekong delta's major arteries.

central highlands, and at An Loc to the north of Saigon. Initially, the NVA drove the ARVN back with overpowering force, particularly along the DMZ, but as the offensive continued ARVN resistance stiffened and the assault ground to a halt. With the help of U.S. air support, ARVN troops eventually pushed back the NVA and succeeded in winning the battle on all three fronts. The ARVN fought well and proved they could defeat the North Vietnamese in big-unit combat with the help of U.S. logistics and air support. However, the next time the NVA attacked, the ARVN would not have either luxury.

The Final Defeat

By the beginning of 1975, the United States had withdrawn all financial and military support from South Vietnam and the ARVN stood alone to face its fate. Therefore, when the final North Vietnamese offensive began in March 1975, ARVN units were paralyzed because of a lack of petroleum and other much-needed supplies. Artillery shells and rifle ammunition were rationed. Used bandages had to be washed and reused due to a lack of medical supplies.

The final North Vietnamese offensive began in March 1975 and ended just two months later, on April 30.

....

South Vietnam no longer had the logistics or finances to keep the ARVN running. Under such dire circumstances, the end came quickly.

Just two months after North Vietnam launched its main offensive, the war was over. ARVN forces quickly collapsed in the face of the enemy onslaught and North Vietnamese troops captured Saigon on April 30, 1975. To many U.S. observers, the final defeat of the ARVN came as no surprise. They had always believed political infighting, cowardice, and incompetence were the defining features of the ARVN. Although these negative characteristics certainly made the ARVN's chances of success more difficult, the final defeat of the ARVN was not predestined. In the Easter Offensive, the ARVN had proved that it had potential; with U.S. air power and logistical support, it had turned back a massive NVA offensive. In the end, U.S. support was key to the ARVN's survival. Without it, South Vietnam simply did not have the ability to defend itself any longer.

December 25 President Johnson orders a halt to Operation Rolling Thunder in another attempt to pressure the North Vietnamese into negotiating a peace settlement. Again, North Vietnam ignores the peace overtures.

December 31 By the end of the year, the U.S. troop presence in Vietnam has reached 184,000 troops. However, Vietcong forces control about half of the South Vietnamese countryside.

The Other War: Pacification

The center of gravity in guerrilla warfare is usually the people, and this most certainly proved to be the case in Vietnam. Guerrillas had to live among the people, so they relied on others for their survival.

The work done by the VC during the first two phases of Mao's guerrilla war formula had given the Communist forces deep inroads into the South Vietnamese rural population, and the establishment of a VC shadow government had helped solidify this hold. The Pacification Program was designed to weaken the control the VC had on the countryside and strengthen simultaneously the confidence the people had in the South Vietnamese government. The first goal

Left: The battleground presented a stark contrast between the agrarian nature of much of South Vietnam and the technology of the American military machine. Right: A Vietnamese farming family.

would protect the rural population from insurgents and help deprive the insurgency of its rural support base. The second goal would be brought about by a host of reforms that would address the needs of the people and win their loyalty to the government. In both areas, the pacification effort would have to overcome a huge VC head start.

The word "pacification" was first used during the French period in Vietnam, so to the Vietnamese it smacked of colonialism and outside interference. Nonetheless, the United States continued to use the term, reflecting a failure to fully understand the Vietnamese situation. This lack of cultural awareness would plague the U.S. pacification efforts, and the South Vietnamese desire to run the program without outside supervision would lead to inefficiency and a lack of accountability.

To refer to a pacification "program" may be somewhat gracious, especially in the war's early years. In reality, there were many programs, often competing and disjointed, and it was not until 1967 that the various efforts were centralized under one office. Even then, pacification consisted of a mind-boggling quantity of initiatives that, although now prioritized and coordinated, were often still

singularly inefficient. In addition to these problems, the program suffered criticism by many military commanders that it detracted from the "Big War." According to this school of thought, the enemy would be defeated by fighting and not by civic action. Therefore, pacification was never really given the priority it deserved and, in the end, this lack of focus and commitment doomed the effort to failure.

Agrovilles

Of all the situations that made South Vietnamese peasants vulnerable to VC exploitation, perhaps the most frustrating was the critical need for land reform. Of all arable land, 45 percent was owned by just 2 percent of the total population. To address this issue of inequitable land distribution and to improve security, one of the earliest pacification initiatives was the Agroville Program. Beginning in 1948, the Diem government used a combination of direct

The Vietnam War blurred the lines between combatant and noncombatant and created serious problems in targeting and security.

1966

JANUARY

January 12 During his State of the Union address, President Johnson notes that in Vietnam, "The enemy is no longer close to victory. Time is no longer on his side. There is no cause to doubt the American commitment."

January 28–March 6 U.S. forces conduct the large-scale search-and-destroy Operation Masher/White Wing. Americans suffer 228 killed and 788 wounded. North Vietnamese army losses are 1,342.

January 31 President Johnson announces the bombing of North Vietnam will resume after the thirty-seven-day pause and stalemated negotiations with North Vietnam.

January 31 Senator Robert F. Kennedy criticizes the decision to resume the bombing, stating that the United States may be headed "on a road from which there is no turning back, a road that leads to catastrophe for all mankind."

The Strategic Hamlet Program sought to concentrate the rural population in a limited number of fortified villages to provide protection against the Vietcong.

force and incentives to relocate peasants scattered throughout the countryside to large communities called Agrovilles. The initial focus area for the Agroville Program was the Mekong delta, where the dispersed pattern of settlement exacerbated the security problem. Villages were strung out for miles along canals and waterways, making them vulnerable to Communist infiltration. In a classic example of denial and oversimplification, Diem believed it was this geographic isolation that made the peasants easy prey rather than considering that the VC might actually be appealing to the people by meeting their social and economic needs. Therefore, in Diem's mind, relocation would free the people from the clutches of the enemy and the problem would be solved. By 1960, there were twenty-three Agrovilles, each consisting of thousands of people.

In addition to relocating the population, Diem wanted to secure people's allegiance by making them aware of their larger national identity. To accomplish this, he emphasized collective action, self-help, and hard work— ideas that were all subject to abuses. Provincial officials conscripted thousands of peasants for construction work without pay. Many more were drafted than were needed and the construction interrupted the farmers' efforts to bring in their harvests. A scarcity of construction equipment forced the projects to be built largely by peasant manual labor.

The relocation schemes often alienated the population and incited antigovernment sentiment ranging from the graffiti shown here to defection to the Vietcong.

However, rather than correcting this problem, the government boasted that because of the absence of machines, "the people should feel that this was something they had done themselves." In another selfish manipulation, Diem argued that the peasants had to build the

---

FEBRUARY

February 1 The 9th Infantry Division is activated at Fort Riley, Kansas, in preparation for riverine operations in the Mekong delta.

February 3 Influential newspaper columnist Walter Lippmann criticizes President Johnson's strategy in Vietnam, stating, "Gestures, propaganda, public relations, and bombing and more bombing will not work."

February 6–9 President Johnson and South Vietnamese prime minister Nguyen Cao Ky meet in Honolulu, Hawaii. Johnson presses for an increase in pacification efforts.

February 18 In televised hearings of the Senate Foreign Relations Committee, Secretary of Defense McNamara testifies that U.S. objectives in Vietnam are "not to destroy or overthrow the Communist government of North Vietnam."

Agrovilles themselves in order to free Vietnam from foreign dependence. Camouflaged in this appeal to self-reliance, Diem was able to protect the project from the U.S. oversight and accountability that he feared would limit his options.

Diem characteristically set a rushed pace for the Agrovilles in spite of providing limited resources. The government allocated the provinces the equivalent of $13,000 for each settlement, even though construction estimates for some centers required two-thirds more than that. The pressure of limited time and money led to additional conscriptions, as officials emphasized signs of physical progress rather than peasant satisfaction. Of course, these increased demands only served to alienate the peasants further. Before long, the Agroville Program had ended up exacerbating the problem rather than helping it.

Under pressure from the United States, Diem finally agreed in March 1960 to slow down the construction of Agrovilles in order to alleviate the program's excesses. This deceleration eventually turned into a gradual abandonment of the program. With construction lagging far

behind, Diem announced in September that the program would be halted after only twenty centers had been built. Diem explained his decision by citing monetary difficulties, but U.S. ambassador Elbridge Durbrow speculated that "Perhaps [Diem] has finally been convinced that the 'real cost' is the loss of popular support for his regime."

The Strategic Hamlet Program

The failure of the Agroville Program left the pacification effort somewhat adrift. Not only had Agrovilles failed to stem the insurgency, they seemed to have contributed to it, and Diem found himself under increasing pressure to adopt the U.S.-style policies he had hoped to avoid. In response, Diem's brother Nhu began plans for a successor to the Agrovilles, which became known as the Strategic Hamlet Program. Based on a scheme that had worked well for the British in Malaya, the idea was to concentrate the rural population in a limited number of fortified villages to provide them physical security against the VC. By focusing on existing settlements, rather than attempting to build new ones, the Strategic Hamlet Program sought to

The ARVN had been built largely to protect the government from a coup rather than to protect the people from the Vietcong. People feared for their lives.

avoid some of the construction problems that had plagued the Agrovilles. Once security was established, social programs that would hopefully foster government allegiance were planned to follow.

The Strategic Hamlet Program was largely a failure. Unlike the Chinese immigrant squatters

1966

MARCH

March 1 Senator Wayne Morse leads an attempt to repeal the Tonkin Gulf Resolution, which fails in the U.S. Senate by a vote of 92–5.

March 7 The MACV completes its Mekong Delta Mobile Afloat Force Concept and Requirements study.

March 9 In an announcement that draws sharp domestic criticism, the United States reports that 20,000 acres of food crops have been destroyed in suspected Vietcong villages.

March 10 South Vietnamese Buddhists begin a campaign to oust Prime Minister Ky after his dismissal of a top Buddhist general. Unrest in several cities in South Vietnam follows.

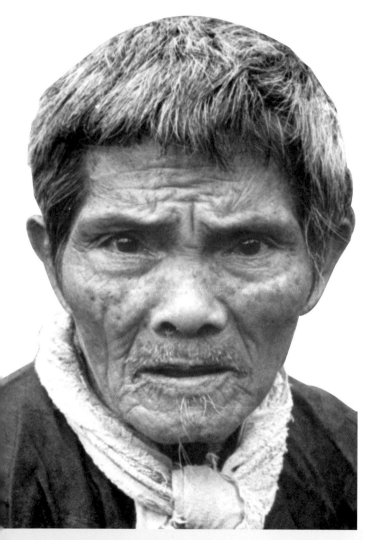

Above and left: A vulnerable population was often forced to choose between loyalty to the government and reprisal from the Vietcong. The Vietnamese people were scared by the ongoing events.

who were the primary subjects of the British relocations in Malaya, the South Vietnamese Buddhists had ancestral ties to the land and moving interrupted their practice of veneration of ancestors. The relocations also caused the peasants to abandon generations of hard work and took vital arable land out of production, hampering economic progress. In the new hamlets, the peasants had to start over from scratch without compensation for their labor or loss. These factors obviously led to a disgruntled population that was ripe for VC exploitation, a situation facilitated by the fact that many VC secretly relocated to the new hamlets with the rest of the population. Many peasants were so alienated by the entire ordeal that they slipped away from the hamlets and returned to their ancestral lands. This greatly hindered one of the goals of the scheme, which was to create free-fire zones in the vacated areas based on the assumption that anyone there now was a VC.

As part of the plan, VC-controlled areas that could not be penetrated by the government were subjected to random bombardment by artillery and aircraft in order to drive the people into the safety of the strategic hamlets. This process

March 26 Antiwar protests are held in New York, Washington, D.C., Chicago, Philadelphia, Boston, and San Francisco.

March 26–April 7 U.S. and South Vietnamese forces conduct Operation Jackstay to attack the Vietcong in the Rung Sat swamp that surrounds the vital shipping channel to Saigon.

created tens of thousands of refugees, which Diem used as propaganda to show political support—the people were voting with their feet as they fled to government-held territory. In reality, the refugees were alienated by this coercion and they resented the government as the instrument of it.

The relocations created other problems as well, including the perception that if relocation was necessary in the first place, security must be weak. Many peasants were left with the impression that if the South Vietnamese government was not able to secure even its loyalists, one had to be cautious in fully supporting it. Finally, by moving the population away from the countryside, a significant, if imperfect, source of intelligence was lost.

All these problems were exacerbated by reporting inaccuracies. By the summer of 1962, the Diem government claimed to have established 3,225 strategic hamlets, which held over 4 million people (one-third of South

Vietnam's population). When the Diem regime collapsed in October 1963, it became apparent that many of these hamlets existed only on paper and the reporting was part of a South Vietnamese misinformation campaign to deceive the United States. As a case in point, the number of "secure" hamlets in Long An province was revised downward from over 200 to about ten after Diem's death. Accurately measuring the success of the effort would be a common difficulty throughout the policy of pacification.

Hop Tac
In June 1964, Henry Cabot Lodge, Durbrow's successor as U.S. ambassador in Saigon, proposed

another pacification program called Hop Tac. In this scheme, pacification would spread outward from Saigon like a "giant oil spot" or concentric "rings of steel." In this way, the capital city would be safeguarded because the enemy could never reach it through the secured outer rings. By September, South Vietnamese troops were

The relocation programs and the fighting created increasing numbers of refugees.

1966

APRIL

April 1 Naval Forces, Vietnam is created to accommodate the direct combat role being played by U.S. naval forces. Rear Admiral Norvell G. Ward is the first commander.

April 12 B-52 bombers are used for the first time against North Vietnam, targeting power facilities, war support facilities, transportation lines, military complexes, fuel storage, and air-defense installations.

April 13 The Vietcong attack Tan Son Nhut airport in Saigon, inflicting 140 casualties and destroying twelve U.S. helicopters and nine aircraft.

MAY

May 2 Secretary of Defense McNamara privately reports that the North Vietnamese are infiltrating 4,500 men per month into South Vietnam.

May 14 South Vietnamese troops clash with Buddhists in Da Nang and Hue. Buddhist monks and nuns renew self-immolations as an act of protest against Ky's regime and its U.S. backers.

implementing Lodge's plan, but a year later little progress had been made.

As officials studied the situation, it became obvious that the Americans were still having problems understanding the situation in Vietnam. Phrases such as "rings of steel" reflected a U.S. attitude that the war could be won by isolating the population from the enemy rather than addressing the fundamental problems that made the population vulnerable in the first place. Progress in this area would be difficult because of the weak commitment of the South Vietnamese government to real reform. Hop Tac made it clear that the ARVN was a largely political organization structured more as a private force designed to protect the regime from a coup than a professional army motivated to protect the population from the VC. Another reason for Hop Tac's failure was that the South Vietnamese perceived it almost exclusively as a U.S. plan. There was little incentive for them to execute it enthusiastically because, even if it succeeded, the credit would go elsewhere. Hop Tac showed that the United States and South Vietnam had still not achieved an appropriate level of cooperation and understanding.

Even more fundamentally, Hop Tac failed to recognize the decentralized nature of Vietnamese society. Although it seemed logical and businesslike to the American mind to work from the center out and to look to the government for centralized solutions, such an attitude was antithetical to the severely localized nature of rural Vietnamese society. The result was almost a reverse oil-spot model. First, VC guerrilla fighters defeated and displaced ARVN units, and then VC political cadres worked out from previously held areas into the newly available territory to expand VC control and influence at the expense of the South Vietnamese government.

Revolutionary Development

With these and other indicators that the pacification scheme was not proceeding as planned, President Johnson convened a meeting with South Vietnamese leaders in Honolulu in February 1966 to discuss the status of economic, social, and political projects for South Vietnam. While in Hawaii, Johnson made it clear that he expected a massive increase in pacification productivity in the upcoming year.

As a result of the meeting, the South Vietnamese decided to give a new face to the program of pacification by renaming it Revolutionary Development. At the core of this new plan were teams of fifty-nine South Vietnamese officials who had been specially trained and financed by the CIA. Thirty of the team members were self-defense experts and the rest were specialists in every kind of village need. The teams, dressed in peasant garb, would move into a hamlet, identify and eliminate the VC secret political cadre, remove corrupt officials from office, organize democratic institutions, and create a hamlet defense force. Once these objectives were accomplished, the team would move on to another hamlet. Meanwhile, the South Vietnamese government would develop programs in education, health, land reform, and financial credit in the first hamlet. To supplement these teams, several U.S. civilian agencies worked at various levels in information, agriculture, and public health programs.

Such an effort was consistent with the "Program for the Pacification and Long-Term Development of South Vietnam" (PROVN), a

JUNE

June 4 A three-page antiwar advertisement signed by 6,400 teachers and professors appears in the *New York Times*.

June 25 Prime Minister Ky arrests Buddhist leader Tri Quang and appeals for calm in the crisis.

June 29 The United States ends its self-imposed restriction and bombs oil depots around Hanoi and Haiphong, citing increased infiltration of Communist guerrillas from North Vietnam into the south.

U.S. Army report commissioned in 1965 and completed in March 1966 that called for a greater focus at local levels. The study argued that "the crucial actions are those that occur at the village, district, and provincial levels. This is where the war must be fought; this is where the war and the object which lies beyond it must be won." Such a strategy, however, conflicted with Westmoreland's vision for a war fought by battalion-sized and larger search-and-destroy operations. Therefore, the recommendations of PROVN were largely ignored until General Creighton Abrams replaced Westmoreland as commander of the MACV in 1968.

Combined Action Platoon (CAP)

The program that probably came closest to the intent of PROVN was the Combined Action Platoon (CAP), created by the U.S. Marines in August 1965. However, although it complied with the intent of PROVN, CAP came to exemplify Westmoreland's negative attitude toward pacification.

A CAP was a combination of a fourteen-man Marine Corps rifle squad and one navy medical corpsman, all of whom were volunteers, and a locally recruited Popular Forces (PF) platoon of thirty-eight men. The resulting CAP was assigned responsibility for a village typically consisting of five hamlets spread out over 1.5 square miles, with an average population of 3,500 people. The marines lived with their Vietnamese PF counterparts and become integral parts of the unit. The effect was synergistic. The marines gained intelligence from the South Vietnamese soldiers' knowledge of the local terrain and enemy, and the PF benefited from

President Johnson requested a marked increase in productivity in the Pacification Program when meeting South Vietnamese leaders in Hawaii in 1966.

1966

JULY

July 5 Secretary of Defense McNamara approves activation and deployment of a Mobile Afloat Force, consisting of two river assault groups.

July 11 The United States intensifies bombing of portions of the Ho Chi Minh Trail in Laos. An estimated 89,000 soldiers infiltrated from North Vietnam to the south via the Ho Chi Minh Trail in 1966.

July 15 Fifteen U.S. marines and South Vietnamese troops launch Operation Hastings against 10,000 North Vietnamese in Quang Tri province.

July 30 The United States bombs NVA troops in the demilitarized zone between North and South Vietnam for the first time.

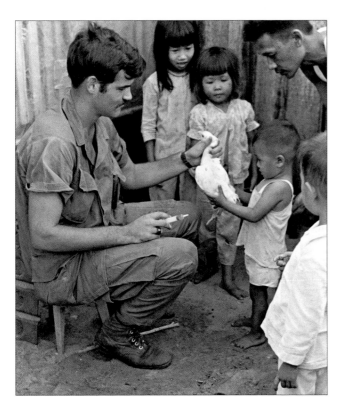

Above and right: Health programs were a significant part of the U.S. civic action effort. In the first half of 1967 alone, American officials performed 4,843,396 medical treatments and administered 1,381,968 immunizations.

the marines' firepower, tactical skills, and discipline. The CAP was a solid and mutually beneficial combination.

Perhaps most importantly, the constant marine presence sent a powerful message that the Americans were there to stay. They did not fly in by helicopter in the morning and fly out at night to leave the villagers at the mercy of the VC. This continued presence was critical because the peasants who cooperated with the government had to carefully weigh the risk of

VC reprisals against themselves, their family, friends, and community with the benefits of improved clothing, food, education, and medical assistance. When the Americans flew in and flew out, the risks to Vietnamese villagers often outweighed the benefits. However, under CAP, the marines shared the same fate as the South Vietnamese soldiers and people. In fact, CAP marines took 2.4 times the casualties of the regular forces in the CAP. The CAP was a strong testimony of U.S. commitment and partnership, and gave the Vietnamese people a sense of enduring security.

In 1966, there were fifty-seven CAPs; by the end of 1967 the number had grown to seventy-nine. Despite these increases and demonstrated successes, Westmoreland was unwilling to adopt the program, arguing that he "simply had not enough numbers to put a squad of Americans in every village and hamlet; that would be fragmenting resources and exposing them to defeat in detail." Although there is some merit to Westmoreland's argument about numbers, his genuine objection lay more in a fundamental strategic difference. He viewed the CAPs as static and defensive employments of his

AUGUST

August 9 U.S. jets accidentally attack two South Vietnamese villages, killing sixty-three civilians and wounding over a hundred.

August 30 North Vietnam announces it will be receiving economic and technical assistance from China.

resources. Instead, he favored the aggressive pursuit and destruction of enemy forces. The focus of the CAP at the small-unit level also violated Westmoreland's quest for scale.

To counter these objections, CAP advocates argued that the real battlefields were the villages and the real enemy were the VC in them. Once the villages were secured, repelling the enemy's main forces would be an easy matter given the U.S. superiority in firepower and mobility. Furthermore, the main enemy forces would be severely weakened by denying them the logistical support they enjoyed from unsecured villages. Such arguments fell largely on deaf ears.

In the end, Westmoreland never put the CAP concept fully to the test and ultimately vetoed the strategic concept. Perceived as competition with the "Big War," CAP was never allocated the manpower resources it required and, lacking a grand strategic direction, its local successes were never able to be replicated on a larger scale. For many,

Left: Special Forces troops were allowed to wear the distinctive Green Beret headgear.

Right: The Combined Action Platoon saw troops assigned responsibility for a village.

CAP showed that the marines, building on their experience in Cuba, Haiti, the Dominican Republic, Nicaragua, and Panama, seemed to understand pacification better than their army counterparts. The difference is exemplified by Marine Major General Victor Krulak and Army Major General Julian Ewell. Krulak, the Special Assistant for Counterinsurgency and Special Activities during the Kennedy administration and a major supporter of CAP, argued that the

1966

SEPTEMBER

September 1 While visiting Cambodia, French president Charles de Gaulle calls for the United States to withdraw from Vietnam.

September 12 Five hundred U.S. planes attack NVA supply lines and coastal targets in the heaviest bombing of the war to date.

September 14–November 24 Some 20,000 U.S. and South Vietnamese soldiers conduct Operation Attleboro, a search-and-destroy operation fifty miles north of Saigon near the Cambodian border. The United States suffers 155 killed and 494 wounded, but destroys significant enemy supplies. North Vietnamese casualties are 1,106.

September 17 A conference begins at Coronado Naval Base, California, to examine the joint training implications that would be imposed on the 9th Division and the army training command by participation in the Mobile Afloat Force.

September 23 The United States announces that jungles near the demilitarized zone are being defoliated by spraying chemicals.

big force engagements "could move to another planet today, and we would still not have won the war because the Vietnamese people are the prize." In contrast, Ewell, commander of the 9th Infantry Division and a major proponent of the body count, had his staff draw up a report that concluded "the most relevant statistical index of combat effectiveness was the average number of Vietcong losses inflicted daily by the unit in question." By and large, most army commanders shared Ewell's point of view.

CORDS and Robert Komer

In the meantime, although it appeared promising at first, Revolutionary Development belied a basic flaw with the South Vietnamese government in that it was not at all committed to the reforms the programs envisioned. The South Vietnamese government viewed a better-educated and empowered peasantry as a threat to its power. This failure led to another reorganization in November 1966, in which

By most accounts, the Pacification Program began too late to be effective. Here a soldier distributes comics to South Vietnamese children.

OCTOBER

October 2–24 The 1st Cavalry Division conducts Operation Irving to clear the NVA from mountainous areas near Qui Nhon.

October 3 The Soviet Union announces it will provide military and economic assistance to North Vietnam.

October 25 President Johnson conducts a conference in the Philippines with Australia, the Philippines, Thailand, New Zealand, South Korea, and South Vietnam. These allies pledge to withdraw from Vietnam within six months if North Vietnam withdraws completely from the south.

October 26 President Johnson visits U.S. troops at Cam Ranh Bay in South Vietnam.

the United States instructed Lodge to create the Office of Civil Operations (OCO) in an attempt to bring more efficient management to the pacification effort. OCO was also short-lived and was the last attempt to have pacification run by the United States mission in Saigon.

In May 1967, the United States replaced OCO with the Civil Operations and Revolutionary Development Support (CORDS), which combined the names of the last two pacification efforts and much more. CORDS represented a unification of the previously fragmented pacification effort, with CORDS under MACV command and including representatives from a host of civilian agencies, including the Agency for International Development (AID), the State Department, the CIA, the United States Information Agency (USIA), and the White House. The military and civilian efforts were now fully integrated at all levels in a single chain of command. At its peak strength at the end of 1969, CORDS had approximately 6,000 military and 1,100 civilian personnel. Although late in coming, CORDS represented a dramatic step in the pacification effort. Robert Komer, a former CIA official who

had served in both the Kennedy and Johnson administrations as an aid expert, was selected to head CORDS and given the title of Deputy to the Commander USMACV for CORDS. In March 1966, Komer had been appointed Special Assistant to the President for Pacification. Now, as head of CORDS, he held ambassadorial rank and became the first ambassador to serve directly under a military command and to have command responsibility for military personnel and resources.

Komer brought with him a reputation for nonconformity, and he had a mix of boundless energy and abrasiveness. He soon was nicknamed "the Blowtorch," both for the fire he brought to the pacification effort and his scorching criticisms of how the South Vietnamese government had mismanaged it. Komer's military deputy, Major General George Forsythe, proved useful in mollifying military officers who were taken aback by Komer's direct and often unconventional methods.

....

Robert Komer, here with President Johnson, helped bring some sense of unity of effort to the Pacification Program when he became head of CORDS in 1967.

1966

November 7 Student protesters confront Secretary of Defense McNamara during a visit to Harvard University.

November 12 The *New York Times* reports that 40 percent of U.S. economic aid sent to South Vietnam is stolen or ends up on the black market.

December 8–9 North Vietnam rejects President Johnson's proposal to discuss the treatment of prisoners of war and a possible exchange.

Tension between South Vietnamese and American officials plagued the Pacification Program as many Americans distrusted South Vietnamese competency and sincerity and many South Vietnamese resented U.S. oversight.

Komer found common cause with Ellsworth Bunker, who had replaced Lodge as the ambassador in Saigon in March 1967. Bunker objected to those who called pacification "the other war," saying, "To me, this is all one war. Everything we do is an aspect of the total effort to achieve our objective here." Komer and Bunker represented a shift in philosophy that pacification would no longer be relegated to a subsidiary role in the war. Komer in particular also sought to improve the South Vietnamese Regional and Popular Forces (RF and PF) and police who were participating in pacification. He provided these forces with additional training and equipment, including M16 rifles, and greatly expanded advisory attention. He established a program to field 353 Mobile Advisory Teams (MAT), each consisting of two U.S. officers and three noncommissioned officers, to give what he called "on-the-job training" to the RF and PF units. By these steps, Komer demonstrated he understood that the South Vietnamese would have to be active, capable, and willing participants in the pacification process.

December 13–14 U.S. bombers level the village of Caudat near Hanoi, generating much criticism from the international community.

December 26 The U.S. Department of Defense admits that civilians in Caudat may have been bombed accidentally.

December 27 The United States mounts a large-scale air campaign against suspected Vietcong positions in the Mekong delta using napalm and hundreds of tons of bombs.

The results of Komer's efforts can be roughly divided into four categories. The first involved a massive effort to produce and disseminate propaganda. Second were initiatives focused on distributing food and other supplies to the countryside. Next were paramilitary schemes designed to control the rural population by improving physical security. Finally, there was a whole host of new ways to measure progress and assess the results in order to determine statistically what percentage of the population had been pacified.

Propaganda

The propaganda campaign was intense but often naively reflective of U.S. cultural bias. Between 1965 and 1972, over 50 billion leaflets were distributed in North and South Vietnam and along the Ho Chi Minh Trail in Cambodia and Laos. In 1969 alone, more than 10.5 billion leaflets, 4 million pamphlets, 60,000 newspaper articles, 24.5 million posters, and almost 12 million magazines were produced in the attempt to influence Vietnamese opinions.

Often, however, the propaganda efforts seemed to be more appropriate for a U.S. than a Vietnamese audience. For example, one program in 1968 involved distributing brown paper grocery bags to merchants, with each bag having a political message on it. The problem

The South Vietnamese became dependent on U.S. weapons, technology, and economic assistance rather than becoming a self-sustaining entity.

1967

JANUARY

January 2 U.S. pilots shoot down seven North Vietnamese MiG-21s in twelve minutes without losing a single aircraft during Operation Bolo.

January 8–26 Some 16,000 U.S. and 14,000 South Vietnamese troops participate in Operation Cedar Falls in the Iron Triangle region twenty-five miles northwest of Saigon.

January 10 President Johnson vows in his State of the Union address, "We will stand firm in Vietnam."

January 13 Senator J. William Fulbright publishes *The Arrogance of Power*, which is highly critical of U.S. war policy in Vietnam. It advocates direct peace talks between the South Vietnamese government and the Vietcong.

FEBRUARY

February 2 Expressing long-standing frustrations with the negotiation process, President Johnson states there are no "serious indications that the other side is ready to stop the war."

February 7 Elements of the 9th Infantry Division begin a one-week operation in the Nlion Trach district of Bien Hoa province, just north of the Rung Sat Special Zone.

was that the Vietnamese traditionally used plastic netting or cloth squares rather than paper bags to carry their shopping. Paper was used to wrap purchases. Therefore, rather than using the bags for their intended purpose, merchants often shredded them to use as wrapping material before the customer even had a chance to read the message. The propaganda campaign, like many other aspects of the Vietnam War, was plagued by the American difficulty in fully comprehending the nature of the situation.

Distribution

In addition to propaganda, Komer had at his disposal a $1.7 billion economic aid fund that he could distribute to the population. Multicrop miracle rice, soybean seeds, fertilizers, cooking oil, pharmaceuticals, cement, corrugated tin, medical and dental supplies, and hygiene items all sat in warehouses waiting to be shipped to the countryside. In the first half of 1967, American officials distributed 10,750 tons of food, performed 4,843,396 medical treatments, and administered 1,381,968 immunizations. But what made this aspect of the pacification

Rather than safeguarding the South Vietnamese population, the United States was lured into the periphery, creating a vacuum for the Vietcong to exploit in the populated areas.

February 8–10 U.S. religious groups stage a nationwide "fast for peace."

February 8–12 Both sides observe a truce for Tet, a Vietnamese holiday celebrating the lunar new year.

February 13 After the latest round of diplomatic negotiations breaks down, President Johnson announces that the United States will resume full-scale bombing of North Vietnam.

February 16–March 20 Operation River Raider I, the first joint operation by the U.S. Army and Navy units that will later constitute the Mobile Riverine Force, is conducted in the Rung Sat Special Zone.

February 22–May 14 U.S. and South Vietnamese battalions conduct Operation Junction City near the Cambodian border, the largest search-and-destroy operation of the war. As part of the operation, the 173rd Airborne Brigade conducts the only U.S. combat airborne assault of the war.

Right: Part of the pacification effort was the distribution of propaganda leaflets.
Below: In a people's war, the objective is the people. By its inability to safeguard the South Vietnamese population, the United States forfeited many of its advantages to the Communists.

program difficult was that security had to precede distribution. The last thing Komer wanted was for his efforts to win the hearts and minds of the South Vietnamese people to end up as logistical support for the VC.

Chieu Hoi

An example of a security program was Chieu Hoi, an open-arms amnesty program designed not only to woo VC defectors without reprisal but to also train them to become productive members of the South Vietnamese economy. It was not a popular program with the South Vietnamese government, who considered the VC better candidates for prison than schooling. Nonetheless, Komer pressed ahead, dropping millions of leaflets by plane and artillery shells that promised "We will be happy to welcome you, feed you well, not put you in prison." The program drew large numbers of defectors; as many as 27,178 by early 1968 and, after being

interrupted by Tet, an additional 17,000 from 1969 to 1970. However, when the North Vietnamese saw that the program was beginning to bear fruit, they countered by unleashing a terrorist campaign that reduced defections from 5,000 to 500 a month, often by killing family members of those who had switched sides.

Hamlet Evaluation System (HES)

Ever since the Honolulu conference, there had been increasing calls to conceptualize pacification in terms of production. Therefore, Komer introduced a variety of means to measure the effort in order to determine if pacification was producing "an acceptable rate of return for [the] heavy investments." As part of this process, he established unified

1967

MARCH

March 8 Congress authorizes $4.5 billion for the war.

March 19–21 President Johnson meets in Guam with South Vietnam's Prime Minister Ky and encourages Ky to hold national elections.

APRIL

April 1 The U.S. Navy forms Helicopter Attack Squadron 3, the Seawolves, to provide close air support and reconnaissance for brown-water (river) operations.

April 1 Units from the 2nd Brigade, 9th Infantry Division make a raid into northern Kien Hoa province on the My Tho River south of Dong Tam using barge-mounted artillery.

April 6 About 2,500 Vietcong and NVA attack Quang Tri City.

civilian-military advisory teams for all forty-four provinces and 250 districts. These teams worked with each of the South Vietnamese ministries associated with pacification at all levels, from hamlet to national. Part of their function was to contribute to periodic reports on the progress of various schemes and on the impact of military operations on pacification. Among the benefits of these "report cards" was the ability to identify corrupt and incompetent South Vietnamese officials and to increase U.S. leverage to eliminate those who were not meeting the standard.

Another notable measurement tool set up by CORDS was the Hamlet Evaluation System (HES), which assessed eighteen development and security indicators according to a five-letter scoring system ranging from A to E. Indicators for development were in the categories of administrative and political activities; health, education, and welfare; and economic activity. Security indicators were in the categories of VC

South Vietnamese and American soldiers often secured a village during the daytime, only to abandon it to the Vietcong at night.

military activity, VC political and subversive activities, and security based on friendly capabilities. An "A" hamlet was excelling in all areas of security and development. A "B" hamlet was still considered high-grade, with effective twenty-four-hour security, adequate development, and no VC presence or activity. A "C" hamlet was relatively secure day and night,

April 14 Republican presidential aspirant Richard Nixon visits Saigon and states that antiwar protests back in the United States are "prolonging the war."

April 15 Nearly 200,000 protestors attend antiwar demonstrations in New York and San Francisco. Martin Luther King Jr. claims that the war is undermining President Johnson's social reform programs.

April 20 U.S. bombers target Haiphong harbor in North Vietnam.

April 24–May 11 U.S. marines kill 940 NVA troops in fighting at Khe Sanh, an isolated air base located in North Vietnam's mountainous terrain less than ten miles from the border of Laos.

April 24 General Westmoreland condemns antiwar demonstrators, saying they give the North Vietnamese soldier "hope that he can win politically that which he cannot accomplish militarily."

VC military control had been broken, and there were no overt VC incidents, although VC taxation was perhaps continuing. Economic improvement schemes in "C" hamlets were under way. In a "D" hamlet, the VC frequently entered or harassed at night, VC infrastructure was largely intact, the South Vietnamese plan was in its infancy, and control of the hamlet was still strictly contested. An "E" hamlet was definitely under VC control, and U.S. and South Vietnamese officials entered only as part of a military operation. Most of the people in an "E" hamlet supported the VC.

When Komer began the HES, there were 12,600 hamlets and he was able to assign U.S. senior military advisers to 222 of the 242 South Vietnamese districts. The advisers made their monthly assessments on worksheets that were then sent to Saigon for computer processing into composite scores. There were, however, a couple of problems. The evaluations took place at the district headquarters, far away from rural

The Australian Army Training Team Vietnam (AATTV) first arrived in South Vietnam in July 1962.

1967

MAY

May 1 Ellsworth Bunker replaces Henry Cabot Lodge as the U.S. ambassador to South Vietnam.

May 9 Robert W. Komer becomes head of the Civil Operations and Revolutionary Development Support (CORDS), an organization designed to unify all the pacification efforts in South Vietnam.

May 13 An estimated 70,000 people march in support of the war in New York City.

May 18–26 U.S. and South Vietnamese troops enter the demilitarized zone for the first time and engage NVA forces.

hamlets. A senior adviser normally visited just one-fourth of the district hamlets in a month. Visits to individual hamlets usually lasted only a few hours, and during that time most advisers were completely dependent on interpreters. The result was evaluations based largely on surface appearances or historical data. To make matters worse, these advisory positions were not considered career-enhancing jobs. Therefore, many military officers cycled through them as quickly as possible in pursuit of more prized combat positions.

Accelerated Pacification Program (APP)

In spite of efforts to make the evaluation as objective as possible, assessment was still subject to manipulation. For example, in October 1968 MACV faced the disconcerting prospect of the United States being subjected to NLF demands for concessions at the Paris Peace Conference based on a Communist claim of representing a large segment of the countryside. To preempt this possibility, the United States inaugurated the Accelerated Pacification Program (APP) in November. The APP modified the criteria, attempting now to establish a minimal

government presence in as many hamlets as possible. Some 1,000 additional hamlets were earmarked but, to accommodate these increased quantities, the quality of the effort was diminished. Where cadres once stayed six months, they now stayed only six weeks. One U.S. adviser said, "The name of the game is planting the government flag." Using these new standards, the number of "relatively secure" hamlets (those with A, B, or C evaluations) shot up to 73.3 percent, an all-time high.

These criticisms aside, the APP was not just a numbers game. The heavy losses suffered by the North Vietnamese during Tet had led the enemy to retreat into its border sanctuaries and avoid contact. In the first half of 1968, there were an average of sixteen attacks per month by enemy forces of battalion size or larger, but in the second half of the year such attacks averaged less than five per month. This reduction in enemy aggressiveness freed more U.S. and South Vietnamese forces for pacification operations. Furthermore, many of the U.S. forces were

General Westmoreland talks to different ARVNs at Co Bi Thanh Tan after Operation Shawnee.

May 22 President Johnson urges North Vietnam to accept a negotiated peace settlement.

JUNE

June 1 The Mobile Riverine Force becomes operational, utilizing U.S. Navy "Swift" boats combined with army support to halt Vietcong usage of inland waterways in the Mekong delta.

June 1–26 The Mobile Riverine Force conducts Operation Coronado I, which consists of coordinated airmobile, ground, and waterborne attacks supported by air and naval forces.

broken down into units of company level and smaller, which were more conducive to pacification operations. U.S. and South Vietnamese forces often conducted joint small-unit operations. The local knowledge of the South Vietnamese soldiers, combined with the new intelligence gained from Tet, proved to be useful in ferreting out the VC infrastructure. In all, the APP improved territorial security, and Komer declared after he had completed his tour with CORDS that he was "prouder of having devised and pressed the [APP]—over considerable objection—than anything else."

Creighton Abrams, Nguyen Van Thieu, and William Colby

Pacification received increased emphasis when General Creighton Abrams replaced Westmoreland as commander of the MACV in 1968. Abrams was not only more committed to the "one-war concept" than his predecessor, but the reality of the phased U.S. withdrawal and Vietnamization limited large combat operations. Instead, Abrams emphasized that "the key strategic thrust is to provide meaningful, continued security for the Vietnamese people

President Nguyen Van Thieu reads a land title being given to a former tenant farmer.

in expanding areas of increasingly effective civil authority."

Abrams was interested in neutralizing the VC infrastructure and separating it from the population; he saw it as the "eyes" of the enemy forces. Without this intelligence, he claimed the main forces "cannot obtain intelligence, cannot obtain food, cannot prepare the battlefield, and cannot move unseen." What Abrams hoped to do was to implement the essential provisions of the PROVN report that were largely ignored when it was published in 1966. Abrams insisted that population security, not enemy destruction, was the definitive mission. One observer called the new approach "Son of PROVN."

Vietnamization also helped convince the South Vietnamese government to get behind pacification, as President Nguyen Van Thieu realized he had to secure a popular base before the U.S. withdrawal. Thieu actively promoted the return of village elections, which Diem had abolished in 1956, and proclaimed what the *New York Times* called "probably the most imaginative and progressive non-Communist land reform of the twentieth century." Although admitting Thieu had many critics in other

1967

JULY

July 7 North Vietnam's politburo launches a widespread offensive against South Vietnam that will eventually become the Tet Offensive.

July 22 The first helicopter barge is delivered to a mobile riverine base.

July 29 In the worst naval accident since World War II, 134 U.S. sailors aboard the USS *Forestall* in the Gulf of Tonkin die in a fire that resulted from a punctured fuel tank.

July 31 General Westmoreland's request for an additional 200,000 reinforcements (on top of the 475,000 soldiers already scheduled to be sent to Vietnam) is reduced to 45,000 by President Johnson.

aspects of his performance, Komer assessed Thieu as "personally the most pacification-minded of all top [South Vietnamese] leaders [who] did more than any other person to promote its growth." Specifically, Komer praised Thieu for chairing the Central Pacification and Development Council and using his personal leadership to make the 1970 Pacification and Development Plan a primarily South Vietnamese–drafted document.

In addition to support from Abrams and Thieu, the new head of CORDS, William Colby, helped guide the Pacification Program in the post-Westmoreland era. Colby was a career CIA official who had previously served in Vietnam, including as the CIA station chief in Saigon. He returned in November 1968 after several years' absence to replace Komer. In contrast to his predecessor's aggressive, outspoken manner, Colby was quiet and thoughtful. However, as head of CORDS, he made it his mission to put "pacification on the offensive."

By operating in the villages with South Vietnamese forces, the United States gained much intelligence with the Combined Action Platoons.

AUGUST

August 9 The Senate Armed Services Committee begins closed-door hearings on the influence of civilian officials on military planning. Secretary of Defense McNamara testifies that the U.S. bombing campaign is failing to stem North Vietnam's ability to fight in South Vietnam.

August 18 California governor Ronald Reagan says the United States should get out of Vietnam, explaining it is difficult to win a war in which "too many qualified targets have been put off-limits to bombing."

August 19–September 9 The Mobile Riverine Force conducts Operation Coronado IV, with operations in Long An, Co Cong, and Kien Hoa provinces.

August 21 China shoots down two U.S. planes that accidentally cross into China during air raids in North Vietnam along the Chinese border.

Left: Cameras such as the one in the background here brought the war into the American living room.

Far left: The controversial Phoenix program used ruthless but effective measures to capture and eliminate suspected Vietcong.

Phoenix

Perhaps Colby's most controversial pacification program was Phoenix, or Phung Hoang. The initiative had been envisioned under Komer's tenure, but its activation fell to Colby, the timing motivated in part by the VC's terror campaign in response to the success of the Chieu Hoi program. Phoenix's objective was to eliminate the VC political organization in South Vietnam, and its methods were ruthless. With CIA and CORDS assistance, Colby tasked the South Vietnamese to target the VC leadership through arrest, conversion, or assassination, and in its first year of operation, Phoenix eliminated 16,000 VC cadres, mostly by defection or capture.

The South Vietnamese implemented the program aggressively, but not without their characteristic corruption and political infighting. Some South Vietnamese politicians identified their political enemies as VC and used the Phoenix hit squads, properly known as "provincial reconnaissance units," to go after them. In a development reminiscent of the body count, pressure to eliminate VC led to a quota system that erroneously labeled many innocent people as VC. Nonetheless, the Phoenix program achieved results. Colby testified before

SEPTEMBER

September 1 North Vietnamese prime minister Pham Van Dong vows that Hanoi will continue to fight.

September 3 Nguyen Van Thieu is elected president and Nguyen Cao Ky vice president of South Vietnam, winning just 35 percent of the vote.

September 11–October 31 U.S. marines are besieged by NVA at Con Thien, 1.8 miles south of the demilitarized zone. Firing 281,000 artillery rounds and launching B-52 air strikes, the marines lift the siege and inflict more than 2,000 NVA casualties.

a congressional committee that between 1969 and 1971, Phoenix had reduced the insurgency by 67,000 people. Of that number, approximately 21,000 were killed while the rest surrendered or were captured.

Revised Hamlet Evaluation System

In a less controversial endeavor, Colby was intimately familiar with the process of relocations and hamlet security, having worked on the plan for the original Strategic Hamlet System with Diem's brother, Nhu. As head of CORDS, Colby built on this knowledge to create a new Hamlet Evaluation System designed to remove some of the subjectivity from the previous scheme.

As part of this process, the army contracted with Control Data Corporation to develop a new survey called HES 70. This was billed as "a highly integrated man-machine interface," which would solve the problem of subjectivity by being "objective and uni-dimensional." The new survey counted such things as television sets, organized activities for youths, motorized vehicles, self-defense forces, and other key indicators of security and development.

However, in a marked departure from the old system, advisers no longer did the rating, and all scoring was done in Saigon using a formula not known to the advisers. The idea behind this arrangement was to remove the impression that the advisers were actually evaluating themselves. Although HES 70 improved the system, it remained better suited to measure quantifiable factors such as control and suppression of the opposition rather than the less tangible but more significant ideas of popular allegiance and the strength of commitment to the South Vietnamese government.

Colby remained with CORDS until 1971, when he returned to the United States to be with his critically sick daughter. He then turned CORDS over to his deputy, George Jacobson, who led the organization until it was dissolved in 1973.

Robert Komer, perhaps the man most associated with the pacification effort in

....

External support from China and the USSR was critical to the Vietnamese effort. The Ho Chi Minh Trail and the Cambodian port city of Sihanoukville were key to the Communist logistical structure.

Vietnam, forthrightly described pacification as "admittedly inefficient." He realistically assessed that the chaotic nature of a half-formed country at war with an ever-present enemy created a difficult environment for dramatic progress. Knowing that no single program could achieve success by itself, Komer opted for quantity over quality. He noted that "there was no one pacification technique that could of itself and by itself be

OCTOBER

October 5 Hanoi accuses the United States of hitting a school in North Vietnam with antipersonnel bombs.

October 21–23 At the "March on the Pentagon," 55,000 people protest against the war.

decisive if we just put all our resources behind it. So as a practical matter we pulled together all the various programs then in operation—civilian and military—that looked as though they could make a contribution." It was not a system that reflected efficiency, a familiar business model, or a traditional approach. Instead, it was a fluid situation that hoped to make gradual progress by trial and error, time, and cumulative effects.

Final Assessment

In spite of these inherent inefficiencies, in the final analysis pacification probably represented the best hope for the achievement of U.S. and South Vietnamese victory in Vietnam. Instead, it succumbed to a variety of issues that caused the effort to be too little, too late. The biggest obstacle to full implementation of pacification was its perception as competition with the "Big War." Ambassador Komer and other pacification advocates favored a "clear, hold,

As William Colby put "pacification on the offensive" between 1969 and 1971, his Phoenix program reduced the Communist insurgency by 67,000 people.

and rebuild" strategy, while General Westmoreland favored a traditional military solution to the war by using large-unit search-and-destroy operations. Therefore, Westmoreland relegated pacification to second-tier status as "the other war." Perhaps the most promising pacification program, the Combined Action Platoon, fell victim to this demand for large-unit offensive operations.

This strategic divergence was part of a larger problem that weakened pacification. All the various initiatives and organizations—Agrovilles, strategic hamlets, the Office of Civil Operations, Chieu Hoi, Phoenix, and many others—implied a disjointed and fragmented approach to pacification. Even after CORDS, innate differences fractured many efforts. The marines and the army viewed pacification differently. As MACV commanders, Westmoreland and Abrams had different strategic approaches. The South Vietnamese often resented U.S. supervision and, in turn, the United States doubted South Vietnamese abilities. Pacification suffered from a lack of common purpose and synchronized effort in its various components.

1967

NOVEMBER

November 3–December 1 U.S. forces repel an attempted NVA attack on the Special Forces camp at Dak To along the Cambodian and Laotian border.

November 5–January 14 The Mobile Riverine Force conducts Operation Coronado IX, a series of operations north of the My Tho River that are directed against enemy bases in Dinh Tuong province.

November 11 President Johnson makes another peace overture to North Vietnam, only to be rejected again.

November 17 Following an optimistic briefing by several of his key advisers, President Johnson goes on television and tells the U.S. public, "We are inflicting greater losses than we're taking . . . We are making progress."

November 29 Secretary of Defense McNamara announces his resignation.

Right: Securing the countryside involved the arduous, dangerous, and frustrating task of searching villages.

Far right: One 1966 U.S. Army publication declared that "a more bizarre, eccentric foe than the one in Vietnam is not to be met." Among the Vietcong ranks were female soldiers such as these.

Pacification also failed to address the needs of the South Vietnamese people. In many cases, South Vietnamese government officials resisted the necessary reforms because to do so would have weakened their power. The South Vietnamese government became increasingly illegitimate in the eyes of the peasants, and the self-serving execution of many pacification programs actually drove many of the South Vietnamese to the VC side.

Perhaps the best way to sum up all these problems is to say that the Americans—and the South Vietnamese—never really understood the nature of the war in Vietnam. In a "people's war," the objective is the people. Thoroughly schooled in Mao's doctrine, the North Vietnamese understood this and waged the war accordingly. The United States did not figure this out until it was too late. By then, the VC had such a head start in winning people's hearts and minds that the pacification effort could not catch up. To be successful, the surge in U.S. interest in pacification that finally gained traction in 1968–69 would have been better started in the late 1950s or early 1960s.

DECEMBER

November 30 Democrat Eugene McCarthy, running on an antiwar platform, announces he will be a candidate for president.

December 4 Four days of antiwar protests begin in New York and result in the arrests of 585 people.

December 6 The United States reports that the Vietcong have murdered 252 civilians in the hamlet of Dak Son.

December 23 President Johnson visits Vietnam for the second and final time during his presidency.

Elusive Enemy: Search-and-Destroy Operations

Although hindsight seems to indicate that pacification would have been the best option for the United States, the overall strategy that ended up being chosen, certainly during the tenure of General William Westmoreland as commander of the MACV, revolved around search-and-destroy operations.

These battalion-sized and larger operations were designed to "find, fix, flush, and finish" the enemy in a way that maximized traditional American reliance on firepower and technology. General Henri Navarre had tried a similar strategy to use rapid mobility to search out the enemy ("harry him and destroy him") during the French years in Vietnam. Westmoreland envisioned that using these search-and-destroy operations would cripple the enemy's main force

Left: The A Shau valley was the site of several search-and-destroy operations.
Right: Secretary of Defense Robert McNamara is often closely associated with America's failure in Vietnam.

units and break the hold that the NLF exerted on the countryside. After these conditions had been established, Westmoreland reasoned, the South Vietnamese could accomplish pacification.

In reality, treating pacification as an addendum proved to be a misunderstanding of the true objective in guerrilla war: the people. Seeking decisive large-unit battles was also problematic against guerrillas who could choose to fight only on their terms. The enemy was often able to elude the big U.S. units, and even when caught and forced to fight, North Vietnam was able to continue to mobilize enough soldiers to thwart the Americans' efforts at attrition. Furthermore, because search-and-destroy did not focus on securing terrain after it had been cleared, the guerrillas were able to reoccupy the

area once the Americans had passed through. Although search-and-destroy produced many tactical U.S. victories, it did not result in the achievement of the U.S. strategic objective.

Technology

Critical to search-and-destroy operations—and therefore perhaps the single piece of equipment most associated with the Vietnam War—was the helicopter. They had seen limited service in the Korean War for logistical resupply and casualty evacuation purposes, but a handful of visionaries soon saw the possibility of a far

Above: The Huey helicopter was the workhorse of the airmobile concept.

Left: Robert McNamara displays a machine gun that had been seized from a Vietcong fighter.

greater role. One such individual was Lieutenant General Hamilton Howze, the Director of Army Aviation from 1955 to 1958.

Shortly after Robert McNamara became the Secretary of Defense in 1961, he called on

1968

JANUARY

January 5 Operation Niagara I begins with the purpose of mapping NVA positions around Khe Sanh.

Left: The helicopter provided the U.S. Army with mobility and quick reaction. It was an essential element of search-and-destroy operations.

Below: Helicopters flew into landing zones that were either natural or man-made clearings. Here men of the 11th ARVN Ranger Battalion prepare to load.

Howze to reexamine the army's position and provide new proposals for helicopter employment. Howze was appointed president of the Army Tactical Mobility Requirements Board, a body best known simply as the Howze Board. The board issued its report on August 22, 1962, and its recommendations became the basis for the army's implementation of the airmobile concept. Howze saw the main advantages of the airmobile forces as mobility, usefulness in delay operations, ability to ambush conventional forces, and direct firepower

January 21 General Giap leads 20,000 NVA troops in an attack against the U.S. air base at Khe Sanh. Some 5,000 U.S. marines become isolated in a seventy-seven-day siege, and are sustained by aerial resupply and heavy B-52 bombardment of NVA positions.

January 25 The senior adviser of IV Corps Tactical Zone warns that during the impending Tet holiday cease-fire period, the Vietcong are expected to resupply and move into position for a post-Tet assault.

January 31 The Vietcong and NVA launch the massive Tet Offensive by attacking thirty-six provincial capitals, five autonomous cities, thirty-four district capitals, and at least fifty hamlets throughout South Vietnam.

January 31–March 7 After initially being caught by surprise, U.S. and South Vietnamese troops win the battle for Saigon.

January 31–March 2 South Vietnamese troops and U.S. marines counterattack into Hue and recapture the city, but not before NVA and Vietcong troops have executed over 3,000 "enemies of the people."

Troops of the 1st Air Cavalry fill a long trench during a lull in battle with the Vietcong near Anthi in January 1966.

capability. A month after the report, the army deployed fifteen armed UH-1 Huey helicopters to Vietnam, as well as a concept team to evaluate their effectiveness in counterinsurgency operations.

In January 1963, the army began forming and testing the 11th Air Assault Division. The test program quickly gained momentum, and in September the army conducted an exercise called Air Assault I. This tested an airmobile battalion at Fort Stewart, Georgia. The results were promising enough to warrant further testing, and by January 1964 the army was actively contemplating the inclusion of an airmobile division in its force structure.

The 11th Air Assault Division was formally activated at Fort Benning, Georgia, on February 11, 1964, for the purpose of expanding the test program. Brigadier General Harry Kinnard, who had served with the 101st Airborne Division in World War II, was designated the commander. Under Kinnard's leadership, the division

conducted its second test, Air Assault II, which demonstrated that the "advantages of increased mobility and maneuverability inherent to the air-assault division offers a potential combat effectiveness that can be decisive in tactical operations." Based on this success, Secretary of Defense McNamara authorized the organization of the 1st Cavalry Division (Airmobile) on July 15, 1965. The division began its deployment to Vietnam in a matter of weeks.

Ia Drang

The first combat test of the new airmobile concept and the first major clash of U.S. and North Vietnamese forces was fought in the Ia Drang valley of the central highlands of South Vietnam shortly after the 1st Cavalry Division arrived in the country. The stage for this battle was set when a PAVN army corps attacked a U.S. Special Forces camp near Plei Me, not far from the Cambodian border. The North Vietnamese strategy was to lure a South Vietnamese relief column to rush to the aid of the besieged Americans and then ambush the South Vietnamese. General Chu Huy Man, commander of the campaign, explained, "We

1968

FEBRUARY

February 1 Photographer Eddie Adams captures the exact moment South Vietnam's police chief, General Nguyen Ngoc Loan, shoots a suspected Vietcong guerrilla in the head. The photograph causes many Americans to question the legitimacy of the South Vietnamese authorities.

February 2 President Johnson calls the North Vietnamese Tet Offensive "a complete failure." Tet is in fact a huge tactical victory for the United States, but strategically it leads to a drastic decline in public support for the war.

Left: The battle of Ia Drang derives its name from the Ia Drang River that runs through the valley northwest of Plei Me, in which the engagement took place.

Below: U.S. artillery fire at the battle of Ia Drang. The battle took place at two landing zones northwest of Plei Me, in the central highlands of South Vietnam.

These three photographs depict scenes from the battle of Ia Drang, a U.S. victory that validated the search-and-destroy concept in the minds of many.

February 21 General Westmoreland approves a reorganization of the Mobile Riverine Force.

February 27 News anchor Walter Cronkite tells Americans during his *CBS Evening News* broadcast, "We have too often been disappointed by the optimism of the American leaders to have faith any longer in the silver linings they find in the darkest clouds. The bloody experience of Vietnam is to end in stalemate."

February 28 Chairman of the Joint Chiefs of Staff General Earle Wheeler, on behalf of General Westmoreland, asks President Johnson for an additional 206,000 soldiers and the mobilization of U.S. reserve units.

February 29 The largest naval engagement of the Vietnam War is fought when four North Vietnamese trawlers attack U.S. Navy and Coast Guard patrol boats.

wanted to lure the tiger out of the mountain. We wanted to attack the ARVN—but we would be ready to fight the Americans." NVA historian General Hoang Phuong adds, "We wanted to draw American units into contact for purposes of learning how to fight them." Phuong got his wish, as U.S. and South Vietnamese forces launched a massive counterattack that involved ground units, artillery, and tactical air support to defeat both the attackers at Plei Me and the force trying to ambush the relief column. The PAVN then withdrew to their Cambodian sanctuary after suffering an estimated 850 killed and 1,700 wounded.

Air and Ground Searches

Hoping to follow up on this initial success, Westmoreland called on the 1st Cavalry Division to conduct a series of air and ground searches throughout the Ia Drang valley, a terrain feature formed as the Ia Drang River runs along the north side of the 2,400-foot-high Chu Pong massif. The heights are full of streams, rivers, and caves, and the massif stretches between ten and thirteen miles. The Ia Drang itself begins as the junction of two

small streams but grows into a swift, deep river that becomes a raging torrent in monsoon season. In all, the division's tactical area of operations covered over 890 square miles. Conducting operations over such large, unforgiving territory previously would have been a nearly impossible task, but extensive communications and helicopter mobility now allowed a single brigade to sweep the area. Furthermore, helicopter mobility precluded the requirement for maintaining a central reserve. Once a battle started, every unit not in contact could be airlifted to the scene. The airmobile concept was changing the way the U.S. Army fought.

The operation began on October 28, and for four days the division's searches yielded no results. Then, on November 1, soldiers found a map on a dead North Vietnamese officer, showing unit locations and the routes designated for both the 32nd and 33rd NVA Regiments. This intelligence allowed the division to focus its search, and enemy contacts increased until a major battle was joined on November 14. On that day the 1st Battalion, 7th Cavalry Regiment, commanded by

Lieutenant Colonel Harold Moore, began landing east of the Chu Pong massif in a small clearing known as Landing Zone (LZ) X-Ray. Nearby were the 66th and 33rd NVA Regiments, which quickly began to descend on the landing zone. Almost immediately, Moore's 450-man battalion was surrounded by 2,000 North Vietnamese. Shortly after noon, the two sides were in mortal combat.

Colonel Moore knew his only chance of survival was to secure LZ X-Ray so that reinforcements could be flown in. "That football field–size clearing was our lifeline and our supply line," he said. "If the enemy closed the way to the helicopters, all of us would die in [that] place." Fighting for their lives, the embattled cavalry defended the landing zone on the ground, while over 8,000 artillery rounds and air force fighter-bombers and B-52s flown in from Guam pounded the North Vietnamese from the air. Having attacked prematurely, the North Vietnamese committed their forces piecemeal and the Americans were able to shift from one threatened position to another to hold on. Despite the heavy fire, supplies and reinforcements were delivered by aircrews that

1968

MARCH

March 1 Clark Clifford replaces Robert McNamara as Secretary of Defense.

March 2 During an ambush at Tan Son Nhut airport in Saigon, forty-eight U.S. soldiers are killed.

March 10 The *New York Times* breaks the news of General Westmoreland's 206,000 troop request. Secretary of State Dean Rusk is called to testify before the Senate Foreign Relations Committee and is questioned for two days about the request and the overall effectiveness of the war effort.

March 11 Thirty-three U.S. and South Vietnamese battalions begin Operation Quyet Thang, a twenty-eight-day offensive in the Saigon region.

March 12 President Johnson defeats antiwar Democrat Eugene McCarthy in the New Hampshire Democratic Primary by just 300 votes, indicating political support for Johnson has been seriously diminished.

Moore credits with offering "service far beyond the limits of duty and mission."

The battle continued through the course of two days but, in the end, U.S. tenacity and firepower turned the tide. In the fighting at LZ X-Ray and later at nearby LZ Albany, the North Vietnamese suffered an estimated 3,000 killed, compared to 300 U.S. losses. As the defeated North Vietnamese withdrew toward Cambodia, five battalions of South Vietnamese paratroopers flew to intercept them. Supported by U.S. artillery, the South Vietnamese were able to inflict further casualties before the North Vietnamese made it across the border to safety.

Ia Drang confirmed in Westmoreland's mind the validity of the search-and-destroy concept and became the harbinger of more and larger such operations. Helicopter mobility allowed the Americans to move an entire brigade into battle just hours after being alerted, while the less-mobile North Vietnamese required weeks to plan and execute their efforts. However,

....

The battle of Ia Drang was the consequence of a North Vietnamese plan to attack a U.S. Special Forces camp and then ambush the relief force sent to the camp's aid.

although it demonstrated the capabilities of an airmobile force, the Ia Drang campaign also indicated the difficulty in encircling and destroying the entire enemy, a problem that

would plague future search-and-destroy efforts. Additionally, after suffering heavy losses at Ia Drang, the North Vietnamese merely reverted to guerrilla warfare, a move that largely negated

---

March 14 Senator Robert F. Kennedy offers President Johnson a confidential proposal to agree to stay out of the presidential race if Johnson will renounce his earlier strategy and appoint a committee, including Kennedy, to chart a new course in Vietnam. Johnson rejects the offer.

March 16 Senator Kennedy announces his candidacy for the presidency.

March 16 Some 300 Vietnamese civilians are slaughtered in My Lai by U.S. troops led by Lieutenant William Calley. The initial report by participants at My Lai states that sixty-nine Vietcong soldiers were killed and made no mention of civilian casualties. The army conceals the incident for a year.

March 23 During a secret meeting in the Philippines, General Wheeler informs General Westmoreland that President Johnson will approve only 13,500 additional soldiers out of the 206,000 requested. Wheeler instructs Westmoreland to urge the South Vietnamese to expand their own war effort.

March 25–26 Secretary of Defense Clifford convenes a meeting of twelve senior statesmen and soldiers, dubbed the "Wise Men," and gives President Johnson a bleak report on the prospects for a U.S. victory in Vietnam.

March 31 President Johnson addresses the nation in a speech that ends with a shocking statement: "I shall not seek, and I will not accept, the nomination of my party for another term as your president."

the United States' ability to create the conditions that had given them the advantage at Ia Drang. Finally, in another thematic problem, by the early summer of 1966, sizable enemy units were returning to the central highlands and again threatening the Special Forces camp at Plei Me. Search-and-destroy operations that had abandoned the battlefield were allowing the North Vietnamese to return to it after the Americans had departed. Unless forces remained to secure the area, the whole process became a vicious cycle.

Operation Junction City

After Ia Drang, search-and-destroy operations continued to grow in frequency and size. Although they still relied on the flexibility of the helicopter, the operations became much more deliberate. Operation Junction City was an example of these more deliberately planned and executed operations that followed the classic search-and-destroy methodology of

....

When soldiers fought from prepared defenses, they dug chest-deep fighting positions with overhead cover to provide protection from indirect fire.

"find, fix, flush, and finish." Its detailed plan to systematically isolate the enemy and then crush him with pressure from all sides made earlier operations such as Ia Drang seem almost ad hoc in comparison.

The controlling headquarters for Operation Junction City was II Field Force, Vietnam, under Lieutenant General Jonathan Seaman. II Field Force was a corps-size headquarters responsible for operations in the III Corps Tactical Zone.

1968

APRIL

April 1 The 1st Cavalry Division begins Operation Pegasus to reopen Route 9, the relief route to Khe Sanh.

April 4 James Earl Ray assassinates civil rights leader Martin Luther King Jr. in Memphis, Tennessee. Racial unrest erupts in over a hundred U.S. cities.

April 8 The siege of Khe Sanh ends as NVA troops withdraw after intensive U.S. bombing and the reopening of Route 9.

Artillery and air strikes accounted for most of the enemy casualties in Operation Junction City.

as well, Operation Junction City was exactly the type of search-and-destroy operation Westmoreland had envisioned.

Operation Junction City's initial effort to find the enemy was based on some extremely accurate intelligence analysis. The geographic focus of the operation was War Zone C, a large, sparsely populated jungle area northwest of Saigon and adjacent to the Cambodian border. The Central Office for South Vietnam (COSVN), the headquarters that controlled all Communist political and military operations in central and southern Vietnam, was believed to be in the area. Operation Attleboro, the largest search-and-destroy operation of the war at that time, had brought more than 22,000 U.S. and South Vietnamese troops there in November 1966. Nonetheless, for the most part, enemy control of War Zone C had been uncontested.

Rather than having confirmed knowledge of the enemy, Operation Junction City planners built on intelligence gathered during Operation

Operation Junction City was the first time II Field Force dispatched to the field, and it established a tactical command post at Dau Tieng.

The U.S. 1st and 25th Infantry Divisions provided the bulk of the forces for Operation Junction City, but other U.S. and South Vietnamese units participated as well. In all, the operation involved four South Vietnamese and twenty-two U.S. combat battalions, and it was the largest military offensive of the Vietnam War at the time. Not just in methodology, but in size

April 11 Secretary of Defense Clifford announces that General Westmoreland's request for 206,000 additional soldiers will not be granted.

April 23–30 Antiwar activists led by the Students for a Democratic Society seize five buildings at Columbia University and hold school officials hostage.

April 30–May 3 U.S. marines halt an NVA effort to open an invasion avenue into South Vietnam in the battle of Dai Do.

Attleboro and used pattern analysis to predict enemy locations. As the operation unfolded, this system proved effective, with slightly less than 40 percent of the enemy positions being located within 1,500 feet of their predicted sites. Just as the captured map provided focus to the search in the Ia Drang valley, all search-and-destroy operations relied on some type of intelligence to focus their search efforts and avoid being just aimless wanderings through the jungle.

Fixing and Flushing Activities

During the first phase of the actual operation, both fixing and flushing activities were conducted. From February 22 to March 17, Operation Junction City forces deployed in the shape of a giant inverted horseshoe around the area of suspected enemy activity. Positions in the east and north portions of the horseshoe were established by Major General John H. Hay Jr.'s 1st Infantry Division. Hay had only two of the brigades from his own division available because

....

More than 22,000 U.S. troops participated in Operation Attleboro in War Zone C in November 1966. The same area was the focus of Operation Junction City in 1967.

one of his brigades was busy conducting pacification operations elsewhere. The 1st Infantry, however, was augmented by the 173rd Airborne Brigade; the South Vietnamese Task Force Wallace, which consisted of the 35th Ranger Battalion and one troop from the 3rd Battalion, 1st Cavalry; and a squadron from the 1st Cavalry Regiment. Later, the 1st Brigade, 9th Infantry Division joined the 1st Infantry as well.

To occupy the area quickly in order to prevent the enemy from escaping, the 1st Brigade, 1st Infantry Division and Task Force Wallace moved by helicopter to establish blocking positions in the north. To block the most likely escape route into Cambodia, the 173rd Airborne Brigade, commanded by Brigadier General John R. Deane Jr., conducted the only U.S. combat airborne jump of the war, parachuting into the northeast portion of the horseshoe and establishing blocking positions from Katum to the 1st Brigade area. Responsibility for the eastern leg of the horseshoe was assigned to the 1st Infantry Division's 3rd Brigade with the help of the attached cavalry squadron. The 3rd Brigade was responsible for attacking north to link up

---

1968

MAY

May 5 The Vietcong launch a series of rocket and mortar attacks against 119 cities and military installations throughout South Vietnam in an offensive nicknamed "Mini Tet."

May 10 An NVA battalion attack forces the evacuation of the Special Forces camp at Kham Duc along the border of Laos.

May 10 Peace talks begin in Paris but soon stall amid U.S. insistence that North Vietnamese troops withdraw from the south, and North Vietnamese demands that the Vietcong be allowed to participate in a coalition government in South Vietnam.

JUNE

June 5 Senator Robert F. Kennedy is assassinated in Los Angeles just after winning the California Democratic Presidential Primary. The assassination, along with President Johnson's earlier decision not to seek reelection, throws the Democratic presidential nomination race into turmoil.

with the 173rd Airborne to seal that side of the horseshoe.

The 25th Infantry Division, commanded by Major General Fred Weyand, was assigned to block the northwestern and western portions of the horseshoe as well as to flush the enemy by driving a force north through the open end. In addition to his own 2nd Brigade, Weyand also had at his disposal the 3rd Brigade, 4th Infantry Division; the 196th Light Infantry Brigade; part of the 11th Armored Cavalry Regiment; and two South Vietnamese units, the 1st and 5th Marine Battalions, which formed Task Force Alpha. The 1st Brigade, 9th Infantry Division, part of the 25th Infantry Division's original task organization, was under the operational control of the 1st Infantry Division later in this phase.

The 3rd Brigade, 4th Infantry Division was already in a position in the far western portion of the operational area from a previous operation, and Weyand directed it to block and continue to conduct search-and-destroy operations from that location. The 196th Light Infantry Brigade would conduct airmobile assaults with its three infantry battalions along the northwest portion of the horseshoe to

During Operation Junction City, the 173rd Airborne Brigade conducted the only combat jump by an American unit in the Vietnam War.

establish blocking positions and seal enemy escape routes into Cambodia. The combined positions of the 25th and 1st Infantry Divisions would fix the North Vietnamese inside the horseshoe and prevent their escape, especially to sanctuary across the Cambodian border. This accomplished, the 25th Infantry Division's 2nd Brigade and elements of the 11th Armored Cavalry would drive north into the horseshoe to flush the enemy. Any enemy troops that were not destroyed by these two units would be crushed against the fixing forces that comprised the horseshoe.

Sweep Operations
Additionally, sweep operations were to be conducted to the west, south, and east of the horseshoe by the units forming it. This level of planning and prepositioning of forces showed how search-and-destroy operations had evolved from the much more fluid Ia Drang operation.

JULY

July 1 Congress passes a 10 percent income-tax surcharge to help defray the growing costs of the war.

July 1 The Phoenix Program is established to crush the secret Vietcong infrastructure in South Vietnam, but the scheme will not begin in earnest until 1969.

July 1 General Creighton W. Abrams replaces General Westmoreland as commander of the MACV. Westmoreland moves on to become the chief of staff of the U.S. Army.

July 3 Hanoi releases three U.S. prisoners of war in a move perceived by many as being an effort to manipulate U.S. public opinion.

July 19 President Johnson and President Nguyen Van Thieu meet in Hawaii.

On February 22, Operation Junction City kicked off as planned. By the end of the day, eighteen battalions, organized into six brigades, and one cavalry regiment were deployed around the horseshoe. Thirteen mutually supporting fire support bases also ringed the operational area. In order to back the ground operation, the air force flew 216 preplanned strike sorties. As the Americans and South Vietnamese moved into their positions, enemy contact was light. Just four Americans were killed and twenty-three wounded. Enemy losses were unknown.

The next day, the combined elements of the 11th Armored Cavalry Regiment and the 2nd Brigade of the 25th Infantry Division moved northward through the open end of the horseshoe to trap the Vietcong, locating and destroying North Vietnamese Army and VC installations and COSVN. Almost immediately, the units began to uncover significant caches of enemy supplies and equipment. Enemy personnel, however, remained elusive, with

American soldiers conducted extensive searches during Operation Junction City and uncovered vast amounts of enemy supplies.

1968

AUGUST

August 5–8 The Republican National Convention chooses Richard Nixon as the Republican presidential candidate. Nixon promises "an honorable end to the war in Vietnam."

August 26–29 The Democratic National Convention in Chicago is marred by violence as 10,000 antiwar protesters are confronted by 26,000 police and National Guardsmen. Hubert Humphrey, President Johnson's vice president, emerges as the nominee.

SEPTEMBER

September 1 Vice Admiral Elmo R. Zumwalt Jr. is appointed Commander, Naval Forces, Vietnam (COMNAVFORV).

September 30 The 900th U.S. aircraft is shot down over North Vietnam.

only four minor contacts made during the day's search. Contact on the perimeter of the horseshoe was also light, but the 1st Brigade, 1st Infantry Division did find a battalion-sized base camp complete with shower facilities and over 6,000 pairs of "Ho Chi Minh sandals," the typical VC footwear made from worn-out truck tires.

On February 24, Operation Junction City forces launched several attacks from the perimeter, while the hammer forces of the 25th Infantry Division continued the attack to the north. Engineers also began to construct an airfield large enough for C-130s at Katum, just south of the Cambodian border, which would be used during Operation Junction City and to facilitate future operations in the area. Although contact was generally light, more enemy base camps were located, including a series of camps in an area 1.8 miles south of the Cambodian border. Elements of the 1st Brigade, 1st Infantry Division had to fight their way into this area,

The vertical metal bar modification to the front of this jeep is designed to protect the driver and passenger from wires the Vietcong might string across the road.

indicating that there was something of value to the enemy there. On closer inspection, it appeared that the camps were part of the military affairs section of the COSVN. There

were large mess facilities, lecture halls, recreational areas, and supply depots that stored radios, batteries, office supplies, and a generator. There were also heavily built

OCTOBER

October 8 COMNAVFORV begins the campaign known as Southeast Asia Lake, Ocean, River, and Delta Strategy (SEALORDS) to block infiltration routes along the Cambodian border and to seek out enemy forces along smaller canals and streams.

October 21 The United States releases fourteen North Vietnamese prisoners of war.

October 27 A war protest in London draws 50,000 people.

October 31 Operation Rolling Thunder ends and President Johnson announces a complete cessation of the bombing of North Vietnam in hopes of restarting the peace talks.

defensive positions, large underground living quarters, camouflaged aboveground quarters, shower points, and table tennis tables. The occupants had apparently departed in a hurry, leaving behind partially prepared food in the kitchens as well as their livestock and chickens.

During the next three-week period that marked the rest of the first phase, the level of activity remained largely the same. More and more base camps continued to be discovered. Documents, food, weapons, ammunition, explosives, and communication equipment were the main items found. Soldiers also discovered facilities believed to be associated with COSVN's public information, cultural indoctrination, and propaganda offices. The only major battles fought during this phase occurred at or near Prek Klok on February 28 and March 10. The February 28 action was a meeting engagement between a battalion from the 1st Infantry Division and elements of the 2nd Battalion, 101st North Vietnamese Army Regiment, 9th VC Division, as the Communist battalion was en route to establish ambushes against U.S. convoys traveling between Suoi Da and Katum on Route 4. By the end of the day,

the Americans had killed 167 enemy fighters and captured or destroyed forty enemy weapons.

The March 10 battle again involved elements of the 1st Infantry Division and two battalions of the 272nd Regiment of the 9th VC Division. This time, the 1st Infantry Division forces killed 197 VC while suffering just three killed and thirty-eight wounded. In both these battles, the Americans were able to use big units and firepower against an enemy that was willing to fight, and in such situations the U.S. troops had the advantage. These were the odds that Westmoreland was hoping for in his search-and-destroy operations, but they were the exception rather than the rule. The first phase's operations started to wind down from March 12 and were officially terminated at midnight on March 17. Enemy losses were reported to be 835 killed, together with fifteen men, 264 weapons, and enormous quantities of supplies and equipment captured.

The second phase of Operation Junction City ran from March 18 to April 15. There were several changes to the task organization and Lieutenant General Bruce Palmer Jr. succeeded

Seaman as the commanding general of the II Field Force, but the basic search-and-destroy nature of the operation remained the same. During the twenty-nine days of the second phase's operations, there were only three major battles, all initiated by the enemy. More characteristic were typical guerrilla tactics such as mortar attacks and mining and ambush activities along convoy routes where VC in small three- or four-man groups maintained continuous pressure.

Ap Bau Bang II

The first big battle of the second phase was Ap Bau Bang II. It began on March 19 when the VC attacked A Troop, 3rd Squadron, 5th Cavalry Regiment in its Fire Support Base 20. After initiating a mortar attack, the 273rd Vietcong Regiment conducted a main attack coming from the south and southwest and a secondary attack from the north. The attacks were coordinated with the mortar fire and, once the enemy emerged from the rubber trees, it was obvious this was a major assault.

As the Americans held their ground, reinforcements were sped their way, together

1968

NOVEMBER

November 1 William Colby replaces Robert Komer as head of CORDS.

November 5 Republican Richard Nixon defeats Democrat Hubert Humphrey in the U.S. presidential election.

DECEMBER

December 2 President-elect Nixon appoints Harvard professor Henry Kissinger as his national security adviser.

December 6 Operation Giant Slingshot, a riverine operation, begins. The operation involves 1,044 firefights, captures 124 tons of weapons and 350 tons of other caches, and kills 1,910 enemy soldiers and captures 232.

with a flareship armed with mini guns and a light fire team of helicopter gunships. With these reinforcements, the Americans were able to plug gaps in their perimeter and expand outward using sweeping operations. At 5:00 a.m. on March 20, the Vietcong launched a final assault. It was met by massive U.S. artillery fire, cluster bombs, napalm, and 500-pound bombs. This impressive display of U.S. firepower halted the attack and by 7:00 a.m. the enemy was in the process of withdrawing. The battle of Ap Bau Bang II resulted in 227 confirmed enemy dead, mostly caused by artillery and air strikes. All told, twenty-nine air strikes had delivered 25.9 tons of ordnance and the artillery had fired nearly 3,000 rounds. The United States suffered just three killed and sixty-three wounded.

The second big battle of this phase was fought at Suoi Tre, near the center of War Zone C and fifty-six miles northwest of Saigon. It was less than two miles away from the area in which, during Operation Attleboro four months

....

The command-detonated charges used by the Vietcong to disrupt landings at Soui Tre reflected the Vietcong's ability to develop new tactics to thwart U.S. operations.

earlier, the 1st Infantry Division had defeated elements of the 272nd Vietcong and 101st North Vietnamese Regiments at the battle of Ap Cha Do. As was a common occurrence in search-and-destroy operations, once the

Americans had departed the area after Operation Attleboro, the VC had returned.

On March 19, units under the control of the 3rd Brigade, 4th Infantry Division helicoptered into a landing zone near Suoi Tre to establish

1969

JANUARY

Fire Support Base Gold. Heavy action was not expected. However, as the helicopters touched down, five heavy command-detonated charges were set off by the VC in the tiny clearing. This new tactic was one example of how the VC adapted to and countered U.S. technology and techniques. Three helicopters were destroyed and six more damaged, and fifteen men were killed and twenty-eight wounded. Five more men were wounded when the VC detonated an antipersonnel mine. Seven more helicopters were damaged when they flew in later that day. In spite of this, the Americans were able to proceed with the construction of the fire base.

The next day, the fire base came under a heavy enemy mortar attack at 6:31 a.m. Simultaneously, a massive VC force, later identified as the 272nd Regiment of the 9th VC Division reinforced by elements of the U-80 Artillery Regiment, attacked and destroyed a night patrol that was returning to the perimeter. Some 650 mortar rounds fell while the VC attacked the fire base, and within minutes the entire perimeter came under heavy attack as waves of enemies emerged from the jungle.

The U.S. artillery responded with countermortar fire. At 7:00, the first forward air controller arrived overhead in a light observation aircraft and immediately began to direct air strikes against the attackers. Simultaneously, supporting artillery batteries from nearby fire bases delivered fire within 300 feet of the battalion's perimeter. In spite of these efforts, at 7:11 one platoon was overrun and surrounded by a human-wave attack. Air strikes were called in all along the wood line to the east

Tuy Hoa Air Base. Bases like Tuy Hoa were vulnerable to attack, but Tuy Hoa's defense succeeded because the Vietcong found the local population difficult to infiltrate.

1969

FEBRUARY

February 23 The Vietcong attack 110 locations throughout South Vietnam, including Saigon.

February 25 An NVA raid kills thirty-six U.S. marines at their base camp near the demilitarized zone.

MARCH

March 4 President Nixon threatens to resume bombing North Vietnam in retaliation for Vietcong offenses in the south.

to relieve the pressure on the company's perimeter, but the forward air controller directing the strikes was soon shot down by heavy automatic weapons fire. At 7:50 the artillery began firing "beehive rounds," canisters filled with hundreds of metal darts, into the southeastern and southern sections of the perimeter, but the enemy was still able to penetrate multiple sections of the U.S. positions. By 8:40 the northeastern, eastern, and southeastern portions of the perimeter had withdrawn to a secondary defensive line around the artillery batteries. The northern, western, and southern sectors were managing to hold despite intense pressure from large numbers of VC who had advanced as close as 50 feet from the defensive positions. The attackers were now within hand-grenade range of the battalion command post and were only 15 feet from the battalion's aid station.

Desperately, the artillery leveled its tubes and fired more beehive rounds. Air strikes were brought within as close as 150 feet of U.S. forces, and supporting artillery batteries threw up a continuous wall of shrapnel around the battalion perimeter. When the artillery inside the perimeter had exhausted its supply of beehive rounds, it began to fire high-explosive rounds at point-blank range. By 9:00 the northern, western, and southern sectors of the perimeter were holding but still under VC pressure. The positions on the east had withdrawn even closer, but the line was still intact.

At 9:00 a relief column from another battalion in the 3rd Brigade broke through and linked up with the battered fire base. Bolstered by these reinforcements, the Americans countered and restored the original perimeter. Still the VC continued to attack. At 9:12 a mechanized infantry and armor column broke through the jungle from the southwest, and in the face of these additional reinforcements, the enemy began to withdraw. By 9:30 the original perimeter had been reestablished, and by 10:00 helicopters began delivering supplies and evacuating the wounded. Mechanized and armored units, as well as artillery and air strikes, pressured the enemy withdrawal, and

Colored smoke helped pilots locate landing zones. Identification of the color of the smoke also thwarted attempts to lure pilots into ambushes.

March 15 U.S. troops launch an offensive inside the demilitarized zone for the first time since 1968.

March 17 President Nixon authorizes Operation Menu, a secret campaign to bomb North Vietnamese supply bases located along the Cambodian border of Vietnam.

March 29 Ronald Ridenhour writes several letters that result in a U.S. Army investigation into the My Lai massacre.

At times the enemy was so close to friendly positions during Operation Junction City that artillery gunners fired rounds at point-blank range.

sporadic contact continued until noon. Enemy losses included 647 killed, together with sixty-five crew-served weapons and ninety-four individual weapons captured. The United States lost thirty-one killed and 109 wounded.

The final big battle of the second phase began on March 30 as the 1st Battalion, 26th Infantry Regiment, 1st Infantry Division, commanded by Lieutenant Colonel Alexander Haig, airmobiled deeper into War Zone C to Landing Zone George near the Cambodian border. On landing, the battalion sent out cloverleaf-shaped patrols to locate the enemy and soon uncovered fortified positions in and around the landing zone. Intelligence reports had expected enemy contact, but no enemy was found, and there were no significant encounters throughout that night.

The next morning, the 1st Battalion, 2nd Infantry Regiment flew into LZ George, also without incident, and began search-and-destroy operations in the surrounding area. Northwest

of the perimeter, the Americans found small signs hanging from trees, warning in English that if the Americans went beyond the signs, they would not return. At 1:00 p.m., a reconnaissance platoon made heavy enemy contact approximately three miles south of

the Cambodian border. The battalion responded with artillery and air strikes. A company of reinforcements, on the company commander's initiative and without battalion coordination, also moved toward the platoon's location. Although this move was necessary to assist the

1969

APRIL

April 9 At Harvard University, 300 students seize the administration building in an antiwar protest, throw out eight deans, and then lock themselves in.

April 30 U.S. troop levels peak at 543,400.

MAY

May 8 The *New York Times* breaks the news of the secret bombing of Cambodia. President Nixon orders FBI wiretaps on the telephones of four journalists and thirteen government officials to determine the source of the leak.

May 10–20 The 101st Airborne Division and ARVN forces overcome fierce resistance in the battle of Hamburger Hill in the A Shau valley, only to then abandon the position.

May 14 Nixon uses a television address to announce a peace plan requiring the United States and North Vietnam to simultaneously pull out of South Vietnam over the next year. Hanoi rejects the offer.

reconnaissance platoon, it committed the company to battle without sufficient preparation. Soon the unit found itself heavily engaged by at least a battalion-sized enemy force.

Reinforcements

As the situation worsened, Haig committed an additional company to reinforce and extract the units in contact. These reinforcements, along with intense and accurate artillery and air strikes, allowed the U.S. troops to break contact. As the VC tried to pursue, they were halted by the bombardment. Seven Americans were killed and thirty-eight wounded. Enemy casualties were unknown at the time.

As the U.S. forces returned to LZ George, an additional battalion of reinforcements was flown in. The two battalions coordinated their defensive plans and established a security plan for the night. At around midnight, listening posts to the north, east, and south began to report some movement to their front, but there was no significant contact. Then, at 4:45 a.m., the VC initiated a mortar attack from a position so close to the perimeter that the U.S. troops could hear the rounds being fired. Twelve men

were wounded in the attack. The heavy mortar attack on the two battalions ended at 5:15 a.m., and seven minutes later the VC launched their initial ground attack against the northeast edge of the perimeter. The enemy was able to create a penetration into the perimeter that was roughly 120 feet deep and 300 feet wide. In the midst of hand-to-hand fighting, the U.S. ground soldiers were able to hold the shoulders of the penetration while air force cluster bombs, helicopter rockets, and guns broke the VC attack. The United States then counterattacked, pushing the VC back into the wall of the aerial bombardment. By 8:00 a.m., the perimeter was restored, and the Americans began sweeping around the area. They found 609 enemy killed, and the attackers were identified as all three battalions of the 271st Regiment of the 9th Vietcong Division and elements of the 70th Guard Regiment. The United States suffered seventeen killed and 102 wounded.

Colonel Haig was quick to identify the air support as the critical aspect of the U.S. success, although he also praised the artillery. Air force jet fighter-bombers had flown 103 sorties and dropped over eighty-nine tons of ordnance.

Artillery units of the 1st Infantry Division had also fired some 15,000 rounds into the battle area.

The second phase of Junction City ended on April 15. Except for the three big battles, efforts to force the enemy to fight on terms where U.S. forces had the advantage were frustrating. For example, the 173rd Airborne Brigade made contact of some form on each of the twenty-two days it participated in this phase, but the contacts were with small groups never larger than platoon size. By the last week of the phase, the enemy became increasingly more difficult to find. However, although enemy soldiers remained elusive, the Americans continued to uncover facilities and supplies. The second phase resulted in nearly 1,900 enemy dead and nineteen taken prisoner, and 240 weapons captured.

Third Phase

The initial plan was for Operation Junction City to cease after the second phase, but the first two phases were deemed so successful that a third phase was added. This last phase would be commanded by the 25th Infantry Division,

---

JUNE

June 8 President Nixon meets South Vietnam's President Nguyen Van Thieu at Midway Island and informs him that U.S. troop levels are going to be sharply reduced under the new policy of "Vietnamization."

June 27 COMNAVFORV activates Operation Sea Float to establish a U.S. and South Vietnamese naval presence in the Cua Lon River on the Ca Mau peninsula.

June 27 *Life* magazine features portrait photos of all 242 Americans killed in Vietnam during the previous week, including the forty-six killed at Hamburger Hill.

which committed a brigade of its own and had two other brigades under its control. Until midnight on May 14, the Americans conducted operations throughout the area, but large organized enemy units became nearly impossible to find. What contacts were made involved relatively small VC groups, but the Americans did locate and destroy many bunkers and military structures. It soon became clear that the enemy had moved on to a new area.

As was often the case, the statistical results of Operation Junction City pointed to a marked success. All the regiments of the 9th Vietcong Division had been badly bloodied, resulting in 2,728 enemy killed and thirty-four prisoners taken. By comparison, the United States lost 282 killed and 1,576 wounded. Equipment losses to the Communists were even more impressive, including the capture of 100 crew-served weapons, 491 individual weapons, and thousands of rounds of ammunition, grenades, and mines. More than 5,000 bunkers and military structures were destroyed, and 723 tons of rice and 35.7 tons of other foodstuffs, such as salt and dried fish, were located and denied to the enemy. Nearly half a million pages of

assorted documents were seized and exploited for their intelligence value.

Less tangibly, Operation Junction City affected the headquarters of the COSVN by causing its forces to withdraw to Cambodia and disrupting its control over VC activity. Along with the destruction of facilities, this forced relocation limited the COSVN's ability to plan and control operations for some time. However, the operation's objective of destroying the COSVN headquarters was not achieved.

One of the most far-reaching effects on the VC was their realization that their bases, even in remote locations such as the outer reaches of War Zone C, were no longer safe from helicopter-borne U.S. troops and U.S. air and artillery firepower. As a result, after Operation Junction City the Communists made increased use of Cambodian sanctuaries for bases, hospitals, training centers, and supply depots. Although this adjustment disrupted the existing pattern of VC operations, it exacerbated the

The enemy often reoccupied the targets of American search-and-destroy operations, such as the A Shau valley, shortly after the Americans withdrew.

1969

JULY

July 8 The phased U.S. troop withdrawal begins with 800 soldiers from the 9th Infantry Division.

July 15 President Nixon sends a secret letter through a French emissary to Ho Chi Minh, urging him to settle the war, while at the same time threatening to resume bombing if peace talks are still stalled by November 1.

July 17 Secretary of State William Rogers accuses North Vietnam of "lacking humanity" in its treatment of U.S. prisoners of war.

July 25 At a conference in Guam, President Nixon unveils the Nixon Doctrine, which advocates U.S. military and economic assistance rather than U.S. ground combat troops to nations struggling against Communism.

July 30 President Nixon visits U.S. troops and President Nguyen Van Thieu in his only trip to Vietnam as president.

problem for the Americans who were reluctant to widen the war by crossing the Cambodian border.

Operation Junction City demonstrated some of the inherent difficulties of search-and-destroy operations. As explained by 1st Infantry Division commander Major General John Hay, these included the sanctuary offered by Cambodia, the challenge of effectively sealing off the area based on the advantage that familiarity with the terrain gave the VC, and the difficulty in achieving surprise. More importantly, Operation Junction City showed the inability of search-and-destroy operations to achieve lasting results. In order to discourage the enemy from regaining freedom of action in War Zone C after Operation Junction City, General Westmoreland had intended to use the 196th Light Infantry Brigade as a "floating brigade" to continue to conduct mobile operations in the area covered in the first phase. However, later developments required him to

Helicopters in Vietnam served varied purposes, such as delivering troops and supplies, evacuating casualties, facilitating command and control, and observation.

AUGUST

August 4 Henry Kissinger conducts his first secret meeting in Paris with representatives from North Vietnam.

August 12 The Vietcong launch a new offensive that targets 150 locations throughout South Vietnam.

withdraw the 196th in April and send it north. Subsequent reconnaissance flights over War Zone C soon revealed that the enemy had returned. Even the airfield at Katum, so painstakingly built by engineers, showed signs of being mined by the VC to prevent its use.

A Shau Valley

After General Creighton Abrams replaced Westmoreland as commander of the MACV, pacification received increased emphasis and huge search-and-destroy operations such as Operation Junction City became less frequent. Nevertheless, U.S. commanders remained dedicated to the concept and sought ways to use it to overcome the enemy. One such opportunity presented itself as the North Vietnamese regrouped from their losses incurred during the Tet Offensive and the level of combat throughout Vietnam dropped perceptibly, giving Abrams the forces necessary for a sustained campaign in the A Shau valley. The A Shau

During April and May of 1968, the 101st Airborne Division conducted Operation Delaware Valley in the A Shau valley.

was a rugged stretch of mountainous terrain along the Laotian border, which had previously been largely controlled by the enemy. It was not that the Americans had never attacked into the A Shau. They had, several times, including Operation Delaware in April to May of 1968. After each incursion, however, the enemy had successfully reestablished itself in the valley, further demonstrating the inherent flaw in the U.S. tendency to vacate an area after a search-and-destroy operation.

Operation Apache Snow was designed to break this enemy grip in the area. On May 10, 1969, elements of the 101st Airborne Division and the 1st ARVN Division helicoptered into a series of landing zones throughout the thirty-mile-long valley. Each landing was preceded by air strikes and artillery and helicopter gunship attacks, so the enemy had ample notice of the operation. As had occurred often during Operation Junction City, the surprise element critical to search-and-destroy operations was lost.

On the second day of the operation, a company from the 101st Airborne located an enemy force on the rugged, densely forested,

1969

SEPTEMBER

September 3 Ho Chi Minh dies of a heart attack at the age of seventy-nine, and is succeeded by Le Duan.

September 4 The U.S. Army brings murder charges against Lieutenant William Calley for his role in the March 1968 massacre at My Lai.

September 16 President Nixon orders the withdrawal of 35,000 soldiers from Vietnam and a reduction in draft notices.

After the costly battle of Hamburger Hill, President Nixon impressed upon General Abrams the need to reduce U.S. casualties in Vietnam.

and heavily fortified Dong Ap Bia, designated as Hill 937 on military maps. The company was unable to dislodge the enemy and was soon provided with reinforcements. Over the course of the next ten days, Americans and South Vietnamese attacked the hill. However, the

OCTOBER

October 15 The "Moratorium" peace demonstrations are held in Washington, D.C., and several other U.S. cities.

October 31 Polling data indicates that 71 percent of Americans approve of President Nixon's Vietnam policy.

North Vietnamese repeatedly repulsed the attacks, and the human carnage soon gave the position the nickname "Hamburger Hill." On May 20, a force of four battalions finally captured the hill. Throughout the ten-day battle, the air force flew 272 attack sorties and dropped more than 446 tons, including sixty-eight tons of napalm. The United States suffered fifty-six dead and 420 wounded while killing 505 North Vietnamese. However, after this horrendous struggle, once the hill was secured and its bunkers searched and destroyed, the Americans and South Vietnamese withdrew. The North Vietnamese reoccupied the hill a month later, but the U.S. military declared the battle a victory based on the favorable casualty figures.

For many, Hamburger Hill epitomized the futility of search-and-destroy operations as well as the larger folly of the war. In explaining the action, Major General Melvin Zais, commander of the 101st Airborne, wrote, "It is true Hill 937, as a particular piece of terrain, was of no tactical significance. However, the fact that the enemy force was located there was of prime significance. Although Allied forces were not oriented on terrain, and had no mission to seize and hold any particular hill, obviously the enemy had to be engaged where he was found if the mission was to be accomplished."

For the American soldier in Vietnam, the continuous effort to bring an elusive enemy to bay proved frustrating and exhausting.

1969

NOVEMBER

November 3 President Nixon delivers a televised speech calling for U.S. unity and support from "the great silent majority of my fellow Americans" for his Vietnam strategy.

November 15 The "Mobilization" peace demonstration in Washington, D.C., becomes the largest protest of the war, drawing an estimated 250,000 people.

November 16 The U.S. Army publicly discusses events surrounding the My Lai massacre.

For many, Zais's explanation begged the deeper question of why the enemy had to be attacked wherever he was found. Hamburger Hill seemed to represent another example of the North Vietnamese successfully luring the Americans into the periphery and creating a vacuum for the VC to exploit in the populated areas. It also showed that even in the Abrams era of "one war," the strategy of attrition still weighed heavily in the minds of many U.S. commanders.

Assessment

Although bankrupt as an overall strategy, search-and-destroy operations had some usefulness, especially early in the United States' involvement in the war. In 1965 and 1966, when North Vietnamese and VC forces threatened to overrun South Vietnam, a major conventional military response was probably unavoidable. Large operations against the enemy's main forces were necessary then to halt the enemy's advance and provide a shield behind which pacification could take root. The original idea was that after U.S. troops had cleared an area of enemy main forces, South Vietnamese troops, police, and pacification cadres would move in to eliminate the VC infrastructure and provide lasting security and development to the hamlet. However, this planned follow-through seldom happened. Instead, search-and-destroy operations rapidly became an end unto themselves. In the strategy of attrition and search-and-destroy, the United States missed the point that this war was about securing the people and not about killing the enemy.

By the war's end, the very name "search-and-destroy" became associated with the ugly side of Vietnam. Major General William DePuy, who as Westmoreland's plans and operations officer was one of the concept's principal architects, traced the evolution: "What it meant back in 1965, long before it became unpopular, was simply that U.S. units or Vietnamese airborne units and marine units would patrol in the jungle—not in the populated areas—to search for the main force Communist units, fight them, and destroy them." However, as the war grew to envelop South Vietnam's 16,000 villages, DePuy lamented that the tactic "became associated with pictures of troops searching villages and setting them on fire. The word 'destroy' became a dirty word. It started out with the best of intentions." Well-intentioned or not, search-and-destroy operations proved to be an ineffective tactic in the guerrilla environment of Vietnam. In fact, they played directly into the hands of the North Vietnamese and their strategy of protracted war.

U.S. soldiers, laden with weapons and equipment, hustle out of a landing zone on their way to a search-and-destroy operation.

DECEMBER

December 1 The first draft lottery since World War II is held in New York City. The lottery eliminates many of the inequities of the previous system.

December 15 President Nixon orders the withdrawal of an additional 50,000 troops from Vietnam.

December 20 Frustrated by the proceedings, Henry Cabot Lodge quits his post as chief U.S. negotiator at the Paris peace talks.

Rolling Thunder: The Air War

Not only through search-and-destroy operations but in almost all aspects of its military strategy, the United States hoped to use its superior firepower and technology to force North Vietnam and the Vietcong to abandon their mission of unifying Vietnam under Communism.

In no other aspect of the Vietnam War did this strategy more clearly manifest itself than in the air war. Developed during the years between World War I and World War II, U.S. air war strategy focused primarily on strategic bombing. The proponents of this strategy believed that a bombing campaign that focused on a country's "war-making potential" rather than its armed forces could destroy the enemy's ability to wage war as well as his will to fight.

Left: Better technology and firepower led to a tactic of strategic bombing against the North Vietnamese. Right: U.S. aircraft sprayed herbicides to defoliate the vegetation that helped conceal the Vietcong.

Despite this confidence in firepower and technology, strategic bombing failed to have the desired effect in Vietnam. Strict rules of engagement, gradual escalation, modern antiaircraft defenses supplied by the Russians and the Chinese, and the ability of the North Vietnamese to recover quickly from air strikes all helped to limit the effectiveness of the bombing campaign. Vietcong practices of "clinging to the belts" of the Americans and "clutching the people to their breasts" also limited the successful application of tactical air support. However, the strategic bombing and the use of tactical air support did have some major successes during the Vietnam War. On many occasions, tactical air missions saved the lives of outnumbered and surrounded GIs and the bombing campaign drove the North Vietnamese back to the peace table after Operation Linebacker II in 1972.

Operation Farmgate

The United States began air operations over Vietnam in late 1961, when President John F. Kennedy made the decision to send equipment and 3,000 military advisers and support personnel to aid the South Vietnamese in their war against the Vietcong. Soon, U.S. helicopters were flying ARVN soldiers and American advisers into combat missions against the VC. U.S. planes transported troops and supplies, and reconnaissance aircraft searched for guerrilla units. All of these operations were grouped under the U.S. Air Force advisory effort, code-named Operation Farmgate. Under special rules of engagement, the aircraft used in Farmgate were flown by U.S. personnel but had to have a South Vietnamese air force officer on board. Using the excuse that they were training the South Vietnamese as their cover story, U.S. pilots were actually flying unofficial combat missions against the VC.

The original Farmgate deployment package had 155 airmen, eight T-28s, and four modified and redesignated SC-47s. The unit later received B-26s like this one.

1970

FEBRUARY

February 2 B-52 bombers strike the Ho Chi Minh Trail in retaliation for increasing Vietcong activity throughout the south.

February 21 While the official peace talks remain deadlocked in Paris, Henry Kissinger begins a series of secret talks with North Vietnam's Le Duc Tho.

MARCH

March 18 General Lon Nol ousts Prince Sihanouk of Cambodia in a coup and begins to establish a pro-U.S. regime. Sihanouk aligns with Cambodian Communists, known as the Khmer Rouge, against Lon Nol.

An F-100 covers for three C-123 ranch-hand aircraft on a spraying mission over the jungle of South Vietnam.

In spite of Farmgate's efforts, by 1963 the VC began to inflict a number of defeats on the ARVN. The insurgency was getting stronger as more troops and better weapons flowed into South Vietnam through the Ho Chi Minh Trail. The Vietcong guerrillas had strong concentrations in the Mekong delta, around Saigon, and in the central and northern sections of South Vietnam. It was near these areas that the United States stationed helicopter companies to ferry South Vietnamese troops into battle. The main detachment operating under Farmgate was based at Bien Hoa near Saigon. Tan Son Nhut hosted another important operation base and additional, smaller airfields supported other aspects of the operation. By the end of 1963, Farmgate pilots were flying more than eighty missions per week, attacking VC troops and base areas. They were credited with killing hundreds of guerrillas.

One component of Farmgate was Operation Ranch Hand, an effort to destroy the jungle

cover so critical to Vietcong operations. Beginning in early 1962, aircraft sprayed herbicides to clear the vegetation alongside highways and rivers so that Vietcong ambushes would be easier to spot. Soon, Ranch Hand's

mission was extended to expose VC trails and base areas and destroy crops that might feed Communist units. This broader effort was accomplished using Agent Orange, a powerful herbicide that contained the deadly chemical

APRIL

March 31 The U.S. Army brings murder charges against Captain Ernest Medina, Lieutenant Calley's company commander, for his role in the March 1968 massacre at My Lai.

April 20 President Nixon announces the withdrawal of a further 150,000 Americans from Vietnam within a year.

April 30 After Lon Nol's coup, President Nixon announces a U.S. and South Vietnamese incursion into Cambodia to help eliminate the country as a cross-border sanctuary for North Vietnam. The decision ignites a new round of war protests in the United States.

dioxin. Between 1962 and 1971, Ranch Hand sprayed about 19 million gallons of herbicide, 11 million of which consisted of Agent Orange. The campaign destroyed approximately 6 million acres of South Vietnamese foliage, but many Vietnam veterans claimed exposure to the chemicals caused them to develop cancer and other health issues later in life. Indeed, a study released in the fall of 1969 presented evidence that 2,4,5-T, a component of Agent Orange, could, in relatively high doses, cause birth defects and stillbirths in mice. These health implications, along with ecological concerns and pending international protocols against chemical and biological weapons, led to Ranch Hand's termination in 1971.

Operations Pierce Arrow and Flaming Dart

The first U.S. bombing operations of the Vietnam War began in early August 1964, soon after the Gulf of Tonkin incident. Following the Congressional approval of the Tonkin Gulf

Aircraft carriers like the USS Coral Sea *and the* USS Ranger *served as platforms for launching air strikes against Communist targets.*

1970

MAY

May 1 A combined force of 15,000 U.S. and South Vietnamese soldiers attack NVA supply bases in Cambodia. The invasion sparks widespread campus unrest in the United States.

May 1 President Nixon derides the antiwar student protests as "bums blowing up campuses."

May 4 Ohio National Guardsmen kill four student protesters and wound nine others at Kent State University. The shootings ignite additional protests at colleges and universities across the country.

May 6 The week ends with 450 civilians killed in Vietcong terrorist raids throughout Saigon, the highest weekly death toll to date.

May 9 In support of the Cambodian invasion, a combined South Vietnamese–U.S. naval task force steams up the Mekong River to gain control of it from North Vietnamese and Vietcong forces. Vietnamese naval units reach the Cambodian capital of Phnom Penh. No U.S. personnel are allowed past Neak Luong, halfway to Phnom Penh.

Resolution on August 7, President Lyndon B. Johnson ordered the commencement of Operation Pierce Arrow, a punitive air strike against the North Vietnamese. The targets for the mission were the naval facilities that supported the patrol boats thought to have been involved in the Gulf of Tonkin attacks and an oil storage facility in the city of Vinh. Aircraft from the USS *Ticonderoga* and the USS *Constellation* succeeded in completely destroying about 25 percent of the intended targets, but the United States also lost four aircraft out of a total of sixty-four sorties. One pilot was killed, and Lieutenant Everett Alvarez was captured, becoming the United States' first and longest-held prisoner of the Vietnam War.

A second bombing mission, known as Operation Flaming Dart, began on February 7, 1965, after Vietcong insurgents had mortared a U.S. air base at Pleiku in the central highlands, leaving nine Americans dead and 128 wounded. The air strikes were launched from the aircraft carriers USS *Ranger*, *Hancock*, and *Coral Sea*, and targeted multiple Communist barracks that had been suspected of supporting recent attacks, such as the one at Pleiku. President Johnson

wanted to use the bombings to demonstrate that attacks on U.S. bases and personnel would not be ignored, and to deter the Vietcong from further attacks but, in spite of the bombings, the Vietcong renewed their attacks on February 10.

Operation Rolling Thunder

The U.S. air strikes of Pierce Arrow and Flaming Dart had been in retaliation for specific Communist attacks. However, in February 1965, Secretary of Defense McNamara began to believe that bombing should play a far more significant role in the Vietnam conflict. The idea was that a sustained bombing campaign could make the North Vietnamese stop supporting the war in the south. McNamara was not alone in these thoughts. General Curtis LeMay, who served as Chief of Staff of the U.S. Air Force from 1961 to 1965, was perhaps the most adamant advocate of the role strategic air power should play in the U.S. war effort in Vietnam. "If you are going to use military force," LeMay

....

Air Force Chief of Staff Curtis LeMay was a staunch advocate of air power and the strategic bombing campaign in Vietnam.

argued, "then you ought to use overwhelming military force. Use too much and deliberately use too much . . . you'll save lives, not only your own, but the enemy's too."

May 14 Two students at Jackson State College are killed by police during a protest against the Cambodia invasion, the Kent State shootings, and racism.

May 28 The National League of Families of American Prisoners and Missing in Southeast Asia is incorporated in Washington, D.C.

On February 13, the White House authorized a strategic bombing campaign code-named Operation Rolling Thunder, which, after a series of delays, began on March 2. Proponents of air power felt that this sustained bombing would interdict supplies and personnel infiltrating into South Vietnam from the north. However, McNamara was not prepared to fully embrace LeMay's strategy of annihilation. In a clear statement that the limited war construct would apply to the bombing effort, McNamara described the purpose of Rolling Thunder: "U.S. objectives are not to destroy or to overthrow the Communist government in North Vietnam. They are limited to the destruction of the insurrection and aggression directed by North Vietnam against the political institutions of South Vietnam."

The initial plan for Rolling Thunder was to launch two to three air strikes a week, for a total of eight weeks but, as the eighth week neared, military planners decided to extend

Arc Light missions were initiated on June 18, 1965, designed "to assist in the defeat of the enemy through maximum destruction, disruption, and harassment."

1970

JUNE

June 3 North Vietnam begins a new offensive toward Phnom Penh in Cambodia, which the United States meets with air strikes.

June 22 The United States halts its use of jungle defoliants in Vietnam. Many veterans later blame the fact that they developed cancers on exposure to the dioxins released by the defoliants, including Agent Orange.

June 24 The U.S. Senate repeals the 1964 Tonkin Gulf Resolution.

June 30 U.S. troops withdraw from Cambodia.

AUGUST

August 11 South Vietnamese troops relieve U.S. forces, occupying defensive positions along the border.

August 24 Heavy B-52 bombing raids occur along the demilitarized zone.

Rolling Thunder indefinitely. They believed that in order to dissuade the North Vietnamese from continuing support for the Vietcong guerrillas, the bombing campaign had to be maintained until the pressure became too great for North Vietnam to withstand. However, Rolling Thunder got off to an uncertain start when the United States immediately began to lose aircraft, and it became clear that the campaign was not having its desired effect on the North Vietnamese. Already, it was beginning to look like the air war over North Vietnam was going to be more costly than originally expected.

Tactical Air Support

President Johnson became increasingly convinced that a bombing campaign alone would not bring an end to the Vietnam War, and in March 1965 he committed combat troops to fight the Communist insurgents. As U.S. troops began flooding into Vietnam in 1965, American pilots were given a new task of tactical support for U.S. troops in the field. Hundreds of transport aircraft and fighter-bombers were used to support U.S. troops on the ground. Air strikes could be called in by

any unit in the field at any time. On numerous occasions, bombs, rockets, and napalm saved U.S. units from being overrun. A perfect example of the effectiveness of tactical air support can be seen in the battle of Ia Drang, where troops from the 1st Battalion, 7th Cavalry Regiment found themselves surrounded and heavily outnumbered by an NVA force of 2,000. With the help of timely and accurate close air support from fighter-bombers and Boeing B-52 Stratofortresses, the U.S. forces were able to survive and inflict heavy casualties on the numerically superior enemy. As the war progressed, however, Vietcong and North Vietnamese commanders tried to limit the effectiveness of tactical air support by ordering their soldiers to get in close to the U.S. forces and "cling to their belts" so that the United States could not call in close air support without running the risk of killing their own troops. Enemy use of this tactic made close air support risky, but the United States continued to successfully use tactical air support to win battles and save U.S. lives throughout the war.

Against enemy troops in the open, tactical air support was an accurate and decisive weapon,

B-52s had been designed not for precision bombing but to carry nuclear warheads against the Soviet Union. Their powerful bombs often resulted in oversaturation.

but it was very ineffective against fortified guerrilla bases dispersed under jungle canopy. Therefore, in order to kill enemy troops before they attacked U.S. forces, MACV commander

General Westmoreland suggested the use of carpet bombing with B-52s to destroy the hidden VC bases. The argument seemed to have merit because a cell of three B-52s could obliterate an area three miles long and two miles wide. The bombers were also accurate enough to support U.S. troops in the field because radar could direct the B-52s and tell the crew exactly when and where to drop their bombs. Such a massive response, however, was not consistent with the restraints imposed by the limited war theory and was initially rejected.

Cold War Concerns and Bombing Halts

As the war in the south began to heat up, Operation Rolling Thunder continued in the north. However, President Johnson and Secretary of Defense McNamara began to fear that the bombing of North Vietnam could lead to a much larger war. China and the Soviet Union, the United States' Cold War enemies, had been providing North Vietnam with monetary aid and military equipment for many years. Therefore, Johnson and McNamara feared that an all-out bombing campaign of North Vietnam could draw the Soviets and Chinese into the war, leading in turn to a third world war. On the contrary, the Joint Chiefs of Staff doubted that China and the Soviet Union would risk war over Vietnam, and military planners pushed for a quick and massive bombing campaign to immediately bring North Vietnam to its knees. However, President Johnson refused to take the risk. Instead, he kept strict control of the bombing offensive himself, including personally approving a weekly list of targets. The bombing campaign was so controlled that Johnson bragged, "They can't even bomb an outhouse without my approval." This severe restraint on the bombing campaign frustrated the Joint Chiefs of Staff, as well as U.S. pilots, and would later limit the overall effectiveness of Rolling Thunder.

For the North Vietnamese, the U.S. bombing raids came as a major shock, but they quickly adjusted to the reality of the situation. The North Vietnamese never considered relenting to U.S. pressure. Instead, the North Vietnamese skillfully manipulated the negotiation process to secure bombing concessions and used the pauses to their advantage. For example, on April 8, 1965, North Vietnamese premier Pham Van Dong replied to a peace overture made by the United States with a list of four points that had to be met before peace could even be considered: Vietnamese independence, political settlement, nonintervention by foreign powers, and reunification of the country. The North Vietnamese knew that the United States would not accept such conditions, and the bombing resumed on May 18. However, during the pause, the North Vietnamese had taken the opportunity to improve their air defenses and rebuild much of the damage from earlier air strikes. Therefore, after the bombing restarted, the United States faced a far tougher air defense system than before. Similarly, after President Johnson called for the first bombing halt, the Soviet Union equipped the North Vietnamese with the SA-2 surface-to-air missile. This high-altitude weapon, known as the "flying telephone pole" by American pilots, made air strikes over North Vietnam a far riskier endeavor. When combined with antiaircraft artillery, which was North Vietnam's primary low-altitude defense weapon, air defenses in North Vietnam became quite formidable. The North Vietnamese never failed to use bombing halts to their advantage.

1970

DECEMBER

December 10 President Nixon warns that more bombing raids may occur if North Vietnamese attacks continue against the south.

December 22 The Cooper-Church Amendment prohibits the use of U.S. ground forces in Laos and Cambodia.

1971

JANUARY

January 4 President Nixon announces, "The end is in sight."

January 9 U.S. planes launch heavy air strikes against NVA supply camps in Laos and Cambodia.

January 30–April 6 Operation Lam Son 719 occurs. About 17,000 South Vietnamese soldiers, backed by U.S. air support, attack into Laos in an attempt to sever the Ho Chi Minh Trail. The ARVN performs poorly, but President Nixon declares the battle—and Vietnamization—to have succeeded.

Despite North Vietnam's improved air defenses, Rolling Thunder's attacks steadily intensified in the weeks that followed the pause. Destroying North Vietnam's transportation infrastructure between Hanoi and Vinh was the top priority, but soon the list of targets approved by the White House was broadened. The United States overcame its initial reluctance to use B-52s for fear of drawing China and

Right and below: U.S. pilots faced North Vietnamese air defenses that included Soviet-built SA-2 surface-to-air missiles introduced after the first bombing pause.

RADAR

BAMBOO MATTING

MARCH

March 1 The U.S. Capitol building is damaged by a bomb, apparently planted in protest of the invasion of Laos.

March 10 China pledges its complete support for North Vietnam in its struggle against the United States.

March 29 Lieutenant William Calley is found guilty of the murder of twenty-two civilians at My Lai. He is sentenced to life imprisonment, but the sentence is later reduced to ten years.

March 31 Monthly opinion polls show President Nixon's approval rating has dropped to 50 percent, while approval of his Vietnam strategy has slipped to just 34 percent. Half of those polled believe the war in Vietnam to be "morally wrong."

Russia into the war and began using the powerful bombers to hit NVA infiltration routes in Laos. Even this escalation in bombing, however, did not achieve decisive results.

Right: A MiG-17 makes a firing pass.

Below: U.S. Marine F-4 fighters land at Da Nang.

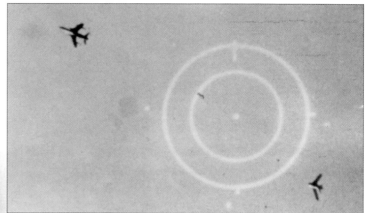

Despite the ability of U.S. air power to deliver heavy ordnance on North Vietnam and the Ho Chi Minh Trail, it was becoming obvious by late 1966 that Rolling Thunder was having a minimal impact on the North Vietnamese war effort. Unlike their U.S. and South Vietnamese opponents, the Vietcong and North Vietnamese needed reasonably small amounts of supplies to continue the war. Given these modest requirements, Operation Rolling Thunder was never able to cut supplies from the north to the point where it really affected the Vietcong.

1971

APRIL

April 3 President Nixon promises to personally review Lieutenant Calley's case.

April 19 An organization called Vietnam Veterans Against the War begin a week of nationwide protests.

April 24 Approximately 200,000 protesters attend an antiwar demonstration in Washington, D.C.

April 29 The 45,000th American dies in Vietnam.

Operation Bolo

Operation Rolling Thunder intensified, with the number of sorties growing to 13,000 in one month in 1967. However, as the United States undertook more bombing missions against the North Vietnamese, more U.S. planes fell victim to antiaircraft defenses and North Vietnamese fighter planes. As a result, it was soon realized that the United States needed to destroy the North Vietnamese air force to reduce the number of U.S. losses. Because of the restricted nature of the air war, U.S. pilots were not allowed to destroy enemy planes on the ground. Therefore, U.S. Air Force Colonel Robin Olds created Operation Bolo, a plan to lure North Vietnamese fighters into battle where they could be destroyed. The mission began on January 2, 1967, when Olds and other members of the 8th Tactical Fighter Wing took off from Ubon air base in Thailand. Once over North Vietnam, Olds's F-4 Phantoms succeeded in drawing North Vietnamese MiGs into battle by assuming the formation of a group of F-105

An F-105 Thunderchief with a bomb load, preparing to go into action.

Thunderchiefs on a bombing run. In what became the greatest U.S. fighter victory of the war, the 8th Tactical Fighter Wing shot down seven enemy MiG-21s in twelve minutes without losing a single aircraft.

Following Operation Bolo, the United States gained further air superiority, expanding Operation Rolling Thunder once again. U.S. bombers began to strike air bases and army bases around Hanoi, as well as several industrial plants in and near the North Vietnamese capital city. Among the most targeted sites was the Thai Nguyen steel plant. U.S. bombers struck these industrial targets many times in an attempt to

MAY

May 3–5 Nearly 12,000 protesters are arrested in Washington, D.C.

HANOI RR/HWY BR OV RED RIVER

27 MAY 68

FLOATING CRANE

hamper North Vietnamese war production, but steel production continued in North Vietnam's rural areas. Other targets, such as the Paul Doumer Bridge, were repeatedly destroyed, but were soon rebuilt by the tenacious North Vietnamese. The North Vietnamese proved resilient and adaptive against seemingly every effort to destroy them from the air.

The End of Rolling Thunder

As Rolling Thunder continued to progress and escalate, Secretary of Defense McNamara began to question the overall success of the campaign. In three years, the United States had dropped more than 892,860 tons of bombs, but the North Vietnamese continued to send more troops and supplies to the south. In fact, military analysts concluded that the amount of supplies and troops coming down the Ho Chi Minh Trail had actually increased throughout Rolling Thunder. For example, U.S. intelligence figures showed that, in 1965, only 35,000

The Paul Doumer Bridge was the principal northern entry into Hanoi. It was made up of two highways and a railway. U.S. pilots raided it on August 11, 1967.

1971

JUNE

June 13 The *New York Times* begins publication of the Pentagon Papers, a secret Department of Defense record of government decision-making concerning Vietnam. The publication of the papers infuriates President Nixon.

June 15 President Nixon attempts to stop further publication of the Pentagon Papers through legal action against the *New York Times* in the U.S. District Court. The case will ultimately go to the Supreme Court.

June 18 The *Washington Post* begins to publish the Pentagon Papers.

North Vietnamese troops infiltrated into South Vietnam, but in 1967 that number had grown to around 150,000. Therefore, it was becoming clear that Operation Rolling Thunder was not seriously hampering the North Vietnamese war effort. To make matters worse, U.S. military analysts discovered that Rolling Thunder was an economic failure as well. Too many U.S. planes were being lost, costing the military millions of dollars. The air strikes simply were not causing enough damage to compensate for the loss of U.S. planes. Some military analysts estimated that it cost the United States $12 for every dollar worth of damage inflicted on the North Vietnamese. As a result, one CIA officer described the bombing campaign as "the most ambitious, wasteful, and ineffective campaign ever mounted."

With these types of returns, the Johnson administration soon determined that Rolling Thunder was no longer worth the effort. In early 1968, President Johnson ordered cutbacks to the operation, and on November 1 he canceled the campaign altogether. All things considered, Operation Rolling Thunder had been a major disappointment for the United

States. The campaign had employed the best firepower and technology that the U.S. arsenal had to offer, but there was little to show for the effort. North Vietnam continued to send troops and supplies down the Ho Chi Minh Trail for the duration of the war. In the wake of this disappointment, the United States would wait three and a half years before again exposing North Vietnam to large-scale bombings.

Operation Menu

Despite the cessation of bombing raids against North Vietnam, the United States commenced a new bombing campaign in Cambodia on March 18, 1969. Known as Operation Menu, the objective of the campaign was to destroy North Vietnamese supply bases and sanctuaries inside Cambodia. During Operation Menu, U.S. and South Vietnamese aircraft dropped approximately 107,140 tons of bombs and successfully destroyed several North Vietnamese base areas and supply depots. Although not all of the Communist base areas were permanently destroyed, the bombing campaign forestalled a planned North Vietnamese offensive against South Vietnam.

Because Cambodia was considered to be a neutral country, the White House tried to keep Operation Menu a secret for as long as possible. However, in May 1970 the *New York Times* wrote a story on the bombing campaign and criticized the Nixon administration for the damage the operation was causing. However, U.S. planes continued to bomb Cambodia until August 1973, when the U.S. Congress passed Public Law 93-55, which prohibited the funding of U.S. operations in Cambodia.

Operations Linebacker I and II

Meanwhile, in May 1972 President Nixon launched a new bombing offensive against North Vietnam in response to the NVA Easter Offensive—an operation designed to defeat South Vietnam in one massive attack. When issuing the order to begin the campaign, Nixon reportedly said, "The bastards have never been bombed like they're going to be bombed this time." Operation Linebacker I had three primary objectives: to cut off land and rail logistical lines from China, to destroy stockpiles of war materials and food, and to interdict supply lines to the south. The United States also

June 22 The U.S. Senate passes a nonbinding resolution urging the removal of all U.S. troops from Vietnam by the end of the year.

June 25 The last U.S. marine ground units leave Vietnam.

June 28 Daniel Ellsberg, the source of the Pentagon Papers leak, surrenders to police.

June 30 The Supreme Court rules 6–3 in favor of the *New York Times* and the *Washington Post*'s publication of the Pentagon Papers.

June 30 George Jackson replaces William Colby as the head of CORDS.

16 BUILDINGS DAMAGED

used B-52s to destroy the attacking North Vietnamese troops in the south.

Operation Linebacker I lasted six months and began when U.S. planes mined Haiphong harbor on May 8. Subsequent raids devastated the North Vietnamese infrastructure around Hanoi. This time, the bombing campaign was very successful. Many military analysts believed this was because Nixon placed few restrictions on the campaign. However, new technology, including laser- and electro-optically guided bombs, also played a key role in making the campaign successful. In the end, the Easter Offensive was quickly blunted and North Vietnam was forced to meet the Americans and South Vietnamese at the negotiating table. A second massive bombing campaign, known as Operation Linebacker II, began on December 18, 1972, when North Vietnamese diplomats walked away from the peace table over disagreements on the sovereignty of South Vietnam. In response, President Nixon ordered

In announcing Operation Linebacker I, President Nixon reportedly said, "The bastards have never been bombed like they're going to be bombed this time."

1971

JULY

July 1 More than 6,000 U.S. soldiers depart Vietnam.

July 15 President Nixon announces that he will visit Communist China in 1972, a major diplomatic breakthrough that helps pressure North Vietnam to negotiate an end to the war.

July 17 President Nixon helps John Ehrlichman and Charles Colson in establishing the White House "Plumbers" unit, which will investigate and plug leaks like those initiated by Daniel Ellsberg. Colson begins compiling an "enemies list" of 200 prominent Americans who are considered to be anti-Nixon.

AUGUST

August 2 The United States admits to having 30,000 CIA-sponsored irregulars in Laos.

August 18 Australia and New Zealand announce that they will withdraw their troops from Vietnam.

SEPTEMBER

September 22 Captain Ernest L. Medina, Lieutenant Calley's company commander, is acquitted of all charges concerning the massacre of Vietnamese civilians at My Lai.

Operation Linebacker II, another massive bombing campaign against North Vietnam. However, unlike other bombing operations, Linebacker II was unique because there were no restrictions placed on target selection.

Final Assessment

The campaign began on December 18 and lasted until December 29. During its eleven days of operation, nearly 2,700 sorties dropped around 17,860 tons of ordnance on North Vietnam. B-52s played a major role in the bombing, striking bridges, railroads, and storage and military facilities. In response to the massive onslaught, the North Vietnamese fired more than 1,000 surface-to-air missiles and succeeded in downing twenty-six U.S. aircraft, including fifteen B-52s. Nevertheless, the operation succeeded in its mission, influencing the North Vietnamese to return to the negotiating table and sign the Paris Peace Accords on January 27, 1973.

The air war over Vietnam produced mixed results. The campaign did have some great successes, such as Operations Linebacker I and II, when the application of U.S. air power had clear goals and was fairly unrestricted. U.S. aircraft also proved to be fairly successful in the role of tactical air support, saving the lives of thousands of U.S. and South Vietnamese troops. But the primary task of the air war—strategic bombing—failed to produce the desired results. Operation Rolling Thunder did not convince the North Vietnamese to discontinue the war effort, and the attacks on the Ho Chi Minh Trail did little to stop North Vietnam from flooding the south with troops and supplies. In World War II, the United States fought a total war against an industrialized enemy with plenty of targets for strategic bombing. The limited guerrilla war against a much less industrialized North Vietnam proved agonizingly frustrating for U.S. bombers. For the U.S. military, the Vietnam War was a painful lesson in the limits of air power.

Operation Linebacker II was unique in that there were no restrictions placed on target selection for nearly 2,700 sorties.

OCTOBER

October 3 Nguyen Van Thieu is reelected president of South Vietnam.

October 9 Members of the 1st Cavalry Division refuse to go on an assigned patrol, an indication of the declining morale and discipline of U.S. troops in Vietnam.

October 31 South Vietnam releases the first of its 3,000 Vietcong prisoners of war.

DECEMBER

December 17 U.S. troop levels in Vietnam fall to 156,800.

December 26–30 In an operation timed to coincide with a period when college students are away from campus, thereby hoping to cut down on protests, the U.S. launches Operation Proud Deep Alpha. The air force and the navy fly 1,000 preplanned sorties against North Vietnam, losing five aircraft and seven airmen.

The Turning Point: Tet 1968

By late 1967, the Vietnam War had reached a decisive point where the battle of attrition had taken its toll on both sides. The Tet Offensive of 1968 was a stunning battlefield victory for the Americans, but on the home front it marked a dramatic shift in support for the war.

The Communists had always been prepared to take massive amounts of casualties to achieve their final victory, but they now feared that if their recent losses continued, their freedom of action would become limited. Therefore, in January 1968 the North Vietnamese decided to deviate from their strategy of protracted war and risk everything on one massive surprise assault on the major urban areas of South Vietnam. In doing so, they hoped to create a

Left: American forces created fortified fire bases that served as fixed locations to conduct operations.
Right: Tan Son Nhut air base, near Saigon, was one of the Communists' targets during the 1968 Tet Offensive.

popular uprising among the South Vietnamese people, which in turn would force the United States to abandon its mission in Vietnam. In the early stages of what would become known as the Tet Offensive, the Vietcong achieved some successes, but the attack allowed the United States and ARVN to bring their superior firepower to bear, which inflicted immense casualties on the attacking Communists. As a result, the Vietcong suffered a major military defeat. In an ironic twist, however, the defeat soon turned into a strategic victory because the attack caused U.S. public opinion to turn against the war.

Prior to Tet, the United States believed it was winning the war in Vietnam. U.S. search-and-destroy missions were racking up an impressive enemy body count and the Americans were starting to feel that their efforts were wearing down the Communist insurgency. However, it was also at this point that the American public started to show its first real signs of weariness with the war. Largely influenced by the images that were being shown on their televisions, more Americans began to protest against the war. To reassure the public, the Johnson administration began a public relations campaign in November 1967 to try to restore U.S. confidence in the war effort. Senators, presidential advisers, and even MACV commander General William Westmoreland held press conferences to tell the country that the war was being won. Westmoreland assured the public that the United States had reached a point "where the end comes into view." He also stated that the recent battles of attrition had weakened the enemy to the point that the Communists could not launch any significant operations in the coming year. However, the events of January 1968 proved him to be completely wrong.

The Communist attack on Saigon was designed not to capture the city itself but to inspire a general uprising of the city's population.

....

The Plan
Around the same time that Johnson was concentrating his effort on drumming up domestic support for the war, General Nguyen Chi Thang (who served as Secretary of the Central Office of South Vietnam until his death in July 1967), Pham Hung (Thang's successor), and General Vo Nguyen Giap were all contributing to plans for a three-stage attack that would become the Tet Offensive of 1968. The first stage was to lure the U.S. forces away from the cities of South Vietnam by drawing them into battles in remote corners of the country. Of particular importance was an NVA buildup around the marine base of Khe Sanh, located in the northernmost reaches of South Vietnam about seven miles from the Laotian border. With U.S. forces focused on these distractions, the Vietcong would initiate the second stage of the offensive, which consisted of secretly moving an assault force of about 85,000 men into position for the

attack. To move undetected, the Vietcong would make use of an extensive system of underground tunnels and jungle trails. The third stage of the plan was the attack itself, which was to take place on the Tet lunar new year, the most important and most celebrated holiday in Vietnam. In previous years, both sides had observed a cease-fire during the celebration, so neither the ARVN nor the Americans predicted the attack. South Vietnamese units sent many soldiers on leave

1972

JANUARY

January 25 President Nixon announces a proposed eight-point peace plan and reveals that Kissinger has been secretly negotiating with North Vietnam. Hanoi rejects Nixon's offer.

FEBRUARY

February 21–28 President Nixon visits China and meets with Mao Tse-tung and Prime Minister Zhou Enlai. The meeting is viewed as a threat by North Vietnam, which fears improved Chinese-U.S. relations may lead to a reduction in Chinese support.

to celebrate the holiday, and the United States remained focused on the developing situation at Khe Sanh. Under these circumstances, the North Vietnamese and VC would enjoy nearly complete initial surprise.

The Attack Begins

The Tet Offensive began in the early hours of January 30, 1968, and focused on the South Vietnamese capital of Saigon, where the Vietcong devoted thirty-five battalions under the command of General Tran Van Tra. Their objective was not to capture the city itself but to strike significant military and political targets throughout the capital. In doing so, they hoped to paralyze the South Vietnamese government's control of the city and inspire an uprising by Saigon's population. Their targets included the presidential palace, the MACV and ARVN headquarters, the national radio station, Tan Son Nhut air base and, most importantly, the U.S. embassy in Saigon.

The spectacle of the U.S. embassy in Saigon being under attack was a disquieting image for Americans at home.

MARCH

March 10 The 101st Airborne Division leaves Vietnam.

March 23 The United States boycotts the Paris peace talks amid charges by President Nixon that North Vietnam is refusing to negotiate seriously.

March 30 North Vietnam launches its Easter Offensive, an all-out attempt to decisively defeat South Vietnam.

The U.S. embassy represented the seat of American power and presence in South Vietnam, and therefore should have been the most secure site in the entire country. However, on the morning of January 30, nineteen Vietcong sappers succeeded in blowing a hole in the embassy walls and gaining access into the compound. Once inside the walls, the Vietcong engaged U.S. military police in a battle that lasted over six hours. In the end, all of the Vietcong sappers were killed before they could make it into the embassy's main buildings. For the defenders of the embassy, the attack ended in victory. The building was secured and order restored fairly quickly. However, for Americans watching on television, the scene looked like a complete disaster. On hearing of the embassy attack, General Westmoreland rushed to the scene and, in a television interview, assured the American people that the enemy had been defeated and that everything was under control. To many viewers, however,

A group of Vietnamese marines transport a body of a marine who had been killed in the Cholon section of Vietnam.

the size and surprise of the Tet Offensive seemed to tell a different story.

Not just in Saigon but throughout the entire width and breadth of South Vietnam, the Vietcong assaulted military and political targets.

Much like in the embassy attack, the Vietcong achieved success in the initial stages of the fighting due to the element of surprise but, as the ARVN and U.S. forces got their bearings, they began to punish the enemy with their

1972

APRIL

April 2 In response to the Easter Offensive, President Nixon authorizes the U.S. 7th Fleet to target NVA troops massed around the demilitarized zone with air strikes and naval gunfire.

April 4 President Nixon authorizes Operation Linebacker I, a massive bombing campaign designed to cut off land and rail logistical lines from China, destroy stockpiles of war materials and food, and interdict supply lines to the south.

April 10 B-52s begin to strike targets as deep as 143 miles into North Vietnam.

April 12 NVA forces attack Kontum in an effort to cut South Vietnam in two.

firepower. The fighting was particularly ferocious in Saigon's Cholon district, where some 10,000 ARVN troops engaged the Vietcong in house-to-house fighting. To stop the Vietcong, the MACV told civilians to evacuate the district and then conducted a massive air strike. Following the bombing, the U.S. 199th Light Infantry Brigade moved into Cholon and pushed the rest of the Vietcong out, destroying a large section of the district in the process. In a similar incident elsewhere during Tet, one U.S. Army officer reportedly explained, "We had to destroy the village to save it." Such was the surreal nature of the war in Vietnam.

The fighting was also bloody at Tan Son Nhut air base on the outskirts of Saigon, where again the Americans were initially caught off guard. Three Vietcong battalions attacked on three sides before the sun came up, taking advantage of the darkness and confusion. The Americans soon recovered, however, and when morning arrived a relief column from the 25th Infantry Division reached the air base and began mopping up the attackers.

Much of the fighting throughout Saigon followed a similar pattern. Surprise gave the

Refugees pass by a tank during Operation Hue City.

April 15 President Nixon authorizes the bombing of Hanoi and Haiphong harbor. Protests against the bombings break out in the United States.

April 19 NVA forces attack An Loc.

April 27 The Paris peace talks resume, an event many credit to the massive Operation Linebacker I campaign.

April 30 U.S. troop levels fall to 69,000.

Vietcong an early advantage, but momentum soon shifted to the ARVN and the Americans. Everywhere in Saigon, the city's defenders drove the attackers off, punishing the enemy by inflicting heavy casualties. The population of Saigon failed to rise up as the Communists had expected. In the battle for Saigon, this miscalculation cost the Communists dearly,

The Perfume River divided Hue into two sections, with the old citadel on the northern side and the new city to the south.

as nearly all of the attackers who launched the assault were either killed or captured.

The Battle for Hue

In much of the rest of Vietnam, the Tet Offensive came to a similar end, with the notable exception of the city of Hue. Unlike the battle for Saigon, which turned out to be a major military victory for the United States and ARVN, the battle for Hue devolved into a bloody and brutal contest. Located on the coast of central Vietnam, the old Nguyen

imperial capital of Hue is divided into two sections by the Perfume River. On the north side of the river is the old citadel, and on the south side of the river is the new city, which contains most of the business and residential areas.

In the early morning hours of January 31, 8,000 North Vietnamese troops from the 4th and 6th NVA regiments invaded Hue and took much of the citadel and the new city. However, units from the ARVN 1st Infantry Division continued to hold out in the northern corner of the citadel, and a few hundred Americans held out in the MACV compound in the new city. The U.S. and ARVN counterattack began when Lieutenant General Ngo Quang Truong, commander of the ARVN 1st Division, ordered his 3rd Regiment to come to his rescue. These reinforcements arrived on the evening of January 31, accompanied by the 2nd, 7th, and 9th ARVN airborne battalions. The next morning, General Truong ordered an attack to retake the entire citadel, but the fight to retake Hue would last nearly a month and would result in the destruction of most of the city.

1972

MAY

May 8 President Nixon announces the mining of Haiphong harbor and the intensification of U.S. bombing in North Vietnam.

May 17 ARVN forces, aided by U.S. air power, retake An Loc.

May 22–30 President Nixon visits the Soviet Union and meets Leonid Brezhnev. Like Nixon's visit to China, this visit raises concerns with North Vietnam about future support from its Communist allies.

May 30 ARVN resistance and massive U.S. air strikes halt the NVA attack on Kontum.

The United States' initial reaction to the NVA attack on Hue showed a lack of understanding of the severity of the situation. On hearing of the attack, the marine commander at nearby Phu Bai dispatched only one company to Hue. After this company came under heavy fire, the commander sent two platoons across the Perfume River to try to connect with the ARVN,

From January 20 to April 8, 6,000 U.S. marines and ARVN rangers were under siege at Khe Sanh.

....

but as these marines neared the citadel they too came into contact with a large enemy unit and were forced to fall back. At this point, the marines finally realized what they were up against and began sending more troops into battle. In the end, it took three marine and eleven ARVN battalions to regain the city.

The plan for recapturing Hue was for the ARVN to assume the responsibility for expelling the Communists from the citadel, while the U.S. marines would take back the new city. After receiving reinforcements, the marines attacked on February 4 and soon found themselves engaged in a vicious house-to-house fight to drive the enemy from the city. As a result, the marines advanced a meager four blocks in six days of fighting. In the first few days of the battle, the United States limited air and artillery

....

Many people feared Khe Sanh would become another Dien Bien Phu, but U.S. B-52s broke the Communist attack.

strikes because of the cultural and historical significance of the city. However, as the intensity of the battle picked up, the United States was forced to call in the heavy weaponry. The result was destruction on a massive scale, but the added firepower helped the marines gain the upper hand. By February 9, they cleared all of Hue south of the Perfume River.

JUNE

June 9 Senior U.S. military adviser John Paul Vann is killed in a helicopter crash near Pleiku.

June 17 Five men are arrested inside the offices of the Democratic National Committee at the Watergate complex in Washington, D.C. The Watergate scandal, which will eventually result in the resignation of President Nixon, begins.

June 30 ARVN forces retake Quang Tri.

June 30 General Frederick Weyand replaces Creighton Abrams as MACV commander. General Abrams moves on to become chief of staff of the U.S. Army.

Located about seven miles from the Laotian border in the northernmost reaches of South Vietnam, Khe Sanh was an isolated target.

Meanwhile, the ARVN 1st Division continued to struggle inside the citadel. When its attacks began to stall on February 12, the 1st Division was reinforced by two Vietnamese Marine Corps (VNMC) battalions and the U.S. Marine 1st Battalion, 5th Regiment. Once again, the Americans and ARVN found themselves involved in a house-to-house fight, and at this point the battle became so intense that the marines took one casualty for every yard they gained. Nevertheless, the allies made steady progress, and on February 21, the 1st ARVN Division linked up with U.S. troops and began to drive the enemy from the citadel. Three days later, on February 24, ARVN Major Pham Van Dinh reraised the South Vietnamese flag over the citadel.

Although the ARVN and Americans had recaptured much of the citadel, some NVA units continued to hold out until March 2. During the month of fighting, over half of the city had been damaged or destroyed and several thousand civilians had been killed. NVA losses were estimated at over 5,000, with approximately 100 killed. U.S. losses stood at 216 dead and ARVN forces lost 384. In addition to these numbers, the NVA executed between 3,000 and 6,000 civilians during their occupation of the city as Communist cadres began rounding up thousands of South Vietnamese government officials, military officers, teachers, Catholic priests, and anyone else who had "committed crimes against the Vietnamese people." During the months and years that followed the battle for Hue, many mass graves were uncovered, and the remains of about 2,800 people were recovered. About 3,000 others have never been accounted for.

Khe Sanh

The final action of the Tet Offensive was fought at Khe Sanh, where the North Vietnamese had launched their initial diversionary attack. Since January 20, some 40,000 North Vietnamese had besieged the contingent of 6,000 U.S. marines and ARVN rangers at the base. Soon after the siege began, NVA artillery began shelling Khe Sanh in hopes of destroying the airstrip there

1972

JULY

July 13 The Paris peace talks resume.

July 14 Senator George McGovern, an outspoken critic of the Vietnam War, is selected as the Democratic presidential nominee.

July 18 During a visit to Hanoi, actress Jane Fonda broadcasts antiwar messages via Radio Hanoi. Fonda becomes known as "Hanoi Jane" and is vilified by supporters of the war.

July 20 The battle of An Loc ends in an ARVN victory.

and cutting off all methods of resupply to the base. Many Americans, including President Johnson, quickly became fearful of Khe Sanh turning into another Dien Bien Phu, but General Westmoreland assured them that the base would hold out. Westmoreland responded to the siege by issuing orders to commence Operation Niagara, a bombing mission that was to continue until the siege was broken. Included in this bombing campaign were the powerful B-52s, each carrying a payload of 36.1 tons.

Despite the extensive bombing campaign, the North Vietnamese continued to tighten their grip on Khe Sanh. At the end of February, the 304th NVA Regiment launched a human-wave attack, but marine firepower, supported by bomber strikes, annihilated the regiment. An NVA survivor of the attack claimed that 75 percent of the 1,800-man regiment was killed by a single B-52 strike, and the sheer destruction of the U.S. firepower convinced General Giap that Khe Sanh could not be overrun. There would be

American firepower proved decisive at Khe Sanh, with the Americans killing 12,000 North Vietnamese compared to just 400 American and ARVN losses.

no Dien Bien Phu against the United States; American firepower was simply too great. Although the destruction of the 304th Regiment effectively halted direct NVA attacks on Khe Sanh, the siege did not end until April 8. At that time, a force of U.S. marines and 1st Cavalry Division troops attacked the remaining NVA troops and forced them to withdraw from the siege. The North Vietnamese suffered 12,000 dead, and the Americans and ARVN lost around

400. Once again, U.S. firepower reigned supreme and the Communists were dealt an emphatic battlefield defeat.

The Aftermath

In the aftermath of the Tet Offensive and the siege of Khe Sanh, it became immediately clear that the Communist offensive was a complete tactical disaster. Of the 85,000 North Vietnamese and VC troops involved in the Tet

AUGUST

August 1 Henry Kissinger meets again with Le Duc Tho in Paris and senses progress.

August 23 The last U.S. ground combat troops leave Vietnam.

August 23 Nixon accepts the Republican nomination for president.

Offensive, some 58,000 were killed. In addition, the South Vietnamese people had failed to rise up against the Americans and the South Vietnamese government as Ho Chi Minh and the Communists had expected. The North Vietnamese had always believed that they were fighting to free the South Vietnamese people from foreign oppression, but the fact that the people did not rise up shattered those illusions. The Tet Offensive also made the North Vietnamese realize that they could never destroy the government of South Vietnam as long as it had U.S. support. In order to achieve victory, they would have to force the United States to leave South Vietnam.

For the United States and South Vietnam, Tet and Khe Sanh represented their greatest tactical victories of the war. Throughout previous engagements, the United States had sought to bring its firepower to bear against the Communists, but was never fully successful in doing so. In almost all earlier battles, the

The VC and NVA standing their ground at Khe Sanh and elsewhere during Tet allowed the Americans to bring to bear the full weight of their firepower.

1972

OCTOBER

October 4 President Thieu opposes the draft cease-fire agreement in a meeting with Kissinger's assistant, Alexander Haig.

October 8 Henry Kissinger and Le Duc Tho break the diplomatic stalemate with a compromise: the United States agrees to allow North Vietnamese units to stay in South Vietnam and North Vietnam consents to the continual existence of the Thieu regime.

Vietcong and the NVA were able to disengage from combat before U.S. air strikes and artillery could punish them. However, during Khe Sanh and the Tet Offensive, the Vietcong and the NVA stood their ground. As a result, the ARVN and the United States were able to fight a classic battle of annihilation. The massive casualty rate suffered by the Vietcong virtually destroyed them as a fighting force. However, the exhilaration of the U.S. victory would not last. The political implications of the Tet Offensive would soon turn victory on the battlefield into a crushing strategic defeat.

A Shift in Public Opinion

Even though the U.S. military had destroyed them on the battlefield, the fact that the North Vietnamese could launch such a massive offensive as Tet alarmed many Americans. Such a display of enemy capability certainly did not square with the recent Johnson administration announcements that progress was being made

....

The remote attack on Khe Sanh served to distract the American high command as the Communists moved forces into position for the Tet Offensive.

October 22 Kissinger visits President Thieu in Saigon to discuss the peace proposal and Thieu rejects the condition that North Vietnamese troops be allowed to stay in South Vietnam. Kissinger returns to Washington, D.C. Radio Hanoi broadcasts the details of the agreement in an effort to pressure Kissinger.

October 22 Operation Linebacker I ends.

October 24 President Thieu publicly denounces Kissinger's peace proposal.

October 26 North Vietnam accuses the United States of attempting to sabotage the peace settlement. With just a week until the presidential election, Henry Kissinger holds a press briefing and declares, "We believe that peace is at hand. We believe that an agreement is in sight."

and victory was near. When *CBS Evening News* anchor Walter Cronkite began to question the United States' ability to win the war, many of his viewers came to agree with him.

Although the American public took a negative view of the events surrounding Tet, General Westmoreland felt confident that he could now achieve victory in Vietnam. He sought to follow up the successful defeat of the Communists' attack by going on the offensive himself, hoping to strike the enemy forces while they still were weakened. By doing so, Westmoreland believed he could destroy the remaining Communist forces and win the war, but he felt he needed an additional 206,000 troops to do so. Such a move would require a large-scale mobilization of the National Guard and the reserves, something that President Johnson had so far resisted and certainly something that would not now be politically expedient. Furthermore, several cabinet members opposed the reinforcements, including Secretary of State Dean Rusk and departing Secretary of Defense Robert McNamara.

Before Johnson would make a decision on the troop request, he sent his new Secretary of

Defense, Clark Clifford, on a fact-finding mission to Vietnam. While in Vietnam, Clifford met General Westmoreland and asked Westmoreland to tell him exactly why he needed the 206,000 new troops, what he hoped to accomplish with them, and when he thought the accomplishment could be completed. Clifford did not like what he heard. On his return from Vietnam, Clifford gave Johnson his assessment: "I could not find out when the war was going to end; I could not find out the manner in which it was going to end; I could not find out whether the new requests for men and equipment were going to be enough, or whether it would take more and, if more, when and how much . . . All I had was the statement, given with too little self-assurance to be comforting, that if we persisted for an indeterminate length of time, the enemy would choose not to go on."

Based on Clifford's report, Johnson decided to deny the troop request and started to develop his own doubts about the United States' ability to win the war. Vietnam had begun to look like

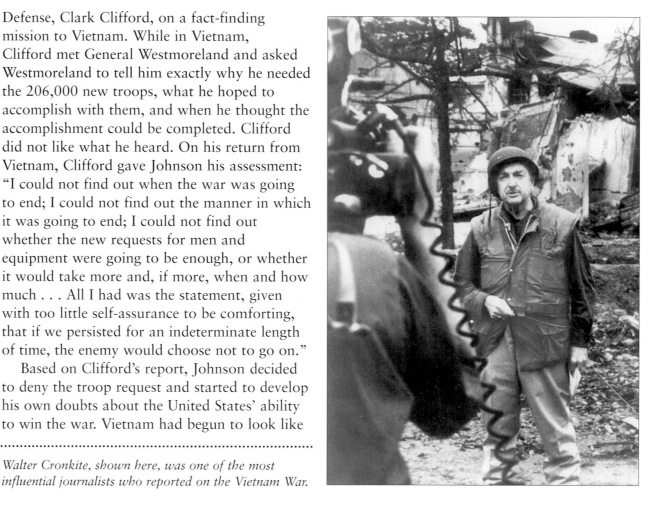

Walter Cronkite, shown here, was one of the most influential journalists who reported on the Vietnam War.

1972

NOVEMBER

November 7 Richard Nixon is reelected president of the United States in a landslide victory.

November 14 President Nixon pledges to President Thieu that he will "take swift and severe retaliatory action" if North Vietnam violates the proposed peace treaty.

November 20 Kissinger resumes talks with Le Duc Tho and presents sixty-nine amendments to the agreement demanded by Thieu.

November 30 The U.S. combat troop withdrawal from Vietnam is completed. Some 16,000 army advisers and administrators remain to assist South Vietnam's military forces.

Clark Clifford with President Johnson; Clifford replaced Robert McNamara as Secretary of Defense in 1968.

U.S. president to lose a war, and the realization of this possibility destroyed his confidence. To make matters worse, 1968 was an election year, and early opinion polls showed that he was losing the support of the American people. On March 31, Johnson informed the country of his decision to limit the war and begin the gradual withdrawal of U.S. forces. He ended his speech with a shocking statement that he would not seek reelection. With this decision, Johnson became yet another casualty of the war.

Tet was the turning point of the Vietnam War. It marked the climactic realization of the superiority of the North Vietnamese strategy of protracted war by showing that battlefield victories could not accomplish the United States' strategic goals. It also marked the point where American popular support for the war turned in a direction where escalation or long-term continuation of the war was politically unacceptable. Tet was the beginning of the end of the U.S. effort in Vietnam.

a bottomless abyss that would continue indefinitely without the United States achieving its strategic objective. In Johnson's mind, 206,000 more troops would not bring about a victory; they would just lead to more American deaths. Therefore, he decided to end the war's

escalation and begin a gradual withdrawal of U.S. involvement in Vietnam. The weight of the decision affected Johnson tremendously, because denying the troop request was tantamount to admitting that the war was unwinnable. Johnson feared he was on his way to becoming the first

DECEMBER

December 13 As a result of the objections raised by President Thieu, peace negotiations between Kissinger and Le Duc Tho collapse.

December 18 When North Vietnam does not respond to President Nixon's demand that peace talks resume, the United States launches Operation Linebacker II, a massive bombing campaign designed to force North Vietnam back to the negotiating table.

December 26 North Vietnam agrees to resume peace negotiations within five days of the end of the bombings.

December 29 Operation Linebacker II ends.

Achilles' Heel: The U.S. Domestic Situation

Carl von Clausewitz, the brilliant Prussian military theorist of the early nineteenth century, described war as "a remarkable trinity" of what his modern interpreters have simplified as the military, the government, and the people.

Grossly overmatched by the combat power, industrial base, and economy of the United States, the North Vietnamese wisely focused on the people as the weak link in the U.S. version of Clausewitz's trinity. The social turbulence of the United States in the 1960s and 1970s made popular support for the war especially vulnerable. Just as the North Vietnamese realized that in a people's war the true objective in South Vietnam was the South Vietnamese

Left: James Meredith became the first African American to enroll at the University of Mississippi.
Right: Martin Luther King Jr. advocated a nonviolent approach to achieving racial justice.

people, they also understood that the best target for their strategy of exhaustion against the United States was the American people.

In the 1960s, the United States saw a marked struggle between those who argued in favor of change and those who wanted to maintain the status quo. The advocates of change were fueled

Elijah Muhammad championed the Nation of Islam, a black separatist group. His most prominent follower, Malcolm X, broke from the group in 1964.

Police commissioner Eugene "Bull" Connor served as a rallying cry for many activists for racial justice.

by a new understanding of social justice exemplified by President Kennedy's promise to lead the nation to a "New Frontier," and President Johnson's effort to create a "Great Society." Many of the resulting changes challenged the established authority and created a period of upheaval and unrest in the United States. The government itself was not immune from this questioning, and the Vietnam War would be waged under unprecedented scrutiny from the U.S. public.

Race Relations

Kennedy did not have an unchallenged mandate when he became president. Not only had he been elected by a razor-thin margin—he received 34,227,000 votes to Nixon's 34,109,000—he also faced a powerful coalition of Republicans

and Southern Democrats in Congress that had dominated domestic policy since 1938. Thus, Kennedy proceeded with circumspection on the New Frontier, but his interventionist response to the sluggish economy helped set the stage for an increasingly active role for the government. Kennedy especially sympathized with those poor who had inherited their poverty and seemed to be consigned to it as a permanent condition. Many African Americans fell into this category

1973

JANUARY

January 8 Henry Kissinger and Le Duc Tho resume talks in Paris and resolve all residual issues by the next day. South Vietnamese president Thieu is left with no choice but to accept the arrangement, although he labels it "tantamount to surrender."

and steps taken toward effecting racial justice would become Kennedy's most important domestic accomplishment.

Nevertheless, in the face of a slim mandate and largely hostile Congress, Kennedy had to move with deliberate caution, relying on executive orders rather than legislative change. Among Kennedy's achievements were the ending of segregated interstate transport, the enforcement of James Meredith's court-assured right to become the first African American to attend the University of Mississippi, and the appointment of an unprecedented number of African Americans to high governmental offices. However, Kennedy was motivated more by pragmatism than morality in his early civil rights efforts as he sought to balance the demands of various political constituencies.

One of the early champions of the moral dimension of the civil rights cause was Martin Luther King Jr., the leader of the Southern Christian Leadership Conference (SCLC). King adopted a nonviolent approach to change, arguing, "The problem with hatred and violence is that they intensify the fears of the white majority, and leave them less ashamed of their

prejudices toward Negroes." Instead of violent confrontation, King led peaceful assemblies such as the "March on Washington for Jobs and Freedom" in August 1963, where a quarter of a million black and white people heard him deliver his famous "I have a dream" speech on the steps of the Lincoln Memorial. King also helped African Americans organize their economic power to instigate changes in transportation, shops, restaurants, and employment. Many times, King's nonviolent tactics were met by heavy-handed police action. In Birmingham, Alabama, police commissioner Eugene "Bull" Connor turned fire hoses, electric cattle prods, and police dogs on King's marchers. Photographs of such brutality helped make the entire U.S. population aware of the poor treatment African Americans received in the South, fueling demands for change and increased federal government action.

Challenging King's philosophy were a host of more militant organizations such as the

....

Malcolm X called for a "working unity among all peoples, black as well as white." He was assassinated in 1965 by a rival Muslim.

January 23 President Nixon announces that the negotiations have resulted in an agreement that will "end the war and bring peace with honor."

January 27 The Paris Peace Accords are signed by representatives from the United States, North Vietnam, South Vietnam, and the Vietcong.

January 27 Secretary of Defense Melvin Laird announces that the draft is ended, and the era of the new volunteer army begins.

January 27 Lieutenant Colonel William Nolde becomes the last U.S. soldier to die in combat in Vietnam.

January 30 Elliot L. Richardson replaces Melvin Laird as Secretary of Defense.

Congress of Racial Equality (CORE) and the Student Nonviolent Coordinating Committee (SNCC). As white responses to black protests became increasingly ruthless, and certainly after King's assassination in 1968, these more radical elements began to carry more sway in the civil rights movement. The center of black protests also began to shift from the South toward the North, where African Americans, often isolated in ghettos and less mollified by traditional influences such as religion, were more hostile to whites. The Nation of Islam, led by Elijah Muhammad but most closely associated with Malcolm X, called for black separatism, self-discipline, and self-defense. Malcolm X broke with the Muslims in 1964 and began calling for a less radical "working unity among all peoples, black as well as white," but he was murdered in February 1965 by a rival Muslim.

Large-Scale Violence

Racial tensions sparked large-scale violence in urban areas, such as the August 1965 riot in the Watts district of Los Angeles, which resulted in thirty-four deaths and $35 million worth of property damage. Chicago, Tampa, Cincinnati, Atlanta, Detroit, and Newark were also sites of major riots. Stokely Carmichael of SNCC and Floyd McKissick of CORE captured this growing radicalization with their demands

Racial tensions exploded into the "Long Hot Summer" of 1965, when riots such as this one in the Watts district of Los Angeles broke out in many urban areas.

1973

FEBRUARY

February 6 The U.S. Navy begins Operation End Sweep to remove mines from Vietnamese waters.

February 12 Operation Homecoming begins the release of 591 U.S. prisoners of war from North Vietnam.

for black power. The most militant of the black power groups was the Black Panther Party, organized around military lines in 1966 with Bobby Seale as chairman, Huey Newton as minister of defense, and Eldridge Cleaver as minister of information. Cleaver and Carmichael both rejected older black organizations such as the National Association for the Advancement of Colored People (NAACP) and even King's SCLC. Gone were the measured slogans like "We shall overcome" of the King era. In their place were threatening calls to "Burn, baby, burn."

Although some groups tried to effect change in the streets and cities, legislative change began to occur as well. After Kennedy's assassination in 1963, Lyndon B. Johnson assumed the presidency and seemingly presented a stark contrast to Kennedy. At fifty-five years old, Johnson was more part of the generation resisting change than the new generation captivated by the youthful Kennedy. As a Texan, Johnson hailed from the state most politically resistant to empowering blacks. Nevertheless, Johnson had a reputation as a reformer who genuinely cared for the poor,

the underprivileged, and the oppressed black population. In May 1964, he called for a "Great Society" in which "the city of man serves not only the needs of the body and the demands of commerce but the desire for beauty and the hunger for community." Johnson also had extensive experience as a legislator, with twenty-three years in Congress and the Senate. He would use these qualifications to codify many of the civil rights advances begun under Kennedy.

Under Johnson's leadership, an impressive body of law would be passed to implement his Great Society. The Civil Rights Act of 1964 prohibited discrimination in the use of federal funds and in places of public accommodation. The law also established the Equal Employment Opportunity Commission. The same year, the Economic Opportunity Act was passed and became a vital part of Johnson's war on poverty. The landmark Voting Rights Act of 1965 brought about an end to the states' ability to disenfranchise African Americans and empowered the federal government to register those whom the states refused to put on voting lists. In addition to these legislative accomplishments, on September 24, 1965,

The draft was plagued by inequities until a lottery system was established in 1969.

Johnson signed an executive order instituting affirmative action, which required federal contractors and institutions receiving federal assistance to make special efforts to employ women and nonwhites.

MARCH

March 29 The last remaining U.S. troops withdraw from Vietnam and the MACV is deactivated.

The counterculture, best represented by the hippies, revolted against traditional culture and authority and became very active in the antiwar movement.

In spite of these initiatives, nothing changed overnight. The United States during the Vietnam era was still a nation deeply divided by race. Part of the tension was the inaccurate but often repeated charge that blacks were being sent to Vietnam and were dying there in numbers disproportionate to the rest of the population. In reality, taking 1967 as an example, African Americans of military age made up 13.5 percent of the total population in the United States but just 9.8 percent of the total population of servicemen in Vietnam. The percentage of blacks in Vietnam was never higher than 12.5 percent.

Nonetheless, racial tension and growing black militancy in the United States naturally followed draftees and volunteers into the army. There were increasingly numerous incidents in the army with racial overtones, and blacks were often the aggressors. In 1969, 9.2 percent of all murders, 50 percent of all attempted murders, 43 percent of all aggravated assaults, and 71 percent of all robberies among army personnel in Vietnam involved a black perpetrator and a white victim. This was at a time when African Americans made up only 9.1 percent of the total population of the army there. During the same period, an average of 58 percent of the army prison population was black. Interestingly, in combat units race relations tended to be the most positive because the need for survival required unity of effort. Most racial problems were among support troops and in rear areas. Responding to these tensions, the army began a Racial Awareness Program in 1973.

Counterculture

In addition to protesting against the status of race relations, many Americans, especially younger ones, challenged traditional culture in general. Many took to the hippie lifestyle, living in rural communes or seedy urban areas such as San Francisco's Haight-Ashbury district. As a voice against authority, the counterculture became a key part of the antiwar movement.

The most visible sign of counterculture revolt was in dress and grooming. Young men began to let their hair grow long and wore sandals. Young women began to wear faded jeans and

1973

APRIL

April 1 Captain Robert White, the last known U.S. prisoner of war, is released.

April 2 President Nixon and President Thieu meet at San Clemente, California, where Nixon renews his earlier secret pledge to respond militarily if North Vietnam violates the peace agreement.

April 17 The U.S. Navy suspends Operation End Sweep, claiming the North Vietnamese are not abiding by the Paris agreement. Operations resume on June 18.

April 30 Top Nixon aides H. R. Haldeman, John Dean, and John Ehrlichman, as well as Attorney General Richard Kleindienst, resign as a result of the growing Watergate scandal.

stopped wearing bras. This new unkempt look was considered offensive by traditional Americans. It certainly contrasted with the short hair and uniformity of the army.

Music was a large part of the counterculture, and much of its agenda was voiced in song. In the early 1960s, many folk musicians such as Bob Dylan, Arlo Guthrie, and Joan Baez began to sing socially conscious songs that asked such questions as "Where have all the flowers gone?"

As the decade progressed, and anger over Vietnam mounted, idealistic folk ballads began to give way to louder and angrier rock protest songs. Many of these were performed at Woodstock, a massive concert at Bethel, New York, in 1969 that attracted around 400,000 people. There, musicians like Country Joe McDonald belted out unabashed war protests like "I-Feel-Like-I'm-Fixing-to-Die-Rag." Among the other performers at Woodstock was Jimi Hendrix, who had served a rather unspectacular tour with the 101st Airborne Division earlier in the decade.

In addition to music, also present at Woodstock was the counterculture attribute of "free love." Concert-goers swam naked in the lake and had sex in the open. The collective, communal nature of the counterculture even extended to sexual partners, and all manner of

Left: Musicians such as Joan Baez fueled the antiwar sentiment with protest songs.

Right: Although not as predominant as the civil rights movement, women's rights activists such as Betty Friedan challenged the status quo of gender relations.

JUNE

June 19 The U.S. Congress passes the Case-Church Amendment by a veto-proof margin. The amendment forbids any further U.S. military involvement in Southeast Asia after August 15, 1973.

June 24 Graham Martin succeeds Ellsworth Bunker as the U.S. ambassador to South Vietnam.

June 25 John Dean, former White House counsel, tells a special Senate committee that President Nixon tried to cover up the Watergate break-in.

sexual taboos fell by the wayside. Premarital sex, birth-control pills, abortions, X-rated films, and sexually explicit magazines all alarmed traditionalists. Along with this loosening of

Increased drug use was one of several discipline problems that plagued the American military in Vietnam.

sexual morals came a reconsideration of traditional gender roles and an increased demand for women's rights. Borrowing from the models of the civil rights and antiwar movements, a women's liberation movement began to gain traction. Betty Friedan championed the women's rights agenda in her 1963 book *The Feminine Mystique* and, with the help of others, founded the National Organization for Women (NOW) in 1966. NOW was soon using the aggressive tactics, such as sit-ins, demonstrations, and protests, that other aggrieved groups had employed. Nonetheless, the women's movement progressed more slowly than the civil rights movement. Throughout the Vietnam War and until 1978, military women served in the Women's Army Corps as a separate corps of the army.

Perhaps above all else, the counterculture mystique was associated with drug use. Marijuana was the most commonly used drug, but many young people experimented with stronger hallucinogens such as LSD. Reflective of this elevated presence of drugs in society, drug use in the army became a serious concern during the Vietnam War, where cheap drugs were readily available. A Department of Defense–sponsored survey in 1971 revealed that 50.9 percent of army personnel in Vietnam had smoked marijuana, 28.5 percent had used narcotics such as heroin and opium, and 30.8 percent had used other psychedelic drugs. Such high rates of drug use were a marked indicator of a serious erosion of military discipline. In 1971 the problem was so prevalent that the army began an Alcohol and Drug Abuse Prevention and Control Program.

The Media

Until the 1965 U.S. intervention in the Dominican Republic, military-media relations had been largely positive. However, during this operation, the Johnson administration and the military issued unclear statements on whether the objective was merely to evacuate U.S. citizens or to stop a Communist takeover. This ambiguity caused the development of tension between the military and the media, based

1973

JULY

July 2 James R. Schlesinger replaces Elliot Richardson as Secretary of Defense.

July 13 Alexander Butterfield, a former Nixon aide, discloses the existence of taped conversations that will establish President Nixon's knowledge of the Watergate break-in.

largely on the media's mistrust of official statements surrounding the intervention. Nonetheless, at the outset of the Vietnam War, the military and the media enjoyed cordial relations.

As the war progressed, however, the divergent agendas of the media and the military, as well as the federal government in general, caused a serious rift. Vietnam became known as the "living-room war" as millions of Americans tuned in to the nightly coverage on their televisions. As they did, they were increasingly exposed to the horrors of war, conditions made even starker by the messy nature of guerrilla warfare. Media images of Vietnamese children burned by napalm, Americans systematically destroying Vietnamese villages, and mounting U.S. casualties alienated the public and made the military feel betrayed by the media.

The climactic moment occurred after the Tet Offensive in 1968 when *CBS Evening News* anchor Walter Cronkite announced, "But it is

....

Media coverage brought images of the horrors of war to the American public in a way that created a serious rift between the military and the press.

increasingly clear to this reporter that the only rational way out [of the war] will be to negotiate, not as victors, but as an honorable people who lived up to their pledge to defend democracy, and did the best they could." In the age before cable news expanded the options

available to viewers, network reporters like Cronkite were enormously influential. Cronkite was personally credited with being "the most trusted man in America." After Cronkite's reversal on the war, Johnson lamented, "If I've lost Cronkite, I've lost the country."

July 16 The U.S. Senate Armed Forces Committee begins hearings into the secret bombings of Cambodia in 1969–70.

July 17 Secretary of Defense Schlesinger testifies before the Armed Forces Committee that 3,500 bombing raids were launched into Cambodia. The extent of the secret bombing campaign angers many in Congress and results in the first call for Nixon's impeachment.

July 18 The U.S. Navy completes Operation End Sweep.

The assassination of Robert Kennedy shocked America's sense of domestic stability in the 1960s.

Feelings between the military and the media were so hardened by the Vietnam War that a popular accusation sprung up in military circles that it was in fact the media that had lost the war. Officers who had served in Vietnam passed these feelings on to the next generation of officers. An adversarial relationship between the military and the media continued throughout the twentieth century and has only recently begun to thaw.

The 1968 Election

The dramatic shift in popular support for the war after Tet severely undercut Johnson's authority. In an emotional address to the nation on March 31, 1968, he announced his plans to limit the war effort as well as to withdraw from the 1968 presidential campaign. "With America's sons in the fields far away, with America's future under challenge right here at home, with our hopes and the world's hopes for peace in the balance every day," Johnson said, "I do not believe that I should devote an hour or a day of my time to any personal partisan causes or to any duties other than the awesome duties of this office—the presidency of your country. Accordingly, I shall not seek, and I will not accept, the nomination of my party for another term as your president." Johnson's withdrawal and the July 5 assassination of the

Richard Nixon won the hard-fought 1968 presidential election and began a policy of "Vietnamization" to end America's involvement in the war.

popular Robert Kennedy threw the Democratic Party nomination process into chaos. The Democratic Convention in Chicago was a disaster, as antiwar activists clashed with Mayor Richard Daley's heavy-handed police. Holding off a challenge from antiwar candidate Eugene

1973

AUGUST

August 14 The United States halts its bombing of Cambodia in accordance with the Case-Church Amendment.

August 22 Henry Kissinger succeeds William Rogers as Secretary of State.

SEPTEMBER

September 22 South Vietnamese troops assault NVA forces near Pleiku.

McCarthy, moderate Hubert Humphrey, Johnson's vice president, emerged with the nomination, but the Democratic Party was in tumult. In his acceptance speech, Humphrey spoke of "the paramount necessity for unity in our country," and also promised to "do everything within my power to aid the negotiations and to bring a prompt end to this war" in Vietnam.

In spite of Humphrey's appeal for unity, many white Southern Democrats, alienated by Kennedy and Johnson's civil rights reforms, flocked to the support of Alabama governor George Wallace's third-party candidacy. Openly racist, Wallace was also an unabashed supporter of the war. His running mate was General Curtis LeMay, a former U.S. Air Force Chief of Staff who was credited with wanting to "bomb Vietnam back into the stone age." Wallace's campaign was an indicator of just how divided the United States had become in terms of politics, race relations, and the war.

In the end, however, Richard Nixon emerged as the winner in a tight popular vote. Hurt by his association with Johnson and the failing war effort, Humphrey garnered 31,271,000 votes.

Wallace captured the far right-wing vote with 9,899,000 voters and carried five Deep South states. Nixon won 31,783,000 popular votes but captured a more impressive 301 electoral college votes to Humphrey's 191.

Nixon brought strong anti-Communist credentials to the White House, and he was a firm believer in containment. In November 1969, he said, "Our defeat and humiliation in South Vietnam without question would promote recklessness in the councils of those great powers who have not yet abandoned their goals of world conquest." In order to preclude this eventuality, but also to "wind down" the war, Nixon proposed a policy of "Vietnamization," to gradually replace U.S. troops and capabilities with South Vietnamese ones.

Campus Unrest

College campuses became especially volatile during the 1960s thanks to large numbers of young people who felt increasingly frustrated by

....

Following the deaths of four students at Kent State University, protests erupted on campuses across the nation, including at Jackson State College.

OCTOBER

October 10 Vice President Spiro Agnew resigns amid allegations of cheating on his income taxes and accepting contractor payoffs. Congressman Gerald Ford becomes the new vice president.

the older generation, the vulnerability of many male college students to the draft, and effective efforts to organize and mobilize the student population. The result was that campuses became the hotbed of the antiwar movement.

Identifying with the youthful vitality of President Kennedy, many college-age students drew a sharp distinction between their idealism and the conservatism that characterized the older generation. The contrast became increasingly doctrinaire with the motto "You can't trust anyone over thirty," which was popularized during demonstrations at the University of California, Berkeley, in 1964. Students began to view the older generation as the impersonal instrument of a corrupt bureaucracy based on greed, abuse of power, and illegitimate privilege.

These feelings were exacerbated by the draft. During the Vietnam War, young men eighteen to twenty-five years of age were eligible for the draft, but college students could obtain a

Political uncertainty, the antiwar movement, civil rights protests, and counterculture activity made the Vietnam era one of domestic turmoil for the United States.

2-S deferment. Therefore, college campuses contained many young men who, for a variety of reasons, were avoiding military service. This college exemption was one of many inequities plaguing the draft system, and in November 1969 the draft lottery law was enacted to improve the procedure. This legislation cut down on many exemptions and reduced student immunity to the draft. Although the new system was fairer, by increasing the number of college students now vulnerable to the draft it also increased campus activism against the draft and the war. Many campus protests involved young men burning their draft papers. Others avoided the draft altogether by fleeing to Canada.

By the mid 1960s, students were manifesting their political and social activism in a variety of organized forms. College students were an integral part of civil rights projects such as the Freedom Summer in Mississippi in 1964. Many young people had gained social consciousness serving in organizations such as the Volunteers in Service to America (VISTA). Others found their place in the radical Students for a Democratic Society, which railed against centralization and elitism, and became very

1973

NOVEMBER

November 7 Congress passes the War Powers Resolution, which requires the president to obtain the support of Congress within ninety days of sending U.S. troops abroad.

DECEMBER

December 3 The Vietcong destroy 18 million gallons of fuel stored near Saigon.

Dr. Benjamin Spock was both a pediatrician and an antiwar activist. His ideas of child-rearing were thought by some to have led to a disregard for law and order.

active in the antiwar movement. The result of all these various influences was a campus population ready to act. Some 12,000 students at Berkeley sat through a continuous two-day "teach-in" organized by Jerry Rubin, where such headliners as Norman Mailer, Isaac

Deutcher, and Dr. Benjamin Spock delivered antiwar speeches. Others took more aggressive actions, including vandalizing Reserve Officers Training Corps (ROTC) buildings and occupying administrative buildings. Clashes between students and National Guardsmen called in to restore order and protect property became common. Between 1968 and 1969, some 4,000 students were arrested.

The most notorious incident of campus antiwar protest and violence occurred at Kent State University in Ohio on May 4, 1970. In response to the U.S. incursion into Cambodia, perceived by many as a widening of the war contrary to Nixon's promise to reduce it, protests involving 1.5 million students erupted on half of the United States' 2,500 campuses. At Kent State, students firebombed the ROTC building and caused other damage that led Governor James Rhodes to call in the National Guard to restore order. At first, it seemed calm would return, but when students threw rocks

An out-of-court settlement in 1979 provided $675,000 to the wounded students and the parents of the students killed at Kent State.

and bottles at the National Guardsmen, the soldiers responded with tear gas. When the tear gas ran out, the National Guardsmen withdrew up a hillside to get out of range of the rocks. In the ensuing confused and tragic set of events, the National Guardsmen opened fire on the students, killing four and wounding nine others.

The deaths at Kent State unleashed a new surge of protests in what Columbia University president William McGill called the "most

1974

MAY

May 9 Impeachment proceedings begin against President Nixon.

JULY

July 24 The U.S. Supreme Court rules that President Nixon must turn over the White House tapes to Watergate special prosecutor Leon Jaworski.

July 30 The House Judiciary Committee votes to recommend impeaching President Nixon on three counts.

disastrous month of May in the history of American higher education." By the May 9 weekend, 100,000 students had flocked to Washington, D.C., to protest. On May 14, two more students were killed in campus unrest at Jackson State College (now University) in Mississippi. May saw demonstrations at more than 400 campuses, and 250 universities had to close before the end of the term.

Nixon showed little sympathy for the protesters, saying that the Kent State students' deaths "remind us once again that when dissent turns to violence it invites tragedy." Nixon contemplated forming a special national security committee headed by FBI director J. Edgar Hoover and composed of representatives from the CIA, FBI, and Department of Defense to break the antiwar movement. When Hoover raised objections to the committee's planned extralegal activities, Nixon instead contented himself to rely on the acrid rhetoric of his vice president, Spiro Agnew, in denouncing the

The Kent State protest against the 1970 incursion into Cambodia turned deadly and became the most enduring image of campus unrest during the Vietnam era.

1974

AUGUST

August 9 Richard Nixon resigns the presidency as a result of his involvement in the Watergate scandal. Vice President Gerald Ford becomes president.

SEPTEMBER

September 8 President Ford signs Proclamation 4311, which grants "a full, free, and absolute pardon unto Richard Nixon for all offenses against the United States which he . . . has committed or may have committed or taken part in during the period from January 20, 1969, to August 9, 1974."

"ideological eunuchs" and "effete corps of impudent snobs" who protested against the war. Vietnam had succeeded in driving the country apart in a way unseen since the Civil War.

Watergate

Perhaps as part of Nixon's increasing paranoia against all forms of dissent, he formed the Committee to Re-elect the President (CREEP) in 1971, which disbursed funds for all manners of dirty tricks to embarrass Nixon's potential opponents in the 1972 election. CREEP also conducted a bungled burglary of the Democratic National Committee Headquarters at the Watergate Hotel, and Nixon was soon involved in a cover-up. As evidence of Nixon's role mounted, he was impeached in July 1974 on charges of obstruction of justice. He resigned in August and was succeeded by Gerald Ford, who had replaced Agnew in October 1973. Agnew had resigned after revelations he had cheated on his income taxes and received contractor

The Watergate crisis led to President Nixon's impeachment and weakened the presidency's ability to influence events in Vietnam.

September 16 President Ford announces a clemency program for draft evaders and military deserters.

September 30 The U.S. Congress appropriates only $700 million for South Vietnam. This drastic reduction in support leaves the ARVN vulnerable and the South Vietnamese economy in shambles.

payoffs. Therefore, Ford assumed a severely weakened presidency and leadership of a disillusioned country without even the benefit of a mandate gained by running in a national election. When North Vietnam launched its final offensive against South Vietnam in 1975, he lacked the sway with Congress or the public to send U.S. assistance to its former ally. In 1972 then-President Nixon had promised South Vietnam's President Thieu that, even after the U.S. withdrawal, the United States would still use its military might to protect South Vietnam against any subsequent North Vietnamese cease-fire violations. This promise went unfulfilled in the wake of the U.S. domestic political crisis.

Impact

The result of all these domestic pressures was a weakening of traditional authority. No longer did U.S. citizens, particularly younger ones, explicitly assume the government to be acting wisely or in the country's best interest. The government and the military were exposed to an unprecedented level of scrutiny and, amid a murky and ambiguous war like Vietnam, answers did not always come easily.

Gerald Ford became president of a disillusioned nation after Nixon resigned and had little mandate to continue America's support for South Vietnam.

1974

OCTOBER

October 24 Leaders at the Twenty-first Plenum of the North Vietnamese Communist Party, held in Hanoi, decide to launch an invasion of South Vietnam in 1975.

NOVEMBER

November 19 William Calley is freed after serving three and a half years under house arrest for the murder of twenty-two civilians at My Lai.

Such a situation was exactly what the North Vietnamese wanted. Knowing that they could not defeat the U.S. military might on the battlefield, they opted instead to drag out the war long enough to erode the United States' public support for the conflict. This enemy strategy of exhaustion coincided with a period in U.S. history when a significant portion of the public was willing to challenge the government. The result was a popular demand to end U.S. involvement in Vietnam that the president simply could not ignore.

The reassessment of traditional norms that so influenced U.S. society also impacted the army. As an American institution, the army has always been a reflection of the society it serves and from which it draws its members. This phenomenon complicated the army's mission in Vietnam because the societal challenges to authority, revolt against bureaucracy, and ascendancy of the individual all warred against traditional military practices and values. Especially in a draft army, there were many soldiers who had previously been members of the counterculture or who had at least been influenced by it. Therefore, the army in Vietnam experienced, albeit to a more controlled degree, the same racial, drug, and discipline problems that plagued the United States in the 1960s and early 1970s. Moreover, some soldiers' morale suffered from feelings generated by the antiwar movement. They felt people did not appreciate their efforts or understand their situation.

The result was that the Vietnam War divided the United States and nearly shattered the army. The pressures the war wrought on a changing U.S. society were more than that society could bear. The consequence was not only U.S. withdrawal from the war but also a legacy that cast a shadow over U.S. foreign policy for decades with the demand for "No more Vietnams." The army suffered from the Vietnam experience beyond mere mission failure. It felt betrayed by a government that had committed it to a war and then seemingly abandoned it. It felt attacked by a media that seemed to delight in its difficulties. It felt unappreciated and alienated by the public after doing its best to execute the policies of politicians who had been elected by the very same public. Finally, it exhibited its own self-destructive behavior with the most severe discipline crisis in its history.

The U.S. struggle in Vietnam cannot be separated from the struggle at home. The North Vietnamese seemed to understand this reality much earlier and better than the United States itself did. The result was a North Vietnamese victory wrought not on the battlefields of Vietnam but on the campuses, streets, living rooms, and polling booths of the United States.

In 1971 the army began its Alcohol and Drug Abuse Prevention and Control Program (ADAPC) to try to halt its serious drug abuse problem.

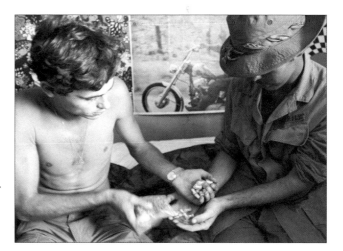

DECEMBER

December 13 North Vietnam violates the Paris peace treaty by attacking Phuoc Long province in South Vietnam. The United States lodges a diplomatic protest but nothing more because of the Case-Church Amendment.

December 18 North Vietnamese officials, after observing the U.S. inaction after the attack on Phuoc Long, meet to develop a plan for final victory.

Vietnamization and U.S. Withdrawal

Amid the tumultuous domestic scene in the United States, the perception of Tet as an indication of a failed war caused the American public to demand a new policy. Therefore, by the middle of 1968, the United States began to extricate itself from Vietnam.

For over three years, the U.S. military had struggled to destroy the Vietcong and force the North Vietnamese to give up their goal of reunifying Vietnam under Communism. However, now the American public had turned against the war and it was time to go in a new direction. By the middle of 1968, the United States began the slow and arduous task of extricating itself from the quagmire of Vietnam. Before it left, the U.S. military embarked on a scheme of "Vietnamization," which was designed to prepare its South Vietnamese allies to face the Communists alone.

After Tet

During the Tet Offensive, the war had come to the cities and towns of South Vietnam, but after Tet it shifted back to the countryside. In April 1968, eighty U.S. and ARVN battalions launched Operation Toan Tang ("Complete Victory"), which was designed to destroy any remaining Vietcong units that had attacked Saigon during Tet. However, the mission proved to be largely unsuccessful because the enemy had slipped back to its sanctuaries in Cambodia. Once the allied offensive subsided, the Vietcong

Left: These American soldiers have just received medals for their service in Vietnam.
Right: Soldiers often endured soggy ground on their patrols due to abundant rainfall, rivers, and rice paddies.

returned to the area around Saigon, and at the end of May began launching rocket attacks against the city.

In the central highlands, General Westmoreland planned to cripple the NVA's ability to function in South Vietnam by launching Operation Delaware, an offensive to destroy the NVA's staging area in the A Shau valley, as it posed a major threat to the city of Hue. The operation began on April 19 when troops from the U.S. 7th Cavalry launched a helicopter assault against the northern tip of the valley. The NVA responded to the attack by firing on the helicopters with intense antiaircraft fire. As a result, ten of the assaulting helicopters were shot down and fourteen others were damaged. However, as the 7th Cavalry advanced, the North Vietnamese began to retreat, leaving only a rearguard to cover their escape. In the short term, the operation was a success because the U.S. forces were able to capture and destroy large quantities of enemy

Many soldiers moved about Vietnam by foot patrols and airmobile operations. Others rode in armored personnel carriers.

supplies. However, in the familiar pattern of search-and-destroy, soon after the Americans left the NVA began to rebuild their staging area.

Farther north, near the demilitarized zone (DMZ), the U.S. 3rd Marine Division engaged the NVA's 320th Division in a fierce battle at

Dai Do. On April 30, the marines discovered the NVA attempting to interdict the U.S. logistical lines and, with the support of tanks and naval gunfire, slowly drove the enemy back. The battle was costly, with U.S. forces sustaining over 300 killed and approximately 1,000

1975

JANUARY

January 6 NVA forces capture Phuoc Long province, north of Saigon.

January 8 North Vietnam's politburo approves the NVA general staff plan for the invasion of South Vietnam.

January 14 Secretary of Defense Schlesinger testifies before Congress that the United States is not living up to its earlier promise to South Vietnam of "severe retaliatory action" in the event of North Vietnamese violations of the Paris Peace Accords.

wounded, but the Americans inflicted over 3,000 casualties on the NVA and managed to forestall an invasion of the south.

These post-Tet battles showed that, while U.S. support for the war at home had diminished, little had changed on the actual battlefield. The United States was still trying to use its massive firepower to fight a war of attrition and the Communists were still refusing to cooperate. By fighting only on their own terms and using their cross-border sanctuaries, the North Vietnamese nimbly escaped the superior U.S. military might. As had been the previous pattern, as soon as the U.S. forces departed an area, the North Vietnamese moved back in. It was a maddening experience for the Americans and exactly what the North Vietnamese had set out to achieve.

Peace Negotiations Begin

As battles such as these raged all over South Vietnam, delegates from the United States and

These Vietnamese women walk through the rubble of Saigon. As in all wars, collateral damage to civilian infrastructure was one of the realities of Vietnam.

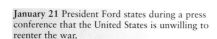

January 21 President Ford states during a press conference that the United States is unwilling to reenter the war.

FEBRUARY

February 5 General Van Tien Duong secretly crosses into South Vietnam to take command of the final NVA offensive.

North Vietnam arrived in Paris to begin peace negotiations. When the talks first began, there was a sense of heightened expectations and a hope for early progress, but the talks quickly stalled as both sides tried to negotiate a victorious peace. There was no give-and-take, especially on the North Vietnamese side, and the talks were marked by tension and frustration. Nevertheless, no one could have thought that five years later they would still be going over the same issues with which they had started. When the U.S. delegation arrived, its members checked into hotels rather than finding apartments or other types of long-term lodging; they simply did not expect the negotiations to last very long.

The main point of contention was over the reunification of Vietnam, and on this key issue neither side would budge. The United States would not agree to a peace treaty unless it allowed for an independent South Vietnam and the North Vietnamese would not give in until they achieved reunification of the country. The talks were deadlocked amid these mutually exclusive positions and, as usual, the North Vietnamese knew time was on their side.

Changes in Military and Political Leadership

In July 1968, General William Westmoreland was promoted to chief of staff of the army and was replaced as MACV commander by General Creighton Abrams. Abrams's mission in Vietnam was to limit U.S. casualties and build

Ambassador Henry Cabot Lodge's prediction that the Mekong delta would be cleared of Communist forces by the end of 1965 proved overly optimistic.

1975

MARCH

March 1 The final Communist offensive begins as five NVA divisions attack into the central highlands.

March 11 Ban Me Thuot falls to North Vietnamese forces after holding out for a week.

up South Vietnamese forces while continuing to hinder Vietcong and North Vietnamese battle plans. He also wanted to continue offensive operations to "kill as many of the bastards as [they] could." However, instead of continuing Westmoreland's large-scale search-and-destroy missions, Abrams focused on smaller-unit actions. He also sought to increase the military's emphasis on the pacification of South Vietnam's countryside. Under Abrams, U.S. combat missions would be smaller and would center on cutting the Vietcong off from the civilians. Abrams's intention was a "one-war strategy" in which pacification and combat operations would work in concert. Newly elected president Richard Nixon also represented a change in the United States' approach to the war. During the campaign, Nixon declared, "Never has so much power been used so ineffectively as in Vietnam. If after all of this time, and all of this sacrifice, and all of this support there is still no end in sight, then I say the time has come for the American people to turn to new leadership . . . not tied to the policies and mistakes of the past." Now Nixon would make good his promise to bring new direction to the war.

By the time Nixon took office in January 1969, there were still more than 500,000 U.S. troops in Vietnam. One of Nixon's goals was to gradually reduce this number while strengthening the ARVN. He also put more pressure on North Vietnam by increasing bombing missions until they agreed to terms that would allow for an independent South Vietnam. However, the North Vietnamese again proved to be obstinate in the face of U.S. firepower. Nixon wished to punish the North Vietnamese by expanding offensive operations, but he could not do so because of adverse U.S. public opinion. The North Vietnamese had succeeded in neutralizing the American military might in an indirect fashion via the home front rather than directly on the battlefield.

Vietnamization

Instead of punishing North Vietnam, Nixon and his National Security Adviser, Henry Kissinger, focused on implementing the

....

President Nixon championed the process of Vietnamization to turn the war over to the South Vietnamese.

program of Vietnamization, a plan to turn the responsibility of ground and air combat over to the South Vietnamese as U.S. troops withdrew. Also as part of the policy, the United States would give the South Vietnamese the equipment and training needed to defend their sovereignty. To support this transition,

March 13 President Thieu meets commanders at Cam Ranh and orders all ARVN forces in the central highlands to retreat to the coastal town of Tuy Hoa so that Saigon and the southern half of the country will be better defended. The withdrawal fuels widespread panic and mass refugee movements.

March 18 In spite of earlier estimates that the fighting would continue for up to two years, NVA leaders realize South Vietnam is already near collapse and decide to accelerate their offensive to achieve total victory.

March 19 NVA forces capture Quang Tri City.

The U.S. incursion into Cambodia was limited to just over nineteen miles, but this apparent widening of the war still touched off numerous antiwar demonstrations.

....

the United States planned to launch several offensive operations to weaken the North Vietnamese and VC so that South Vietnam would have more time to build up its military. Once complete, Vietnamization would allow the United States to execute Nixon's promised "honorable end" to its involvement in Vietnam.

The first step toward Vietnamization came in June 1969 when President Nixon announced the reduction of U.S. troop presence by 25,000. As troops began to withdraw, Nixon compensated for the reduction by increasing air strikes and stepping up delivery of the latest weaponry and equipment to South Vietnamese forces. The South Vietnamese government also issued a major mobilization order that expanded the size of the South Vietnamese military to over a million men. As a result of these actions, South Vietnam's armed forces gave the appearance of being a formidable military, but problems with leadership, morale, and training continued to undermine their effectiveness.

The War Spills Over

As the Vietnamization plan continued, an unforeseen situation arose in the neighboring country of Cambodia. In March 1970, the neutral Cambodian government of Prince Norodom Sihanouk was overthrown by the pro-U.S. forces of General Lon Nol. This was an important development because, in spite of Cambodia's official neutrality, the country had long been a base of external support for the North Vietnamese. Lon Nol ordered the expulsion of North Vietnamese forces from Cambodia and moved to shut down the Ho Chi Minh Trail. However, the North Vietnamese refused to leave and soon joined Communist Cambodian forces, the Khmer Rouge, to attack the Lon Nol regime.

The Nixon administration responded to the situation by planning a cross-border operation to destroy Vietcong bases in Cambodia and to help in the survival of Lon Nol's government. Many of Nixon's advisers warned against launching a full-scale attack, fearing that the U.S. public would see the assault as a hostile invasion of another country and a widening of the war, and would react with large-scale

1975

MARCH

March 24 NVA forces capture Tam Ky.

March 25 South Vietnamese troops flee Hue and leave it to the North Vietnamese forces.

March 26 The South Vietnamese evacuate Chu Lai.

protests. Taking these concerns into account, Nixon chose not to attack deep into Cambodia, but instead issued the order to launch a limited incursion into the Fishhook and Parrot's Beak border areas near Saigon.

In an attempt to forestall massive protests by Americans, Nixon addressed the nation in the final hours before the invasion, explaining, "I have concluded that the time has come for action. Tonight, American and South Vietnamese units will attack the headquarters for the entire Communist military operation in South Vietnam. This key control center has been occupied by North Vietnamese and the Vietcong for five years in blatant violation of Cambodian neutrality. This is not an invasion of Cambodia." Despite Nixon's words, violent protests erupted all over the United States, the most notable of which was the Kent State University protest where four students were shot and killed by the Ohio National Guard.

As the protests raged in the United States, American and ARVN forces moved into Cambodia and, on April 29, the incursion into the Parrot's Beak began. Soon after the South Vietnamese and U.S. forces crossed into

Cambodian territory, the Communists fell back and abandoned their supply bases. A few days later, they retreated again when U.S. and ARVN forces entered the Fishhook region. However, the attacking forces were unable to pursue the fleeing Communists because Nixon had limited their incursion to nineteen miles within Cambodia in an attempt to reduce concerns at home. As a result, U.S. and South Vietnamese forces exited Cambodia on June 30 without fully destroying the Communist infrastructure. Soon after the withdrawal, Communist forces returned to the region and rebuilt their logistical system.

Operation Lam Son 719
After the incursion into Cambodia, South Vietnamese president Nguyen Van Thieu began to press for a second attempt to destroy Communist bases across the border. He knew that U.S. support for the war was rapidly

....

Right: The Communist Khmer Rouge forces attacked the pro-U.S. government of Lon Nol in Cambodia. The Khmer Rouge later unleashed a reign of terror when they came to power.

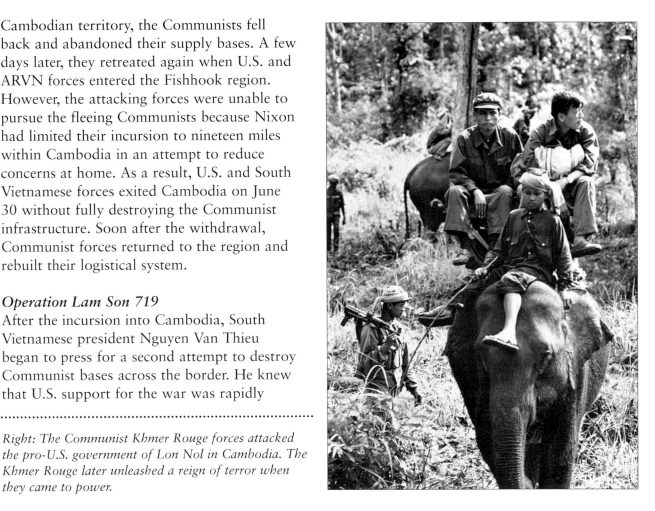

March 29 NVA forces capture Da Nang without a fight.

March 31 The NVA begins the Ho Chi Minh Campaign, its final push toward Saigon.

waning, and he hoped to convince the United States to launch one more major strike against the sanctuaries. This time the target was Laos

and, although the U.S. military approved of the plan, it insisted that the ARVN forces do most of the fighting. The cross-border assault, known as Operation Lam Son 719, called for 15,000 ARVN troops to advance into Laos and attack Communist logistical bases on the Ho Chi Minh Trail.

Left: Vietnam continued to divide America even as President Nixon worked to bring the country "peace with honor."

Right: American aviators were forced to rescue the ARVN in Laos during Lam Son 719. U.S. helicopter losses were staggering.

1975

APRIL

April 7 Le Duc Tho arrives at the Communist headquarters at Loc Ninh to oversee the offensive.

April 9 NVA forces close in on Xuan Loc, thirty-seven miles from Saigon, and encounter stiff resistance from the ARVN 18th Division.

The operation began on January 30, 1971, when U.S. forces reoccupied the Khe Sanh marine base as the logistical and fire support base for the attack into Laos, followed by an ARVN ground and airmobile assault on February 8 that was designed to capture the town of Tchepone. Soon after the mission began, ARVN forces began to run into trouble. Unlike in Cambodia where NVA troops fled in the face of the attacking forces, the North Vietnamese chose to stand and fight in Laos, where the logistical lines were absolutely vital to their war effort. Lieutenant General Phillip B. Davidson noted, "The Ho Chi Minh Trail was in 1971 the only means of supplying the entire enemy force in South Vietnam, southern Laos, and Cambodia. If the ARVN could cut the trail, they would deal a devastating blow to all Communist operations in South Vietnam. Therefore, the North Vietnamese had to oppose Lam Son 719 with every resource they could bring to bear."

Right: ARVN forces would be called upon to bear the brunt of the Lam Son 719 invasion. Their objective was to interdict Communist logistical lines in Laos.

April 10 President Ford makes an emotional televised plea for $722 million in emergency aid to South Vietnam, but Congress does not respond.

Because Laos was so critical, the North Vietnamese refused to retreat. Instead, General Giap gathered a force of 40,000 NVA soldiers to oppose the ARVN attack. Facing such a large and determined enemy, the ARVN began to take heavy casualties and was soon forced to abandon its effort to control Tchepone and

withdraw from Laos. However, as the South Vietnamese began to retreat, NVA forces moved to cut off and destroy the invaders.

Lam Son 719 was turning into a complete disaster, and soon U.S. helicopters had to come to the rescue of the beleaguered ARVN. As discipline and order waned, the battle became

an "every man for himself" fight for survival, with panic-stricken South Vietnamese soldiers swarming the evacuation helicopters and clinging to their skids. In the end, the ARVN invasion force escaped Laos with the help of U.S. air support, but the damage had been done. Some 7,682 ARVN soldiers became casualties, 1,764 of whom were killed. The Americans suffered 1,402 casualties, including 215 killed, and 108 helicopters were destroyed. Exact NVA casualties are unknown but are estimated to be around 16,000.

On April 7, 1971, President Nixon announced to the U.S. public that, based on Lam Son 719, "I can report that Vietnamization has succeeded." In reality, the ARVN forces, when faced with a determined enemy, had been defeated and suffered a breakdown in discipline. The success of Vietnamization itself now looked questionable, as it became clear to the U.S. military that the South Vietnamese were not yet ready to stand on their own. Despite these misgivings, the die had been cast, and the United States continued to reduce the numbers of its troops in South Vietnam.

ARVN soldiers like the ones shown here drilling on a soccer field performed poorly in Lam Son 719, but the withdrawal of U.S. forces continued.

1975

APRIL

April 12 The United States begins Operation Eagle Pull to evacuate U.S. and allied personnel from Phnom Penh, Cambodia.

April 17 Phnom Penh falls to the Khmer Rouge.

The Easter Offensive

Following Lam Son 719, the Vietnam War settled into a relatively quiet period. For the rest of 1971, no large-scale operations took place as the United States and ARVN only engaged the enemy in limited small-unit actions. At the peace talks, U.S. and North Vietnamese diplomats continued to work toward an end to the conflict, but the negotiations still showed no significant progress. Therefore, Kissinger and Nixon chose an alternative plan to bring an end to the Vietnam War. Seeking to exploit strained Sino-Soviet relations, Nixon and Kissinger made plans to travel to China and Russia to discuss the situation in Vietnam. By opening relations with Communist nations, Nixon and Kissinger hoped to dissuade them from continuing to provide support for North Vietnam.

This new development greatly concerned the North Vietnamese, so Giap decided to launch a massive conventional assault to win the war on the battlefield. An immediate victory would negate any gains that the United States made in its diplomatic endeavor and bring about the fall of the South Vietnamese government. The assault, known as the Nguyen Hue Offensive or Easter Offensive, was to be a three-pronged attack: a strike across the DMZ to capture Hue, an attack in the central highlands to take Kontum, and an attack from Cambodia to seize the provincial capital of An Loc near Saigon.

The offensive began on March 30, 1972, when four NVA divisions, backed by tanks and heavy artillery, crossed the DMZ and slammed into the 3rd ARVN Division in Quang Tri province. Faced with overwhelming firepower, the 3rd Division immediately lost ground and began to crumble. Fire-support bases collapsed quickly and the NVA forces captured the town of Dong Ha. The remaining ARVN defenders were soon surrounded in the province capital of Quang Tri City. With the aid of South Vietnamese marine and ranger units and U.S. air support, Quang Tri City held out against a two-division NVA assault for several days. However, NVA artillery barrages and tank attacks forced the South Vietnamese to abandon their defenses on May 1.

....

Kontrum was one of the objectives of the three-pronged Communist Easter Offensive of 1972. ARVN defenders and U.S. air support forced the attackers back.

After taking Quang Tri City, the NVA turned its attention to the city of Hue, which was defended by the 1st ARVN Division together with marine and airborne units. Under the leadership of General Ngo Quang Truong, the commander of I Corps, the ARVN units not

April 17 Lon Nol's forces surrender to the Khmer Rouge in Cambodia. Pol Pot begins an unprecedented reign of terror.

April 20 U.S. ambassador Graham Martin meets President Thieu and encourages him to resign.

April 22 Xuan Loc falls to NVA forces.

only held their ground but soon went on the offensive. With the help of U.S. air power and the effective leadership of Truong, three ARVN divisions successfully pushed back six NVA divisions and recaptured Quang Tri City by the end of June. Therefore, despite early losses, the battle for Quang Tri turned out to be a resounding victory for the South Vietnamese.

Meanwhile, farther south, two NVA divisions drove toward the central highlands town of Kontum. The advancing North Vietnamese quickly seized the town of Dak To and began to attack Kontum itself by mid-May. The ARVN defenders of the city, aided by U.S. B-52 strikes, fought valiantly to fend off the NVA assault. By the end of May, NVA losses became so high that they were forced to call off the attack.

The situation also unfolded in a similar fashion in the battle of An Loc. There, the North Vietnamese quickly advanced across the Cambodian border and launched their attack on the province's capital. By April 7, the NVA had

Under the able leadership of General Ngo Quang Truong, the ARVN performed well at Quang Tri and recaptured the city after initial losses.

1975

APRIL

April 22 President Thieu resigns. The presidency passes to Vice President Tran Van Huong, who also resigns. Eventually, General Duong Van Minh will become president of South Vietnam.

April 23 Speaking in New Orleans, President Ford calls the Vietnam War "finished."

April 25 Nguyen Van Thieu flees Saigon for Taiwan.

Left: By April 13, An Loc was surrounded by Communist forces and the defenders had to be resupplied by helicopter and parachute drops.

Right: Against the odds, the defenders of An Loc held their ground and by May 17 the siege was lifted.

completely surrounded An Loc and began to lay siege to it. Once again, the North Vietnamese sent waves of tanks against the city's defenders but, as in Kontum, U.S. air power and infantry antitank weapons blunted the NVA assault. However, the Communists did succeed in taking the northern half of the city and the battle turned into a street-by-street fight. In early May, the NVA launched their final attempt to take An Loc, but once again B-52 raids destroyed the attacking NVA forces. By May 17, all of An Loc was in ARVN hands and the remaining NVA forces withdrew back into Cambodia.

On all fronts, the Easter Offensive was a major victory for the ARVN forces, as they stood firm in the face of the enemy's best attempt to destroy them. However, the decisive factor in the battle had been U.S. air power, with B-52 strikes shattering the NVA's attacking divisions and bringing an end to the Easter Offensive. In total, the North Vietnamese suffered more than 100,000 dead but, in spite of the massive losses, the NVA will was not broken. Nevertheless, it would be another two years before North Vietnam was ready to try to conquer the south again.

In addition to providing tactical air support to the ARVN forces in the Easter Offensive, U.S. planes renewed the strategic bombing offensive. President Nixon ordered Operation Linebacker I, a large-scale bombing offensive on North Vietnam that, unlike previous bombing campaigns such as Operation Rolling Thunder, had few restrictions. U.S. B-52s now targeted Hanoi and Haiphong, pounding North Vietnam's military infrastructure and cutting

April 27 NVA forces have Saigon surrounded.

April 28 Tran Van Huong transfers authority as chief of state of South Vietnam to General Duong Van Minh.

their logistical lines. The bombing campaign devastated North Vietnam and forced the North Vietnamese delegates in Paris to make concessions in the peace negotiations.

The Paris Peace Negotiations

By July 1972, U.S. and North Vietnamese delegates were beginning to make serious attempts to bring an end to U.S. involvement in Vietnam. Both sides agreed to compromises, and it seemed as if the war would finally be over for the United States. American delegates agreed to allow North Vietnamese units to stay in South Vietnam and North Vietnamese delegates consented to the continued existence of the Thieu regime, but only in coalition with the Vietcong. On October 8, Henry Kissinger accepted a proposal that called for a cease-fire, prisoner exchange, and the withdrawal of U.S. troops within two months of the agreement.

Despite the fact that an agreement had been reached between the United States and the

The victory at An Loc was cause for celebration among ARVN soldiers, but observers were quick to point out that American air power was critical to their success.

1975

APRIL

April 29 The United States initiates Operation Frequent Wind, the helicopter evacuation of Americans and South Vietnamese from Saigon.

April 30 The last Americans, ten marines from the embassy, depart Saigon. North Vietnamese troops pour into the city and seize control. The war is over.

North Vietnamese, the South Vietnamese government failed to consent to the arrangement. The South Vietnamese had not been included in the negotiations and were therefore shocked by the concessions. President Thieu refused to sign the treaty and the peace negotiations stalled again as the North Vietnamese walked away from the peace table in December 1972. In response, Nixon threatened North Vietnam with a new bombing campaign. When North Vietnam refused to return to the talks, Nixon ordered the commencement of Operation Linebacker II, which lasted from December 18 to 29. During the eleven-day operation, B-52s struck bridges, railways, and storage and military facilities throughout North Vietnam. The North Vietnamese reacted to the bombings by firing over 1,000 surface-to-air missiles at U.S. aircraft. In the end, twenty-six U.S. aircraft, including fifteen B-52s, were shot down, but the operation succeeded in driving the North Vietnamese back to the bargaining table.

On January 8, 1973, the Paris Peace Accords, which differed little from the October 8 treaty, were signed by all sides. As events would soon prove, the peace accords were only a temporary truce between North and South Vietnam but, for the United States at least, the Vietnam War was finally over. Some 58,000 U.S. soldiers had died in the conflict and over 153,000 others had been wounded. In spite of this sacrifice, the United States exited the conflict without resolving the question of South Vietnamese sovereignty and the Paris Peace Accords would only forestall South Vietnam's fate.

The Paris peace talks were tense, on-again-off-again affairs, but on January 8, 1973, an agreement was finally reached that ended U.S. involvement in the war.

MAY

May 12 The U.S. merchant ship *Mayaguez* is seized by Cambodian Communists in the Gulf of Siam. U.S. planes bomb Cambodia. Thirty-eight U.S. marines later die in the rescue of thirty-nine sailors.

The Conclusion and Aftermath

Although the Paris Peace Accords ended the Vietnam War for the United States, for the Vietnamese people the war was far from over. The time had come to see if the program of Vietnamization had succeeded in equipping South Vietnam to continue the war on its own.

In the end, a combination of paper, insufficient preparation, spotty battlefield performance, and U.S. domestic developments conspired to doom the South Vietnamese to defeat. By 1975, the war was over. On paper, however, the situation looked hopeful for the South Vietnamese and their military looked formidable. Armed with the latest U.S. weapons and equipment, the ARVN fielded a force of 450,000 soldiers, supplemented by 525,000

Left: The withdrawal of U.S. forces from South Vietnam left the South Vietnamese to continue the fight alone. Right: In 1975, five NVA divisions attacked into the central highlands to try to split South Vietnam in two.

regional forces. In addition to these numbers, the South Vietnamese air force mustered 54,000 members and the navy had another 42,000. South Vietnam's President Thieu had been given clear assurances by President Nixon that if North Vietnam broke the peace treaty, the United States would retaliate with force. However, in the summer of 1973, in the wake of revelations about secret bombing missions in Cambodia and other political considerations, Nixon no longer had the power to fulfill his promise. In June, Congress passed the Case-Church Amendment, banning combat operations over Vietnam, Laos, and Cambodia.

As the ARVN crumbled in the wake of the North Vietnamese onslaught, countless South Vietnamese became refugees caught in the chaos of war.

battles and instead tried to regain important ground with small attacks in areas where South Vietnamese presence was minimal. At the same time, they would get ready for a future offensive that would aim to destroy South Vietnam once and for all. As part of these preparations, they began laying a pipeline along the Ho Chi Minh Trail that would transport fuel from the demilitarized zone down the length of South Vietnam. They upgraded the trail so that trucks and tanks would have an easier time traveling to southern battlefields. As was always the case, the North Vietnamese had a long-term view.

Economic Crisis in the South

Meanwhile in Saigon, President Thieu began to make plans to go on the offensive. In the days that followed the U.S. withdrawal, South Vietnamese forces had held up well, and Thieu was confident that his regime could survive. In reality, a major crisis loomed on the horizon. The withdrawal of U.S. troops had severely

In Hanoi, the North Vietnamese decided that the first priority was to rebuild their weakened forces. The Easter Offensive of 1972 had been a complete disaster for them, resulting in the loss of more than 100,000 men. In addition to heavy casualties, nearly half of their tanks and large-caliber artillery pieces had been lost in the fighting. Therefore, they opted to avoid big

1976

NOVEMBER

November 2 Jimmy Carter is elected president of the United States.

damaged a South Vietnamese economy that had been buttressed by the United States' presence. Now, a world oil crisis worsened the situation by quadrupling the cost of fuel, making it almost unaffordable for even the South Vietnamese military. The U.S. government also cut the amount of aid to South Vietnam from about $2.3 billion in 1973 to $1.1 billion in 1974. Much of what little aid did arrive was siphoned off by corrupt politicians and military officers. The drastic reduction in foreign aid caused inflation to soar to over 200 percent, and poverty and unemployment rose as well.

As a result of these economic woes, the effectiveness of South Vietnam's military plummeted. The South Vietnamese could not afford ammunition, spare parts, or fuel. Jets, tanks, trucks, and artillery sat unused because the military lacked sufficient funds to operate them. Therefore, when North Vietnam decided to attack, South Vietnam could not employ much of its high-tech weaponry and equipment. To make matters worse, soldiers could no longer support their families as prices rose and corrupt officers embezzled funds. As a result, morale collapsed as well. It seemed as if North Vietnam

would not need to do much to bring about the destruction of South Vietnam. The country was collapsing under the weight of its own economic problems.

The Beginning of the End

By the beginning of 1974, North Vietnam had almost fully recovered from the damage done by its defeat in the Easter Offensive. The NVA used the spring and summer of 1974 to improve its position in South Vietnam, launching a series of strategic raids to regain the initiative and seize several important pieces of territory. In five months of fighting, the North Vietnamese succeeded in gaining most of the territory they targeted. Their troops also gained valuable combat experience, which would aid them tremendously in future operations. Meanwhile, northern leaders argued about the timetable for the main offensive. At the Twenty-first Plenum, a meeting of the Communist party leadership held in Hanoi in October 1974, North Vietnam

....

Le Duan, first secretary of the North Vietnam Communist Party, had the idea of a limited offensive to test ARVN strength and American commitment.

decided to give immediate priority to a military rather than a political offensive. However, some politburo members still feared that a large-scale military offensive would be too costly. They believed that the ARVN would put up fierce resistance and they also feared the return of U.S. air power.

1977

JANUARY

January 21 On the day after his inauguration, President Carter pardons most of the 10,000 Vietnam War draft evaders.

MARCH

March 1 Assistant Secretary of State Richard Holbrooke begins talks with Vietnamese officials to explore U.S. recognition of Vietnam.

After the loss of Ban Me Thout, President Thieu ordered a withdrawal that resulted in widespread panic. Several ARVN divisions simply dissolved without a fight.

In the end, a politburo member named Le Duan suggested that the attacks on South Vietnam should begin with a limited offensive to test the strength of the ARVN and to see if the Americans would return. In mid-December 1974, two NVA divisions moved against the South Vietnamese province of Phuoc Long. Initially, ARVN troops fought well, but after only three weeks the entire province was lost to the Communists. Shortages of fuel and ammunition hampered ARVN efforts to fight back, and the South Vietnamese lacked the firepower that the United States had previously brought to battle. In the wake of the renewed Communist offensive, President Thieu turned to the United States for help, but none was forthcoming. The Case-Church Amendment prohibited any further U.S. military involvement in Southeast Asia and the Communists took this inaction on the part of the United States as a green light to launch an offensive that would end the war.

Catastrophe in the Central Highlands

The first phase of the North Vietnamese general offensive began on March 1, 1975, when five NVA divisions attacked into the central highlands. Supported by armor and artillery, these units sought to drive through the highlands to cut South Vietnam in two. The ARVN forces at Pleiku, almost numerically equal to those of the NVA, tried to resist, but they soon found themselves outflanked. General Van Tien Duong, commander of the NVA forces, maneuvered around the ARVN and attacked the town of Ban Me Thout to the

1978

DECEMBER

December 25 Vietnam invades Cambodia.

1979

FEBRUARY

February 17 China invades Vietnam.

south of Pleiku. The much smaller force of ARVN defenders at Ban Me Thout held out for a week but were soon forced to give up the town.

Following the loss of Ban Me Thout, President Thieu ordered all ARVN forces in the central highlands to retreat to the coastal town of Tuy Hoa. This move was part of his new strategy to surrender the northern half of South Vietnam above Tuy Hoa so that Saigon and the southern half of the country could be better defended. However, as word of the plan spread, panic gripped South Vietnamese soldiers and civilians. Soon, everyone was rushing to the coastal towns in the attempt to travel to ARVN-held territories further south. The roads that led to coastal cities became packed with soldiers and civilians, and NVA troops began lobbing mortar and artillery rounds into the fleeing crowds, killing thousands. The decision to abandon the northern half of country turned out to be Thieu's most disastrous decision of

Careful not to do anything to cause the U.S. to reenter the war, the North Vietnamese delayed their assault on Da Nang to allow any Americans left there to evacuate.

the entire war. In the retreat from the central highlands, several ARVN divisions simply dissolved without a fight.

As the crisis unfolded in the central highlands, a similar calamity occurred in the northern provinces. There, five NVA divisions attacked the ARVN defenders of Quang Tri, Hue, and Da Nang. Once again, some ARVN defenders fought hard to fend off the NVA advance, but many simply deserted in the face of the enemy. On hearing of Thieu's order to abandon the central highlands, thousands of South Vietnamese soldiers and civilians raced to the coastal towns of Hue and Da Nang in a last-ditch effort to escape the advancing Communists. Soon, the cities became overcrowded with refugees and deserters. Hue fell on March 26, and the NVA next turned their attention on Da Nang. However, instead of attacking immediately, the NVA waited a few days to allow any Americans left in the city to escape. The North Vietnamese did not want to

In spite of a valiant defense from the ARVN 18th Division, North Vietnamese forces overran Xuan Loc on April 22.

do anything, such as inflicting U.S. casualties, that might cause the United States to reenter the war. After this postponement, NVA forces captured Da Nang on March 29 without a fight. During the delay, South Vietnamese forces attempted to rescue as many soldiers and civilians as they could, but in the end they only succeeded in getting 50,000 out before the city fell.

Everyone, including the North Vietnamese, was surprised at the rate South Vietnam was collapsing. North Vietnamese military strategists had predicted that it would take at least two years for the south to fall. Now, after just a few

1982

NOVEMBER

November 13 The Vietnam Veterans Memorial is unveiled in Washington, D.C. While the design was originally controversial because of its nontraditional architecture, the memorial will later enjoy widespread popularity as "the wall that heals."

After Xuan Loc fell, President Thieu resigned from office and fled Vietnam. General Duong Van Minh then became president.

....

support Thieu, had been forced to resign after the Watergate scandal. On April 10, Nixon's successor, Gerald Ford, went on television to make an emotional request for $722 million in emergency aid for the South Vietnamese, but Congress and the U.S. people were not interested. Tired of war and disillusioned by Watergate, the United States left its former South Vietnamese allies to their fate.

The Ho Chi Minh Campaign

As hope faded for the South Vietnamese, the NVA hurried its preparations to finish the war, motivated by a desire to capture Saigon before the monsoon season. The final drive for Saigon began in early April, but before the Communists could capture South Vietnam's capital they had to get through the ARVN 18th Division at Xuan Loc. In perhaps its finest moment, the ARVN held firm against four NVA divisions. For nearly two weeks the battle raged, with NVA artillery pounding the ARVN defenders relentlessly.

months of fighting, the south was on the verge of complete collapse. Once again, President Thieu made a desperate plea for American help, but President Nixon, who had promised to

When the smoke cleared, thirty-seven NVA tanks were shattered and 5,000 NVA soldiers lay dead. Nonetheless, the valiant defenders of Xuan Loc were overrun on April 22, 1975. Throughout the war, the 18th Division had been considered mediocre, but as South Vietnam fell around them, they rose to the occasion.

On the day that Xuan Loc fell, President Thieu resigned from office, railing in his farewell address that the United States had abandoned South Vietnam. A few days later, Thieu also abandoned the country, taking with him millions of dollars in U.S. aid money. On Thieu's resignation, power passed to his vice president, Tran Van Huong, who quickly resigned as well. The presidency then fell to General Duong Van Minh, who was chosen based on the belief that he could negotiate a truce with the Communists. However, with their armies already on the outskirts of Saigon, the North Vietnamese had no need to negotiate.

Operation Frequent Wind

As the NVA stood poised to capture the South Vietnamese capital, the United States began to make an effort to rescue U.S. personnel and thousands of Vietnamese who had worked for the United States during the war. The rescue mission was delayed until the last minute because U.S. ambassador Graham Martin believed there was still a chance that the South Vietnamese could hold on. However, as this hope evaporated, the evacuation—named Operation Frequent Wind—finally began on April 29. The operation called for the transportation of evacuees to staging areas where helicopters would take them from rooftops to the U.S. fleet waiting just offshore. Originally, planes from Tan Son Nhut air base were also supposed to transport people out of the country, but heavy NVA shelling forced that part of the mission to be canceled. The helicopter airlift lasted until 5:00 a.m. on April 30, when the last evacuees were transported from the roof of the U.S. embassy. The helicopter mission, along with a naval rescue operation, saved around 77,000 people. Tens of thousands more were left behind to face the wrath of the North Vietnamese.

A few hours after Operation Frequent Wind concluded, North Vietnamese units entered Saigon. At noon, a group of tanks stormed through the gates of the presidential palace and lined up on the lawn. Inside, General Minh, the last president of South Vietnam, awaited them. The ranking NVA officer, Colonel Bui Tin, a

Operation Frequent Wind, the evacuation of remaining American personnel and selected South Vietnamese who had worked for the United States, began on April 29.

1984

MAY

May 7 A federal judge announces a $180 million settlement against seven companies that had manufactured Agent Orange, on behalf of Vietnam veterans who claimed exposure to the chemical had left them with health problems.

May 28 President Ronald Reagan presides over the burial of the Vietnam unknown soldier at Arlington National Cemetery.

military newspaper reporter, entered the palace to receive the surrender. General Minh greeted him, saying, "I have been waiting since early this morning to transfer power to you." Tin replied by saying, "There is no question of you transferring power. Your power has crumbled. You cannot give up what you do not have." The Vietnam War was finally over.

The Boat People

For many South Vietnamese, the end of the Vietnam War meant the end of a way of life.

Fearing Communist oppression, economic hardship, and the possibility of death, hundreds of thousands of Vietnamese fled the country by boat. By the late 1970s, more than 300,000 "boat people" had landed on the shores of Thailand, Malaysia, and other Southeast Asian

....

Right: The fall of Saigon ended the Vietnam War.

Below: On April 30, just hours after Operation Frequent Wind had ended, North Vietnamese units began to roll into Saigon.

nations in the vicinity of Vietnam. An estimated 250,000 more arrived between 1980 and 1984. In fleeing their homeland, these refugees risked everything for freedom. Thousands died on the open sea as overcrowded boats sank in high waves and others were killed by pirates who preyed mercilessly on the refugees. The exact number of boat people lost in their flight from Vietnam is unknown, but some estimate the numbers to be in the hundreds of thousands.

For those who were lucky enough to make it to shore, uncertainty and hardship awaited. Many refugees soon found out that their host countries did not want them, and others spent years in refugee camps in Thailand or Malaysia before being resettled. Some agreed to voluntarily return to Vietnam, but many chose to remain in the camps, risking an indefinite stay rather than returning to their homeland. The lucky ones were resettled in France, Canada, Australia, and the United States.

Even the refugees who made it to the United States found they had more challenges ahead of them. In some cases assimilation was difficult, especially for those who did not speak English. Moreover, refugees faced the complex task of maintaining Vietnamese culture and tradition while becoming Americans. However, as the years passed, many became successful members of the U.S. middle class and valuable contributors to society. Today, the Vietnamese-American community is over 1.1 million strong.

On April 30, a group of tanks broke through the gates of the presidential palace. General Minh surrendered to the ranking NVA officer, Colonel Bui Tin.

1990

AUGUST

August 10 The U.S. Congress recognizes the National League of Families' POW/MIA (prisoner of war/missing in action) flag and designates it "as the symbol of our Nation's concern and commitment to resolving as fully as possible the fates of Americans still prisoner, missing, and unaccounted for in Southeast Asia, thus ending the uncertainty for their families and the Nation."

The South Vietnamese who chose to stay and live under the new regime faced their own perils. Those who supported the Americans or worked for the South Vietnamese government or military were in the most danger. Because of the Hue massacre of 1968, many people predicted that the Communists would slaughter hundreds of thousands of South Vietnamese, but the large-scale massacre did not occur. Nonetheless, 60,000 "undesirables" were executed in the days after the war ended, and most of the South Vietnamese who had opposed the Communists in the war were sent to "reeducation camps," where they were subjected to horrible acts of torture and indoctrination. Some prisoners were released within a short time, but many were kept in the camps until the 1990s.

In neighboring Cambodia, the situation was far worse. On gaining power, the Marxist Khmer Rouge slaughtered about 30 percent of the population in a horrendous massacre known as the "killing fields." Anyone who was even suspected of holding anti-Communist sentiments was put to death. Even those who wore glasses were executed for being "intellectuals." The killings lasted until 1978, when the Vietnamese went to war with Cambodia over an unrelated political dispute.

After the defeat of South Vietnam, thousands of people fled to avoid Communist persecution and other hardships. Many set sail in rickety boats.

The Price of Victory and Defeat

For the victorious Vietnamese Communists, the conclusion of the Vietnam War did not bring an end to hardships. The North Vietnamese and Vietcong had suffered terribly in the war, losing some 1.1 million dead and another 600,000

1991

FEBRUARY

February 12 Colonel Millard Peck resigns as Chief of the Special Office for Prisoners of War and Missing in Action in protest of what he feels is government inefficiency and deception in attempting to recover living POWs and MIAs.

MAY

May 9 The U.S. Senate passes a resolution recommending the establishment of a U.S. POW/MIA Office in Hanoi that will serve as a liaison between the families of POW/MIAs and the Vietnamese government.

While a large-scale massacre did not occur, the victorious North Vietnamese did send many thousands of South Vietnamese to "reeducation camps."

rice to feed its own people. As a result of this program and others, the Vietnamese economy plummeted, and by the late 1970s Vietnam was almost completely reliant on the Soviet Union for survival. Pham Van Dong, prime minister of Vietnam, summed up postwar Vietnam's difficulties succinctly, saying, "Yes, we defeated the United States. But now we are plagued by problems. We do not have enough to eat. We are a poor underdeveloped nation. Waging a war is simple, but running a country is very difficult."

For the United States, the fall of Saigon and the end of the Vietnam conflict meant that the United States had lost its first war. Even though U.S. forces had not been truly bested on the tactical battlefields, the United States had failed in its strategic bid to save South Vietnam and contain Communism in Southeast Asia. Americans who supported the war believed the defeat came as a result of political interference with the military's prosecution of the war. They

wounded. A million civilians are estimated to have died in the war. In addition to this enormous loss of life, Vietnam faced major economic problems because the nation's infrastructure was almost entirely destroyed in the war. To make matters worse, the Communist leadership compounded the

problems by implementing ill-conceived cooperative programs.

For example, soon after achieving victory, the leaders of Vietnam initiated a program of agricultural collectivization. This interference in farm production caused rice yields to decline and soon the country was not growing enough

1995

JULY

July 11 The United States establishes diplomatic relations with Vietnam.

believed political concerns got in the way of winning and as a result the military's hands were tied so tightly that victory became unachievable. On the other hand, those that opposed the war felt that the United States never should have been involved in Vietnam and that the tragedy of Vietnam came as a result of misguided and arrogant foreign policy. The war's divisive effect on U.S. society continued long after its conclusion.

Regardless of the causes of defeat, the loss in Vietnam deeply wounded the American psyche. Before Vietnam, citizens of the United States believed in U.S. exceptionalism. To them, the United States was a good country and was well-meaning in its actions. In previous wars, Americans had always been the good guys, fighting on the side of democracy and freedom. After Vietnam, many Americans began to question this idea. The experience of the Vietnam War taught Americans to distrust their government and question the United States'

In Cambodia the Khmer Rouge embarked on a horrific massacre known as the "killing fields." Thirty percent of the population was killed between 1975 and 1978.

international role. For many years, a "Vietnam Syndrome" made the nation reluctant to become militarily involved in world affairs. Memories of Vietnam were often cited as a caution against U.S. involvement in Nicaragua and Honduras in the 1980s. Only after success in the Persian Gulf War in 1991 did President George H. W. Bush exclaim, "By God, we've kicked the Vietnam Syndrome once and for all!" However, recent events have called that analysis into question,

and Bush's proclamation appears to have been premature. As the initial success of Operation Iraqi Freedom gave way to the frustrations of nation-building, inevitable comparisons with Vietnam began to emerge. In April 2005, Senator Chuck Hagel spoke for many when he said, "We are locked into a bogged-down problem not . . . dissimilar to where we were in Vietnam. The longer we stay, the more problems

1996

MAY

May 14 President Bill Clinton signs an executive order terminating the designation of Vietnam as a combat zone.

we're going to have." In August 2007, President George W. Bush evoked Vietnam comparisons again, cautioning that a hasty U.S. withdrawal from Iraq could lead to chaos similar to that which occurred after the U.S. withdrawal from Vietnam. Vietnam remains the yardstick by which Americans measure their wars.

A Time to Grieve

Because the Vietnam War was so divisive, many Americans chose to ignore or forget the conflict and its related political upheavals soon after the United States disengaged from Vietnam. As a result of this prevailing attitude, many veterans were forgotten and ignored, shunned lest they serve as reminders of tragedy and defeat. Many veterans found themselves alone in a country that would not remember them or their sacrifices. However, the United States' attitude toward its Vietnam veterans began to change in the early 1980s. The dedication of the Vietnam Veterans Memorial in 1982 has done much to change that attitude. Called "the wall that heals," the polished black granite wall bears the names of 58,256 American men and women who died in Vietnam. For many Americans, including veterans themselves, the wall has become a place to grieve and a place to remember the sacrifices of the Vietnam generation. As a result of the memorial and long-belated welcome-home parades, Americans have finally begun to come to terms with the Vietnam War and to heal from it.

Vietnam has begun to heal as well. Although it is still a Communist country, it is rapidly

Known as "the wall that heals," the Vietnam Veterans Memorial has been a key factor in America's effort to come to grips with the Vietnam War.

1998

JULY

July 10 The remains of First Lieutenant Michael J. Blassie, a twenty-four-year-old air force pilot who was shot down on May 11, 1972, near the southern Vietnamese village of An Loc, are returned to his family. Blassie had been the Vietnam War's unknown soldier buried in the Tomb of the Unknowns in Arlington National Cemetery until DNA testing revealed his identity.

The trauma of Vietnam left America with a "Vietnam Syndrome" that caused it to be reluctant to become militarily involved in world affairs.

turning to capitalism. In fact, an April 2005 article in the *Economist* about postwar Vietnam was aptly titled "America Lost, Capitalism Won." As a result, business is booming and the country boasts one of the strongest economies in Asia. Vietnam has also benefited from improving relations with the United States. In 1995 the United States and Vietnam restored diplomatic relations and since then cooperation between the countries has grown steadily. With the support of the United States, Vietnam became a part of the World Trade Organization in early 2007. The two nations are cooperating on issues such as recovering the remains of missing U.S. soldiers, and dozens of remains have been repatriated to the United States since the joint effort began. Relations are strengthening in other areas as well. Each year, thousands of American tourists, including Vietnam veterans and former boat people, travel to Vietnam to see the sites and meet old friends. Because of these strengthening

ties, the scars left by the Vietnam War are beginning to heal. The Vietnam War will never be forgotten, but Americans and Vietnamese are getting beyond old anger and hatred and moving toward a future of cooperation and friendship.

Index